# The Bedside, Bathtub &
# Armchair Companion
# to
# Mark Twain

# The Bedside, Bathtub & Armchair Companion to Mark Twain

## Pam McAllister

continuum

NEW YORK • LONDON

2008

The Continuum International Publishing Group Inc
80 Maiden Lane, New York, NY 10038

The Continuum International Publishing Group Ltd
The Tower Building, 11 York Road, London SE1 7NX

www.continuumbooks.com

Printed in the United States of America

Library of Congress Cataloging-in-Publication Data

McAllister, Pam.
     The bedside, bathtub, and armchair companion to Mark Twain / Pam McAllister.
     p. cm.
   Includes bibliographical references and index.
   ISBN-13: 978-0-8264-1813-5 (pbk. : alk. paper)
   ISBN-10: 0-8264-1813-9 (pbk. : alk. paper) 1. Twain, Mark, 1835-1910—Handbooks, manuals, etc. I. Title.

PS1331.M2215 2008
818'.409—dc22
[B]
                              2007049878

# Contents

Contents

Contents

# Preface

The summer I was eight, my parents packed my two sisters and me into the back of the station wagon for a cross-country trip. Every night we camped in state parks; by day we toured historic sites, which included "America's hometown," Hannibal, Missouri. In a snapshot, my sisters and I are reaching out to touch the *actual* fence of the *fictional* boy. Nearby, a marker bears this legend:

> *HERE STOOD THE BOARD FENCE WHICH TOM SAWYER PERSUADED HIS GANG TO*
> *PAY HIM FOR THE PRIVILEGE OF WHITEWASHING. TOM SAT BY AND SAW THAT IT*
> *WAS WELL DONE.*

I was none too impressed with Tom Sawyer or Huck Finn; my heart belonged to the London pauper, Tom Canty, and to his long-suffering double, Prince Edward. When I was an adolescent, a teacher handed me the recently published(!) outlaw book, *Letters from the Earth*, in which Twain bills Satan as a curious visitor to God's wacky little experiment, planet Earth. Written in 1909, it was withheld from publication until 1962, when it made the *New York Times* bestseller list. Like America, I was ready for all the social satire Twain had to offer, his dark edge of despair at the human condition, his disdain for the hypocrisies of church and state.

I was sixteen when Hal Holbrook appeared on our black-and-white television set in *Mark Twain Tonight!* (The next time I saw this show, it was live, on Broadway. Holbrook and I were both thirty-eight years older. Holbrook dropped the Twain persona and reappeared in a red bathrobe for the post-show "Talk Back.") I let Twain dance me through the minefield of my angst-ridden teenaged years. At college, I was handed another bit of outlaw lit; a copy of Twain's *The War Prayer*. This antiwar fable was read aloud at peace demonstrations and in smoky coffeehouses, while Joan Baez and Bob Dylan albums played in the background.

Twain's writings continue to blow my mind. One day, while working on this book, I turned on my laptop, glanced at the day's news, and read that First Lady Laura Bush was lauding Twain and his work. My computer screen immediately froze: it took a full day to get it working again.

## I Love Twain, but Would I Like Him?

I love Mark Twain for never allowing himself to be boxed in. Not for him the neat and tidy résumé: the shape of his life was as full of twists and turns as the river he loved. All my maternal instincts rise up to warn him: Watch out! But he slips out of my reach just as neatly as Tom slips away from Aunt Polly, living ten lifetimes to my one safe one.

Mark Twain understood that humor is rooted in sorrow. Though he repeatedly sank into a funk of loneliness, guilt, and despair, he could always crack up a room with his deadpan drawl. People waited patiently for his punch lines, which often had an aftertaste, a profound point that wormed its way into awareness hours later. He could have remained on safe ground as "the humorist," but when he had the ear of the whole world, he spoke out against mindless patriotism and insincere religiosity. He wrote daily for long hours, through the severe pain of rheumatism and, often, through the even more debilitating pain of an aching spirit. Reading Mark Twain is like watching television with a friend who has Attention Deficit Disorder and is holding the remote control. Twain boldly free-associated. "Formlessness" is a hallmark of his writing; he let his mind and heart run wild, unfettered and uncensored across time and space.

Twain wrote, "Life: we laugh and laugh, then cry and cry, then feebler laugh, then die," and it was true. His life was no more tragic than most, with its series of losses and failures, recoveries and triumphs; it is only that, as the world's first celebrity, his was more public. Contrary to the popular imagination, he lived fully to the end. Even in the months before he died, he was not shut off from the world, staring at the wall in stony depression: instead, he was laughing, albeit feebly, in sunny Bermuda and playing miniature golf with Woodrow Wilson.

I love Twain, but wonder, would I actually *like* him? He smoked forty cigars a day. He had an unpredictable temper and abrupt mood swings. His colossal ego and limitless insecurities (in equal measure) fed his humor and loosened his tongue. I cannot imagine feeling relaxed in his presence, burdened with an ego and insecurities of my own. Following dutifully behind the docent while on a tour of his Hartford home, I sensed Twain standing in the corner, smoking a ghostly cigar and shaking his head at the tourists who ooohed and aaaahed at *his* desk, *his* telephone, *his* billiards table, *his* lamp, just like the people he mocked in his travel books. I was embarrassed.

"IT COULD PROBABLY BE SHOWN BY FACTS AND FIGURES THAT THERE IS NO DISTINCTLY NATIVE AMERICAN CRIMINAL CLASS EXCEPT CONGRESS."

— Pudd'nhead Wilson's New Calendar

@Tom Tenney

I wonder if I would like this man, so often "politically incorrect" by today's standards, who publicly worked through his thoughts on slavery and racism, inching along in his personal growth and holding up a blood-drenched mirror, as if to say, "Look at who we really are!" His use of the words "nigger" and "savage" make me cringe, even when I understand his intentions. He was committed to disentangling his adult life from the race prejudices he had learned in the slaveholding South of his childhood, and, like Huck Finn, made demonstrative progress. He was far less committed to working on his prejudices against Native Americans, Roman Catholics, or the French. His struggle of a century ago touches a raw nerve in an America that is still burdened by discord and division; watching him stumble along so publicly, I am simultaneously uncomfortable with and impressed by the relentless but unfinished effort.

He grew increasingly outspoken on American imperialism, Christianity's mistreatment of native peoples, war (strangers killing strangers), cruelty against animals, but his inconsistency about class, simultaneously loving and loathing wealth, bewilders me. Sometimes decadent and wasteful, he wrote powerfully about the sin of greed and the pitfalls of capitalism and was embraced as "the People's Author," cheered by masses of working-class people who saw themselves as heroes in his work. Would I like this man who seemed to have it both ways?

He was, by all accounts, faithful to his wife, a real one-woman man, but his lifelong affection for young girls makes me wince, and his discomfort with adult sexuality is unsettling. I love Mark Twain, but would I *like* him?

## Acknowledgments

My family and friends have patiently listened to me chatter on about Twain, appreciating in varying degrees the books and stories I pushed on them. My parents, Helen and Arden McAllister, first exposed me to the man and his world. My sister Lois and her husband Greg Baum have been encouraging all along, and my cousin Richard (Ricky) Cottrell called every few weeks for the past two years to ask, "Well, how's Mark?"

Evander Lomke is not only my editor but my friend, and our meetings at the Housing Works Bookstore and Café in Soho are the happiest times of my life, second only to long mornings working beside other writers at the Cocoa Bar in Park Slope, Brooklyn. Day after day, the counter staff greeted me with, "Hey, Ms. Twain, how's it going?"

I am grateful to my friend Joyce Pyle, who took me to see Hal Holbrook on Broadway and toured Mark Twain's home in Hartford with me on the anniversary of Susy Clemens's death in that house. I am thankful to Edward Nathan, who made sure that I knew about Twain's more obscure works, and grateful to Carol Scott for several creative suggestions. Finally, I thank the secret admirer who left a first edition of *Roughing It* on the organ bench at the church where I am employed as Music Director.

## My Favorite Books about Twain

There are several books beyond Twain's works that I found indispensable in writing this overview book. I hold them near and dear to my heart with deepest thanks to the authors.

*Mark Twain A to Z: The Essential Reference to His Life and Writings,* by R. Kent Rasmussen. New York: Oxford University Press, 1995. Foreword by Thomas A. Tenney, editor of the *Mark Twain Journal.*

This hefty volume, remarkably readable and comprehensive, is a godsend to any student of Twain, whether serious or casual. Accurately described as "one-stop shopping," it has over five hundred pages full of artwork, photographs, biographical sketches of real people and fictional characters, and synopses of Twain's titles arranged alphabetically.

*Lighting Out for the Territory: Reflections on Mark Twain and American Culture,* by Shelley Fisher Fishkin. New York: Oxford University Press, 1997.

Written in first-person, this book explores Twain's landscape, from Hannibal to Hartford, from outer space to cyberspace. Fishkin focuses a sharp eye on the American tendency to whitewash our history as a slaveholding society and our continuing struggle with a legacy of racism and makes a powerful case for embracing *Adventures of Huckleberry Finn* as an anti-racist work. Fishkin has a gift that most academics do not: the ability to write lively, passionate prose, informed by long years of careful research, but not weighed down by it.

*Around the World with Mark Twain,* by Robert Cooper. New York: Arcade, 2000.

Cooper left Elmira, New York on July 14, 1995, exactly one-hundred years after Twain departed from Elmira at the start of his around-the-world lecture tour and carefully retraced Twain's itinerary across North America, to Fiji, Australia, New Zealand, India, Ceylon (Sri Lanka), and South Africa. It is an enlightening companion to Twain's *Following the Equator.*

*Mark Twain: A Life,* by Ron Powers. New York: Free Press/A Division of Simon & Schuster, 2005.

Pulitzer Prize-winning Powers reigns as the current Twain biographer extraordinaire. Like his subject, Powers writes with humor and scathing honesty, debunking myths and unearthing details missed by others. His prose is scholarly and elegant, thorough, insightful, and illuminating.

*Mr. Clemens and Mark Twain: A Biography,* by Justin Kaplan. New York: Simon and Schuster, 1966.

In this essential biography, which begins with Twain's thirty-first year, Kaplan analyzes the complex nature of the beloved literary giant, who endured in the face of tragedy, his comic spirit intact.

## But There Is More I Want to Say

In a letter to a friend Twain wrote, "A successful book is not made of what is in it, but what is left out of it." I should have heeded his advice, but I did not want to stop writing. The *Bedside* series comes with a word limit: in the end, I had to cut over two hundred pages from my manuscript, having gotten entirely carried away with the world, wit, and wisdom of this über author who burrowed his way deep into my heart and soul.

I close, feeling grateful for this opportunity to study the Twain canon and write this book. I hope that it will open aspects of Twainiana to a world of readers ready to delve, wherever they may be: in their armchairs, beds, tubs, libraries, favorite coffee bars, or cafés.

Pam McAllister
Brooklyn, New York

# Riding the Tail of the Comet

· · · · · · · · · · · ·

Halley's comet was fading in the Missouri sky on November 30, 1835, the night Samuel Langhorne Clemens was born, twenty-seven years before he would adopt the pen name Mark Twain. The comet's visibility may have been taken as a good omen by his worried mother, who took one look at her premature baby and despaired.

By the close of this life, Twain was first and foremost a storyteller. He knew that a good ending reflects back on the beginning, picking up a common thread that neatly ties everything together. A comet that is visible on a seventy-five year cycle was the perfect thing. Suspecting that his recurrent chest pains would be his undoing and tired of loss and loneliness, he wistfully predicted his demise:

> I came in with Halley's comet in 1835. It is coming again next year, and I expect to go out with it. It will be the greatest disappointment of my life if I don't go out with Halley's comet. The Almighty has said, no doubt: "Now here are these two unaccountable freaks; they came in together, they must go out together." Oh, I am looking forward to that.

Twain jumped the gun a little, as if too eager to "light out for the territory," but his blithe, bitter, tobacco-weathered heart stopped beating at sunset on April 21, 1910. Halley's comet was at the outer edges of visibility, and, according to news reports, it was spectacular that year.

Because he had framed it with his storyteller's eye, the synchronized cycle of the man and the comet have seemed like remarkable cosmic coincidence, the stuff of legend. Who wouldn't want to claim a comet for a personal insignia? Twain was fiery and fierce, with a blazing wit and mesmerizing personality. When he was in the room, all eyes were on his bright presence. The neat coupling with the comet became a lasting image in the popular imagination, easily cited by biographers and remembered by school students.

The comet connection was used to great effect by David Carkeet in his novel *I Been There Before* (Harper & Row, 1985), in which Twain returns with the 1985 sighting of Halley's comet. In an episode of

*Star Trek*, entitled "Time's Arrow," Mark Twain appears as a character who, on encountering the crew of the *USS Enterprise* in the 24th-century, asks, "So, this is a space ship! . . . Did you ever run into Halley's comet?

# Designation of a "National Mark Twain Day" by the President of the United States

Excerpts from Proclamation 5414, issued on November 26, 1985

Like the comet that startled the night sky at his birth and returned as a bright chariot to "carry him home" 75 years later, the literary achievements of Mark Twain can truly be called an "astronomical" phenomenon.

Born Samuel Langhorne Clemens, November 30, 1835, in Florida, Missouri, he enjoyed an idyllic boyhood in Hannibal, Missouri. There by the banks of the mighty Mississippi, he came to know and love the common people of America. . . .

Today, as we commemorate the 150th anniversary of Mark Twain's birth – and as Halley's Comet again brightens the skies of our planet – the wit, the wisdom, and the inimitable style of Mark Twain continue to delight and instruct young and old – in more than 50 languages....

He was American to the core and he was also a sophisticated world traveller. He evoked the concrete details of his own time and place as no one else could, and he was also deeply versed in history.

He relished the innocent joys of childhood and the storybook adventures of his young manhood. He knew the fulfillment of a happy marriage and the heady wine of wealth and adulation. The dons of Yale and Oxford honored him with exalted degrees, and when he died the common people wept.

Twain also knew the shattering humiliation of betrayal and bankruptcy. He endured the soul-searing desolation of bereavement, and in the depths of his grief he could sometimes rail like the proverbial village atheist.... He would probably have been amused at all the fuss that has been made over him and chuckle at some of the theories the critics have spun about him and his works. Self-deprecation was the hallmark of his humor; he loved to puncture pomposity – even his own.

New York, Connecticut, California, and Hawai'i are only some of the States that can claim to have shaped his life, but Hannibal, Missouri, where he grew up, will always have a prior claim....

The Congress, by House Joint Resolution 259, has designated November 30,1985 as "National Mark Twain Day" and authorized and requested the President to issue a proclamation in observance of this event.

Now, Therefore, I, Ronald Reagan, President of the United States of America, do hereby proclaim November 30, 1985, as National Mark Twain Day. I call upon the people of the United States to observe such day with appropriate ceremonies and activities.

In Witness Whereof, I have hereunto set my hand this twenty-sixth day of November, in the year of our Lord nineteen-hundred-and-eighty-five, and of the Independence of the United States of America the two hundred and tenth.

~ Ronald Reagan

# The Boy from H — L (Hannibal, of Course)

· · · · · · · · · · ·

## (1835–47)

The luckiest thing that happened in young Sam Clemens's life was that his father failed to make a go of it in the "almost invisible village" of Florida, Missouri. If the town had had a motto, it might have been, "If you *can't* make it here, you probably *can't* make it anywhere." Both sides of the family tree were cursed with big dreams and bad luck. Fickle Fortuna (a.k.a. Lady Luck) turned her Wheel of Fate very fast indeed. Twain was in for a notoriously wild ride. He would win at the game of life, lose everything, win again, and lose, while the whole world watched.

John Marshall Clemens, named after the republic's first Chief Justice, always thought of himself as a gentleman from Virginia, bound to help shape this new world. In 1823, living in Kentucky, John married Jane Lampton, a red-haired and witty storytelling woman who loved to dance. Together they would have seven children. Hard, humorless, and honest to a fault, John would be immortalized as the judge in a number of his son's stories and books,

most famously as Judge Thatcher, Becky's father, in *The Adventures of Tom Sawyer*.

As if in search for the elusive pot of gold at the end of the rainbow, John Clemens spent his adult life investing in various business and real-estate schemes. He purchased seventy-thousand acres of timberland in Tennessee, but he was the anti-Midas; everything he touched turned to IOUs. As each new venture failed, he uprooted his wife and children and hauled them farther into a wilderness of broken-dreams: Kentucky-Tennessee-Missouri.

### Little Sammy's Hardscrabble Life

Sammy, the sixth child of the mismatched couple, was born two months premature in a rustic, two-room shack in Florida, Missouri, as Halley's comet faded from view. Decades later, the shack would be carried to higher ground, with a historic marker tacked on, MARK TWAIN'S CABIN, located in Mark Twain State Park, not far from Mark Twain Lake. When the

Clemens family and their slave girl, Jennie, lived there, Florida had only two streets, two stores, one log church that doubled as a schoolhouse, lots of pigs and dogs, and about one-hundred people. "I increased the population by 1 per cent," Twain would write. "It is more than many of the best men in history could have done for a town."

As if he knew from the start that he didn't belong there, Sam began life little, blue, and as sickly as the town itself. Against all the odds, he lived, but, as a toddler, was frequently bedridden. He earned the nickname "Little Sammy" and would remain slight, small-shouldered and fine-boned. It was a hardscrabble life for this still growing family, where Henry, the last child, was born in 1838. There was always talk of that Tennessee land that John Clemens believed held the promise of wealth: it would, instead, become a family curse. Later, Twain would write;

*It is good to begin life poor; it is good to begin life rich – these are wholesome; but to begin it "prospectively" rich! The man who has not experienced it cannot imagine the curse of it.*

Florida was bleak and poor, but there was one saving grace; Sammy's Uncle John Quarles. He had a farm ("a heavenly place for a boy") and a supply of humorous folk tales, including one about an unfortunate but prize-winning frog. There were slaves at Uncle John's farm, just like there would be later in the re-created farm of the Tom Sawyer and Huck Finn books. There, Sam would go out beyond the orchard to the tobacco fields and Negro quarters, and listen attentively, soaking up the dialect, bits of wisdom, superstition, ghost stories, tall tales, and stories of survival and despair. He

would listen to the songs, later known as *spirituals*, the weaving of moans, dreams, and biblical lore. These remained with him for a lifetime. As Twain, he would recall time spent listening to the man who would be immortalized as Huck's companion, Jim:

*I can see the white and black children grouped on the hearth, with the fire-light playing on their faces and the shadows flickering upon the walls, clear back toward the cavernous gloom of the rear, and I can hear Uncle Dan'l telling the immortal tales.*

It never occurred to Sam to question slavery. Like Huck Finn, he accepted what was considered natural by everyone he knew. And, like Huck, he would eventually grow to question, reject, and then loath the "peculiar institution."

John Clemens, gaunt and aloof, set up shop with the hearty, good-natured Quarles, but the alliance was doomed from the start. Sam's father turned to his practice of law and became the Monroe County judge and worked on plans for a future railroad connection and an academy.

Sam seemed to exist on a diet of castor oil and "allopathic" medicines. He suffered from convulsions, nightmares, and sleepwalking. One summer night when he was three, he got out of bed and, as if in a trance, walked into the bedroom of his ailing sister, Margaret, began plucking at the bed covers, then turned around and went back to bed. "Plucking the covers" was considered a sign of impending death in Victorian America. Nine-year-old Margaret died of bilious fever several days later, and the family declared that Sam had "second sight."

That autumn, John heard poverty knocking at his family's door and death breathing down his neck. Margaret had

5

been the second of their children to die; the first was a baby boy, Pleasants Hannibal. John's slim fortune was dwindling fast and his big dreams had dried up; he moved his family thirty-five miles to Hannibal the month Sam turned four. Here was a bustling town on the banks of the Mississippi River; the town would be immortalized in Twain's famous "boys' books" as "St. Petersburg," named, significantly, for the saint who guards the pearly gates of paradise. Hannibal would feed Sam's soul for the rest of his life and, through his writings, become "America's hometown."

The family's first home there was a hotel, the Virginia House. Like Judge Clemens's delusions of grandeur, the hotel sounded good but was, in reality, rundown. The plan was to fill the place with paying guests. Instead, within a few years, John had to declare bankruptcy. Later, Twain would write, "When I was a boy everybody was poor but didn't know it." This was not quite true: his father knew and resented it.

Red-haired Sam remained a sickly child, but whenever he had strength, he was the spittin' image of the fictional daredevil he would later hand the world, Tom Sawyer. A smoker by age seven, he played endless tricks on his ever-gullible mother and always had a collection of boy-things in his pockets: teeth, dead bats, live toads.

The year the Clemenses arrived in town, Hannibal boasted almost one thousand residents. There was no electricity, and the streets were made of mud, but new buildings were going up beside aging shacks. Within a decade of the family's arrival, Hannibal would boast four stores, three saloons, and two churches. There were tobacco and hemp-processing factories. Ten thousand pigs a year were forced through the streets to the slaughterhouses.

When Sam was six, he saw his parents kiss for the first (and last) time in his life. It was at the deathbed of his brother Ben, who did not live to see his tenth birthday. Jane insisted that the children touch Ben's cold cheek. Sam cooperated, but was traumatized. Wildly mourning the loss of another child, Jane turned to religion and dragged Pamela, Sam, and Henry to the Presbyterian church where they sat through long sermons on hellfire and damnation. Jane was a forgiving woman with a charitable heart and a soft spot for anything caged or condemned. Stray and abused cats followed her from the streets into the house; at one time the family shared its tight quarters with nineteen felines.

John and Jane Clemens moved their family again, down the street, to a small, wooden house at 206 Hill Street, the one tourists know as the "Boyhood Home of Mark Twain." Orion and Pamela were old enough to have rooms of their own, but Sam and Henry shared a room. It was under the little window of that room that poor-boy Tom Blankenship would meow like a cat in the night and through which bad-boy Sammy would slip for his moonlit adventures; good-boy Henry watched, deserted and forlorn.

Hannibal was defined by the Mississippi River that kept the lifeblood flowing. Boats brought goods and all kinds of colorful characters: peddlers, healers, con men, gamblers, trappers, politicians. They also brought and carried away slaves, like Jennie, who was eventually sold "down the river" in a last-ditch effort to ease the family's financial strain. The steamboats, themselves, were as exciting as their passengers, with their banners flapping in the breeze.

With no public schools or laws requiring parents to educate their children, families had to pay twenty-five cents a week per pupil. In his autobiographical musings, Twain would remember the "dame school" at the end of Main Street where the teacher began the class with a prayer and Bible reading. His first day in school, he broke a rule and got a whipping. He would attend only three other schools before he was through with the whole scene. Sam was fascinated with words and languages. Even when he played hooky from school, which he did often, he spent his time reading: *Robin Hood, The Arabian Nights, Gulliver's Travels, Don Quixote,* Shakespeare.

His school chums would be cherished for a lifetime and given immortality on the page. There was Tom Nash, the postmaster's son, who went with Sam for a midnight skate on the frozen Mississippi and fell into the water; and Tom Blankenship, the penniless child of a drunken drifter from South Carolina, the model for Huckleberry Finn. Golden-haired Will Bowen, from one of Hannibal's upscale families, was Sam's co-conspirator in numerous adventures and misadventures. There were sweethearts, too, like blue-eyed Annie Laurie Hawkins, the model for Becky Thatcher.

Frontier America was a violent place. Hannibal was a place of rough language, rude humor, blood sports, drunken brawls, outlaw bands, infant death, and slavery. Before Sam was twenty, he encountered his share of corpses and witnessed a number of murders.

- When he was seven, Sam climbed through the window of his father's office and was shocked to see a corpse laid out on the floor. It was the body of James McFarland, a farmer destined to be remembered as Hannibal's first recorded murder victim, stabbed after an argument about a plow.
- When he was nine, Sam saw William Owsley, fed up with relentless harassment, pull out his pistol and wound "Uncle Sam" Smarr, an obnoxious drunk. Smarr was laid out on the counter at a drugstore and a heavy Bible was placed on his bleeding chest, its weight adding to the torture of his dying.

- When he was ten, Sam watched a black slave die an agonizing death after a white overseer threw a chunk of slag at the man, punishment for "some small offense."
- He blamed himself when a drunken tramp burned to death while imprisoned in the village jail. Earlier, Sam had given the man some matches.
- The nightmare-wracked boy happened to be in the wrong place at the wrong time again and witnessed the murder of a Californian emigrant, stabbed in a drunken brawl.
- Another night, Sam joined a crowd that followed a raging drunk up a hill to a house where an elderly widow stood, cradling a rifle. The drunk carried on like a fool, while the woman slowly counted to ten. Too late, he realized she was not kidding; the woman shot a gapping hole in the man's chest. Sam "went home to dream and was not disappointed."
- Sam knew a storekeeper, a "hunchback," who would give out cigars in exchange for a bucket of water drawn from the village pump. One day, Sam and some pals brought water and, finding the storekeeper slumped over on the porch, sat down to wait for him to wake up. "He was dead. I remember the shock of it yet," Twain would write.
- When he was eleven, Sam and his friends spent an afternoon collecting pecans and berries on an island. The boys were wading through shallow water when the mutilated corpse of a runaway slave rose up out of the water. The boys ran for their lives.

- The river could be cruel. By his own count, Sam almost drowned seven times, but was saved each time by ever-vigilant slaves. Two of Sam's friends were not so lucky.

Is it any wonder that Twain's writings would be littered with corpses, graveyards, and lynch mobs? Sam was destined to become a humorist with his finger on the pulse of a violent society.

Perhaps it is not surprising that Sam's childhood came to an end the way it did. After a complicated series of lawsuits and countersuits, the Clemenses sold their furniture, gave the Hill Street house to a relative, and moved into some barren rooms above a drugstore. It was in this condition of utter defeat that John Marshall Clemens traveled by horseback twelve miles through a sleet storm one night in March 1847. When he got home, he was chilled to the bone and quickly developed pneumonia. John's cycle of big dreams and bad luck ended two weeks later. As the family gathered awkwardly around his bed, he reached out, not to his wife, but to his twenty-year-old daughter, Pamela, whom he kissed in a rare display of affection. Ten minutes later, Judge Clemens was dead at the age of forty-nine.

Over his father's corpse, opposite his mother, Sam was made to promise that he would be a "better boy" and not break his mother's heart. Soon after, eleven-year-old Sam positioned himself to catch a glimpse of his father's autopsy and saw Dr. Meredith turn toward the cadaver, knife in hand. With that slice of the scalpel, Sam's childhood came to an end.

# Short Works of the 1860s

· · · · · · · · · · ·

It is unlikely that we will ever see a bound volume entitled *The Complete Writings of Mark Twain*. Such a book would have to be the size of a small car. Behind the mask of his slow drawl and lazy cigar smoke, Twain was a disciplined (albeit haphazard) writer. The result was his enormous output of free-range imagination, enough to keep any reader happy for a lifetime.

1863 **"Curing a Cold"** (Sketch)
The narrator follows every bit of unsolicited advice he gets for how to get rid of a cold and lives to tell about it.

1864 **"The Killing of Julius Caesar 'Localized'"** (Sketch)
After covering the 1864 presidential election, Twain parodied the sensationalism with this faux report on the assassination of Julius Caesar, using modern political jargon.

1864 **"Aurelia's Unfortunate Young Man"** (Sketch)
A young woman's wedding has been repeatedly postponed while her beloved endures smallpox, scalping by Indians, the loss of both arms and legs to accidents, and an eye to disease. The young woman is beginning to waver, but is advised not to give up.

1864 **"Lucretia Smith's Soldier"** (Short story)
In this spoof of sentimental Civil War stories, Lucretia spurns her fiancé, Reginald. After he goes off to war, however, Lucretia regrets her rebuff. When Reginald is wounded, Lucretia hurries to nurse him back to health and finds that his head is wrapped in bandages. After three weeks, the doctors remove the bandages, and Lucretia is appalled to learn that she has been nursing the wrong man.

1865 **"The Story of the Bad Little Boy"** (Short story)
Countering Sunday School lore, little Jimmy is remarkably free from consequences as he grows from a prankster into a murderer and a respected member
of the legislature.

1867 **"The Celebrated Jumping Frog of Calaveras County"** (Short story)
This story was celebrated as the birth of a new literary tradition unique to the
American West *(see separate summary).*

1868 **"The Facts Concerning the Recent Resignation"** (Sketch)
With tongue-in-cheek, Twain claims that he quit his job as a private secretary
for a senator in Washington, D.C., because he was not given a billiards partner
and his advice was rudely ignored by the secretaries of the Navy, War Department, and the Treasury.

1868 **"Cannibalism in the Cars"** (Short story)
In this satire on legislative procedure, a train is stranded in a snowstorm. After
a week without food, the passengers began nominating each other for dinner.

1868 **"My Late Senatorial Secretaryship"** (Sketch)
Twain lampoons the tendency of our lawmakers to skirt the issues and dupe
the voting public, by describing four offensive letters he wrote on behalf of a
senator.

1869 **"Journalism in Tennessee"** (Sketch)
In this parody of both Southern journalism and the tradition of dueling, the
narrator inadvertently becomes a part of an exchange of insults between newspaper editors. The situation escalates from a war of words to a general riot, and
the narrator concludes that Southern hospitality is "too lavish" for him. He
checks into a hospital.

1869 **"Only a Nigger"** (Essay)
Twain recounts the news that a black man in Memphis, lynched several years
earlier after an accusation of rape, was decreed innocent when another man
confessed. "Ah, well! . . . A little blunder in the administration of justice by
Southern mob-law."

1869 **"A Medieval Romance"** (Short story)
Twain spoofs romance novels in this gender bender, set in 1222, in which a
German baron brings up his daughter as a son so that she might inherit the
throne.

1869 **"Legend of the Capitoline Venus"** (Short story)
Inspired by a petrified-man hoax, the Cardiff Giant, unearthed in 1869 near
Syracuse, New York, Twain penned this story, set in Rome, about a penniless
American artist, who benefits financially from an art hoax.

1869 **"The Personal Habits of the Siamese Twins"** (Sketch)
In this meditation on conjoined twins, Chang and Eng Bunker (1811–74),
Twain mixes fact with fantasy and imagines that the brothers fought on
opposite sides in the Civil War.

# The Cat-Lover's Mark Twain

· · · · · · · · · · · ·

Twain considered himself an "expert" in cats; he probably was, having spent his entire life enjoying their company. Precocious daughter Susy observed, "The difference between papa and mama is that mama loves morals and papa loves cats."

*Papa is very fond of animals particularly of cats, we had a dear little gray kitten once that he named "Lazy" (papa always wears gray to match his hair and eyes) and he would carry him around on his shoulder, it was a mighty pretty sight! the gray cat sound asleep against papa's gray coat and hair.*

Susy also noted the fun her father had in naming cats: Stray Kit, Abner, Motley, Fraulein, Buffalo Bill, Cleveland, Sour Mash, Pestilence, and Famine. Once, while summering in New Hampshire, catless, Twain "rented" three kittens from a farmer down the road; he nicknamed both of the black kittens Sackcloth ("they cannot tell each other apart") and called the little gray one Ashes. There was also a mother cat named Satan, and her offspring, Sin.

Toward the end of his life, Twain's favorite cat was Tammany. One of her lively kittens had a penchant for billiards and, while still small enough to be tucked into a side pocket of the table, would happily remain there, wide-eyed and alert, watching the game and darting out a little paw to bat at the balls passing by.

It is little wonder that a cat's "meow" was the signal used by that free spirit, Huck Finn, to call Tom Sawyer out into the night for some adventure. Actual cats rarely faired well at the hands of the boys, however. Who can forget Aunt Polly's cat, Peter? He did somersaults across the room after Tom fed him some nasty-tasting painkiller. The first time we meet Huckleberry Finn, the boy is carrying a dead cat by the tail, and a central adventure will revolve around the boys' attempt to bury it in a graveyard that night.

In *Roughing It,* "slenderly educated" Dick Baker, a pocket-miner at Dead-Horse Gulch, often talked about his cat, Tom Quartz, who was "the remarkablest cat I ever see."

*He had more hard, natchral sense than any man in this camp – 'n a* power *of dignity – he wouldn't a let the Gov'ner of Californy be familiar with him. He never ketched a rat in his life – 'peared to be above it. He never cared for nothing but mining.*

Baker rendered a tall tale about old Tom, claiming that the cat knew more about mining than any man. One unlucky day, however, the miners blasted a shaft where Tom was taking a nap on a gunny sack. The cat was blown into the sky and came tumbling down, covered in soot. From that day on, he was steadfastly "prejudiced" against quartz mining.

TOM QUARTZ.

What if cats ruled the world? In *A Connecticut Yankee in King Arthur's Court,* 19th-century Hank tried to persuade Clarence, his 6th-century protégé, that a republic would be a better form of government than a monarchy, because kings were dangerous. Clarence would not hear of it and proposed the rule of cats. They might be laughably vain and absurd, but no worse than human royalty and, as a rule, "the character of these cats would be considerably above the character of the average king."

Twain made up bedtime stories for his young daughters, and in "A Cat-Tale," he re-creates such a scene, complete with the girls' questions and comments. The story concerns a short-tailed Manx cat named Catasauqua (a soprano) and her catlings, Cattaraugus (bass) and Catiline

(tenor). When Twain doodled a crude sketch of the cats singing, Susy accused her father of exaggerating one cat's tail: Twain replied that he had taken poetic licence and drawn a long tail on a short-tailed cat to illustrate joy.

In *Personal Recollections of Joan of Arc,* the brave teenager finds a kitten shortly before she leaves her village to fight the English and save France. Later, after leading her army to victory in a number of battles, she is reunited with her dear uncle, who tells her that people come from miles around to look at Joan of Arc's cat; the villagers hanged a man who dared to throw a stone at it.

In "A Fable," an artistically sophisticated house cat is the only animal that understands how to look at a painting. After the ass, bear, cow, tiger, lion, leopard, camel, and elephant all fail to appreciate an artist's work, the house cat states the moral of the story.

In *No. 44, The Mysterious Stranger,* a young magician turns a maid into a cat. At first, she is distressed until she realizes that her life in the castle will be much better lived as a cat than as a slave. "I've never caught a mouse," she says, "but I feel it in me that I could do it." A boy, hearing her speak, asks the magician to teach him to speak a cat language, either *catapult* or *cataplasm*. Instantly, he begins reciting a poem in cat talk.

## What Twain Had to Say about Cats

- Next to a wife whom I idolize, give me a cat – an *old* cat with kittens. (letter to Livy)
- Of all God's creatures there is only one that cannot be made the slave of the lash. That one is the cat. If man could be crossed with the cat it would improve man, but it would deteriorate the cat. (notebook)
- By what right has the dog come to be regarded as a "noble" animal? The more brutal and cruel and unjust you are to him the more our fawning and adoring slave he becomes; whereas, if you shamefully misuse a cat once she will always maintain a dignified reserve toward you afterward – you will never get her full confidence again. (autobiographical writings)
- Hardly any cats are affected by music, but these are; when I sing they go reverently away, showing how deeply they feel it. (autobiographical writings)
- I believe I have never seen such intelligent cats as these before. They are full of the nicest discriminations. When I read German aloud they weep. . . . French is not a familiar tongue to me, and the pronunciation is difficult, and comes out of me encumbered with a Missouri accent; but the cats like it, and when I make impassioned speeches in that language they sit in a row and put up their paws, palm to palm, and frantically give thanks. (autobiographical writings)
- A home without a cat – and a well-fed, well-petted and properly revered cat – may be a perfect home, perhaps, but how can it prove title? (*Pudd'nhead Wilson*)
- You may say a cat uses good grammar. Well a cat does – but you let a cat get excited once; you let a cat get to pulling fur with another cat on a shed, nights, and you'll hear grammar that will give you the lockjaw. Ignorant people think it's the noise which fighting cats make that is so aggravating, but it ain't so; it's the sickening grammar they use. (*A Tramp Abroad*)
- Cats are loose in their morals, but not consciously so. Man, in his descent from the cat, has brought the cat's looseness with him but has left the unconsciousness behind – the saving grace which excuses the cat. The cat is innocent, man is not. ("The Damned Human Race")
- A cat may err – to err is cattish; but toward even a foreigner, even a wildcat, a catacaustic remark is in ill taste. ("A Cat-Tale")

"A HOME WITHOUT A CAT— AND A WELL-FED, WELL-PETTED, AND PROPERLY REVERED CAT— MAY BE A PERFECT HOME, PERHAPS, BUT HOW CAN IT PROVE TITLE?"
—Pudd'nhead Wilson, ch. 1

© Tom Tenney

# The Apprentice

. . . . . . . . . . .

## (1847–61)

After his father died in 1847, everything changed for eleven-year-old Sam Clemens, except financial desperation and nights full of bad dreams; those remained constant. Sam would have a few more months of playing boyhood pranks and of enduring the miseries and humiliations of formal schooling, but, at age twelve, all that came to an end.

Pale Pamela helped support the family with income earned by teaching piano and guitar lessons. Orion sent money from his printer's job in St. Louis. It was Sam's turn to contribute, and he tried but, long before a real-estate tycoon named Donald Trump made "You're fired!" his signature phrase, Sam Clemens heard it at the conclusion of a string of odd jobs.

The family moved out of their rented rooms above the pharmacy and back to the little house at 206 Hill Street, but they had long since hit rock-bottom. Jane became increasingly eccentric: smoking a pipe, crying day and night, prophesying. When she was no longer able to support him, she sent Sam to live in the home of Joseph Ament, publisher of the *Courier*. Here, Sam began a long stint as a "printer's devil." He was to tend the fire, sweep the floor, go for water from the town pump, wash the rollers, learn to set type, fold the newspapers, and help deliver them. At times, Sam's reality was like a chapter out of *Oliver Twist*; he was paid nothing for his long hours of work, and the food rations were so slight, he stole onions and potatoes from the cellar to survive. Often, his bed was a straw pallet on the floor.

Sam puffed on cigars during the tedious hours of work, his delicate fingers picking out tiny letters from a case of metal typefaces to make the lines of words. When one line was done, he placed it on a tray, and slowly the page of a newspaper would begin to take shape, until it was ready to be inked and pressed. The work was precise, repetitive, and excruciatingly slow. Sam would spend his life fascinated by any machine that could speed up the process. He viscerally learned the wisdom of choosing just the best word, later saying, "The difference between the *almost right* word and the *right* word is really a large matter – 'tis the difference between the lightning-bug and the lightning."

In 1849, Hannibal started bleeding people, as if it had been caught in a cosmic knife fight with an invisible foe. It began that spring with the California Gold Rush; hundreds left town and headed for John Sutter's place with dreams of instant wealth. That summer, other citizens departed for new digs, six feet under, victims of a cholera epidemic. This was followed by an outbreak of yellow fever, then cholera again. Red-haired Sam held on against both greed and death. He managed to quit smoking long enough to join the Cadets of Temperance and wear the showy red sash in several parades, but, as summer heat set in, his willpower gave out.

In 1850, his mother, perhaps not as distracted as people thought, heard a rumor that the publisher of Hannibal's *Journal* was getting ready to leave town and join the Gold Rush. She alerted Orion, who moved home and, after a year of publishing an interim paper, was able to merge that paper with the *Journal*. Shy Henry came on board right away, and Sam left the *Courier* to join his brothers. He was fifteen and a hard worker: though Orion promised to pay him $3.50 a week, it never happened. Sam did manage, however, to get published. The first trickle of "fillers" widened into a small stream of sketches published in a variety of papers. In May, 1852, he got his first byline, "S.L.C.," with "The Dandy Frightening the Squatter," published in Boston's comic weekly, *Carpet-Bag*. The next week, his initials appeared at the end of a short piece in Philadelphia. The byline didn't seem to matter as much as the thrill of getting published. Sam tried on his first pen name, writing as "W. Epaminondas Adrastus Perkins." Days later, he changed "Perkins" to "Blab."

In 1853, when their newspaper became a daily, Sam, bored from tedious hours of setting print, was on the lookout for space that needed filling, and manufactured a mock dialogue. First, as "Rambler," he submitted a flowery ode dedicated to "Miss Katie of H — L." The next day, writing as "Grumbler" in a faux letter-to-the-editor, he protested the ode, saying that "Katie in Hell is carrying the matter too far." As "Rambler" he then replied that it was not meant to be Hell but Hannibal. Readers enjoyed the fun so much that Orion gave Sam a regular assignment: OUR ASSISTANT'S COLUMN. Was it that this was a reward Sam deemed too little, too late or that the title of the column was so dull? Or was it just a feeling in the air, as Sam watched the flow of travelers heading West? Whatever inspired it, in May he abruptly quit the paper and left Orion and Hannibal in the dust.

## New Horizons

At seventeen, it was time for Sam to see the world. For two months he soaked in the big city ways of St. Louis, staying with Pamela, now married and a mother. He set type at the *Evening News* long enough to buy a one-way ticket out of town.

Next stop was New York City, but this was long before one could simply board a red-eye flight and arrive the next morning in the city-that-never-sleeps. Sam had to navigate a complicated combination of boats, trains, and stagecoaches to get there. He found a room to rent in lower Manhattan and spent the next weeks walking the streets. He would write over fifty thousand letters in his lifetime; his first were ones to his mother describing the city. "I am borne and rubbed and crowded along, and need scarcely trouble myself about using my own legs." Typesetting was just as tedious here as it had been in St. Louis and Hannibal, but after work, he walked, then took refuge in the free printer's library.

After two months, his letters arrived from Philadelphia, where he was a substitute typesetter at the *Inquirer*. On his off-hours, Sam played tourist; Orion began publishing his descriptive letters. By February 1854, Sam was writing from snowy Washington. He stayed only long enough to take a good look at the Senate and find it wanting.

Sam returned to the Midwest in the late spring, working again in St. Louis. A year later, he was ready to retreat from the whole city scene and settled for the deadly calm of Keokuk, Iowa, where his brothers were now setting up the Ben Franklin Book and Job Office. By now, Orion was married and starting a family, but Sam and Henry were bored and lonely boys. Finally mature enough to become friends, they confided in each other. Sam practiced the piano and began keeping a notebook, filling it with lists of things to do and descriptions of pretty girls and their addresses.

It seemed to Sam that sometimes the universe gave him signs and directions. One October day, the wind blew a piece of paper past him and up against a wall. It was a fifty-dollar bill, "the largest assemblage of money I had ever seen in one spot." Sam advertised the lost money, but, after four days, he bought a ticket for Cincinnati, where he found work in a printing office. He moved into a cheap boarding house and later claimed that he spent hours there with a philosophizing Scotsman named Macfarlane, who read the Bible and the dictionary. Scholars now suspect that Macfarlane was a fictional creation.

Wanderlust gripped Sam's soul. After reading about explorers on the Amazon River, he decided to go to Brazil and harvest coca from which was derived cocaine, said to have miraculous powers. He bought a ticket to New Orleans and boarded the *Paul Jones*, piloted by Horace Bixby.

## The Riverboat Pilot

The Big Easy wasn't easy on Sam Clemens. There were no ships leaving for Brazil and, Sam learned, "there probably wouldn't be any during that century." Broke, sick of typesetting, and clueless about what to do next, he begged Bixby to teach him to be a riverboat pilot.

Steamboats, during this "Golden Age of Riverboating," were referred to as "floating palaces" or "mountains of light." For two years, Sam served as a cub pilot, learning the lower Mississippi. He wrote, "A steamboat is as pretty as a wedding cake, but without the complications," and filled his notebooks with descriptions of the notoriously winding river and of the various characters he met along the way. Top of the list was Bixby, whom Sam idolized. Just ten years Sam's senior, Bixby was temperamental, charming, and small like Sam. Devoted to the river, the veteran pilot dressed for work wearing his finest silk neckties and starched collars. His student, too, began to pay attention to clothes, strut along the "texas deck," and smoke cigars. Sam was happy at last. He would write: "A pilot, in those days, was the only unfettered and entirely independent human being that lived in the earth."

One May evening in 1858, when Sam's boat docked at New Orleans, he was happy to see the *John J. Roe* in the next slip. He knew its crew well. Sam leapt onto the deck of the *Roe* to greet his friends. Suddenly, fourteen-year-old Laura Wright appeared on deck. The angelic Missouri girl took Sam's breath away and, for the next three days, became his "instantly elected sweetheart," one he would remember for the rest of his life.

Shortly after those unexpected three days of heavenly infatuation, Sam descended into hell, as if he were streaking through the sky on the back of a comet, riding from one pole to another. On the morning of May 30, Sam awoke from a nightmare of his brother Henry, laid out in an open casket, white roses splayed across his chest, with one red rose in the center. Later that same day, the Clemens brothers set sail for New Orleans aboard the *Pennsylvania*, piloted by the sadistic William Brown. Sam endured Brown's bullying, but when the pilot turned his abuse on sweet Henry, it was more than he could take. Sam's only known occasion of physical violence lasted five minutes, while the boat drifted. He had to take another boat back upriver from New Orleans, while Henry maintained his lowly position as "mud clerk" on the *Pennsylvania*. The brothers, now separated, planned to meet again in St. Louis.

A few days later, Sam heard the terrible news shouted from the shore; that the *Pennsylvania*'s boilers had exploded and the boat had gone down with a great loss of life. It was June 13, one month before Henry's twentieth birthday. It must have seemed to Sam that he was on a slow boat through hell. An early edition of a paper listed Henry as a survivor, but the next edition listed him as "hurt beyond help." Sam's boat floated through water littered with bloated corpses and pieces of the ship. When it docked in Memphis, Sam rushed to his brother's side. Though he was horribly burned and had massive internal injuries, Henry's sweet face had been untouched by the accident. Wracked with "survivor's guilt," Sam tormented himself with a long list of "what-ifs?" For several days, he begged God to spare the life of his brother and take his life instead, but, on June 21, Sam saw his brother laid out in a suit, a bouquet of white roses on his chest, with one red one in the middle. Henry would live on in books, notably as Sid in *Tom Sawyer*. Fateful June 21 would play a part in *A Connecticut Yankee* as the date that Hank Morgan, lashed to the stake in King Arthur's court, was saved from a fiery death by an eclipse of the sun.

Within a month, Sam was piloting steamboats along the Mississippi. He was granted his pilot's license in April, 1859. At twenty-three, he had learned to speak a new language: river. He would write, "The face of the water, in time, became a wonderful book . . . it had a new story to tell every day."

## The Soldier

Sam could have been happy as a steamboat pilot on the Mississippi River for the rest of his life, but reality intruded. Though he had not been paying attention, the rest of the new nation was tearing itself in two, North versus South, with divergent dreams. At the dawn of 1861, several southern states seceded from the Union and, in February, formed the Confederate States of America with Jefferson Davis as president. After the first shots were fired at Fort Sumter, the nation was officially at war with itself. Sam remained oblivious until May, when he was sailing on the last boat allowed across the Union blockade of the river at Memphis. The Mississippi River would remain closed to commerce and pleasure for the duration of the war.

The Civil War not only divided the nation, but families and friends, who struggled to pick a side and defend it. Bixby and some of the other pilots signed up as Union soldiers. Sam's brother Orion, long an abolitionist with a deep hatred of slavery, had campaigned for Abraham Lincoln and knew which side he favored. Sam's mother, on the other hand, hated the damned Yankees and loved the South, and his boyhood friend, Sam Bowen, signed up as a Confederate soldier. The state of Missouri never officially joined the Confederacy, but its young men were urged to fight Union forces. Like the state that spawned him, Sam could not make up his mind. He basically wanted to avoid the whole mess, but in mid-June, Sam's friends dragged him along to St. Louis to be sworn into the Missouri State Guard, then returned to form a militia. Now, instead of pretending to be Robin Hood's Merry Men romping through an imaginary forest with pretend weapons, they called themselves the Rangers and the weapons were real.

The Rangers were a sorry, ragtag crew of reluctant warriors. Union forces roamed the streets with the support of the majority of the town's citizens, but when a rumor spread that the Blue and Gray were preparing to march south, the Rangers got jittery. They disbanded after only two weeks. Sam would later fictionalize his experience in "The Private History of a Campaign that Failed," in which his narrator would famously say, "I knew more about retreating, than the man that invented retreating."

# Sam and His Siblings

· · · · · · · · · ·

The boy who became Mark Twain was born into a house crowded with love and competition. His mother had already given birth to five children. The first child, born in Tennessee during the hot summer of 1825, was given the name of a cold winter constellation, **Orion**, but his name was oddly pronounced with the accent on the "or." Perhaps this was psychically significant, since, for most of his life, (deemed "pathetic" by Twain and his subsequent biographers), Orion, a dreamer, seemed to say "either" to this and "or" to that. In a formal photograph taken when he was fifty-five, he looks bewildered, as if he could not believe that he had inherited his father's bad luck on the wheel-of-fate; he was, after all, hardworking, intelligent, and generous. He left home while still a teenager and moved to St. Louis where he learned to be a printer, taking an idealized version of Ben Franklin as his role model. For the rest of his life, he would be involved in typesetting, printing, and newspaper production. Like an unskilled boxer who doesn't know when to quit, Orion would get pummeled by the competition and knocked out cold time and again, only to stagger to his feet, bloody and humiliated.

When he was twenty-nine, he married Mollie Stotts and settled in Keokuk. In his mid-thirties, after working on the Lincoln campaign, he was made secretary of the Nevada Territory. This was the high point of his professional life, but this taste of prestige and power didn't last long. First, came the death of his eight-year-old daughter Jennie. Then, Orion abruptly began advocating temperance, an unpopular position in the Wild West, and failed to be elected to a position in the new state. He headed back East, where he tried his hand at writing, raising chickens, and practicing law. His now-famous brother repeatedly bailed him out of financial disasters and resentfully provided a regular stipend for living expenses. Twain alternately chided and cherished Orion, noting that it was Orion's habit "to change his religion with his shirt" and that he was "as unstable as water." Even Orion's death, at the age of seventy-two, lacked finality: he died with a pencil in his hand, "in the middle of an unfinished word."

The second child born to Jane and John Marshall Clemens was **Pamela**. Her name, too, was oddly pronounced, and she was nicknamed "Mela." Sickly for much of her life, she is inevitably described as pious, melancholy, and musically gifted. After their father died, Pamela gave piano and guitar lessons to help support the struggling family. Several years later, she married William Moffet and moved to St. Louis where the couple had two children, Annie and Samuel. Sam, following in his uncle's footsteps, grew up to be a writer. Pamela's children were still young, when her husband died in 1865. Shortly after Twain married, he urged Pamela to move the children to Fredonia, New York. An advocate of temperance and a widow on a tight budget, she supported her children and aging mother and frequently urged her famous brother to send money when he could.

The frontier was a hard place for children, who easily succumbed to illness, harsh conditions, and inadequate medical care. The third Clemens child, a boy with the odd name of **Pleasants Hannibal**, died at the age of three months and was left off the family's written records. **Margaret**, the fourth child, grew sick with bilious fever and died just months before the Clemens family moved to Hannibal. **Benjamin**, sweet and mild-mannered, was also destined for a short life, dying just weeks before his tenth birthday.

Only one child was born after Sam. **Henry**, the baby of the family and his mother's favorite, was thoughtful, gentle, and good. The model for Tom Sawyer's younger brother, Henry was not nearly as obnoxious as the fretful, goody two-shoes we know as Sid. Henry and Sam grew closer as they grew older and made their way in the world. They lived together and worked side by side for their big brother Orion in his various print shops and newspaper offices. When Sam turned from typesetting to piloting a riverboat on the Mississippi, Henry eagerly tagged along, something Sam would eventually regret after the fatal steamboat explosion.

# Twain's Illustrators
# and Their Artwork

· · · · · · · · · · · ·

One of the first illustrators of Mark Twain's work, and the most prolific, was **Truman (True) W. Williams.** An untrained artist and unreliable alcoholic, he nevertheless almost always got it right, capturing the sense of ludicrous adventure and tourist naiveté for *The Innocents Abroad,* the testosterone-saturated world of *Roughing It,* and the greed and pride satirized in Twain's first novel, *The Gilded Age.* Williams drew two-hundred illustrations for *Tom Sawyer.* The one of the barefooted boy in a wide-brimmed hat and holding a fishing pole would endear American readers to Tom forever. He was also the first to render the ragged Huckleberry Finn, wearing patched trousers miles too big. Williams usually, but not always, remembered to sign his illustrations with either a signature or a monogram of the initials T.W.W. A Civil War vet and loner, he had a wicked sense of humor that Twain appreciated. Illustrating a "clever liar" named Williams for *Roughing It,* he sketched a self-portrait, and, in *Tom Sawyer,* he inscribed his own name on a headstone in the cemetery scene. Increasingly self-destructive, the

last artwork Williams contributed to the Twain canon were forty illustrations for *A Tramp Abroad.* Twain wrote of him, "Poor devil, what a genius he has & how he does murder it with rum."

**Daniel Carter Beard** drew several hundred illustrations for *A Connecticut Yankee in King Arthur's Court.* Twain had sought out Beard as an illustrator after admiring his magazine work, and he wasn't disappointed. The witty artist incorporated the

likenesses of real people into his drawings for *Connecticut Yankee*. Looking closely, readers could recognize the face of actress Sarah Bernhardt on a young page, a notorious robber baron's sinister likeness on the slave driver, and the artist's own face on an inebriated partygoer. He also worked into the illustrations the faces of Queen Victoria (an old sow), Kaiser Wilhelm II (for both a "chucklehead" noble and a knight), and author Alfred, Lord Tennyson (Merlin). Sometimes, though, Beard could get carried away with his ornate and expansive drawings. When he designed the cover, his art so crowded the title that he boldly dropped the word "Connecticut." In spite of this, Twain was delighted and later proclaimed the artwork better than the text. He said Beard was "the only man who can correctly illustrate my writings, for he not only illustrates the text, but he also illustrates my thoughts." In addition to *A Connecticut Yankee in King Arthur's Court,* Beard illustrated several of Twain's short writings as well as *The American Claimant, Tom Sawyer Abroad,* and portions of *Following the Equator.*

Twain was less pleased with the work of **Edward Windsor Kemble,** the illustrator for *Huckleberry Finn.* He was hired when True Williams became too erratic. Kemble was a young man from sunny California. He worked fast, producing almost two hundred drawings in just a few weeks. Perhaps he should have taken more time; although the pictures captured boyish energy, they seemed carelessly drawn and unfinished. Twain found the boys' faces "forbidding & repulsive." What was worse, Kemble's depictions of Jim and other African Americans approached offensive caricatures. Kemble redrew a number of illustrations, softening his angular lines, and produced over thirty new ones, which Twain proclaimed "most rattling good." Unfortunately, one of his illustrations was mutilated so that it depicted Uncle Silas with an erection, his pelvis tilted toward Huck. The presses were stopped, and two hundred and fifty advance copies of the book were recalled.

In 1904, when Twain's comical 1893 *Extracts from Adam's Diary* was re-published, New York City artist **Fred Strothmann** was chosen to illustrate the text. Reflecting Twain's claim that the text was a translation of Adam's original hieroglyphics, the illustrations look as if they were crudely carved on rock tablets, some broken or chipped. They depict a Stone Age Adam, looking like something that would later appear in a *Flintstones* cartoon.

**Lester Ralph's** elegant and flowing lines show Eve, lithe, naked, and free, "Garden of Eden style," romping with tigers, dancing under the stars and willow trees, naming each and every new thing she sees. These exquisite drawings got the book into trouble when it was published in 1906. The librarians at the Charlton Public Library in Massachusetts objected to the nudity and banned the book.

When Twain wrote *Eve's Diary* in 1905, a tribute to Livy who had died a year earlier, he sought a very different New York City artist to illustrate this more lyrical text.

# The Treasure Hunter

· · · · · · · · · · ·

## (1861–67)

While the Civil War ravaged the East, splitting North from South, twenty-five-year-old Sam headed West with his brother Orion, who had accepted the position of Secretary of the Nevada Territory. The brothers had to travel light and packed only the bare necessities: warm clothing, blankets, a pistol, some tobacco, and, famously, a six-pound dictionary. After sailing down the Missouri River, the pair took off in a stagecoach, crammed in beside bags of U.S. mail. Sam later recalled in *Roughing It* that he felt "an exhilarating sense of emancipation." Three weeks after beginning their trip, the Clemens brothers reached Carson City. Sam had loved being on the move. "A flying coach, a fragrant pipe and a contented heart – these make happiness," he wrote. "It is what all the ages have struggled for."

The days of slowly floating down the Mississippi River past lush and steamy foliage while languorously smoking his pipe were over. The Wild West was the rough-and-ready world of men in a hurry to get rich quick, peopled by wheelers and dealers, fast-talking speculators, and

INCIPIENT MILLIONAIRES.

gun-slinging gruff-talkers looking for silver. Sam promptly traded in his pilot's blue serge jacket for a blue woolen shirt and found himself a "damaged slouch hat."

While Orion set up his office in Carson City, Sam headed for Lake Bigler, later renamed Lake Tahoe, to stake out timber claims. He and a friend spent a few carefree days swimming and fishing. Dreams of instant wealth went up in smoke when Sam left the campfire unattended and accidently started a forest fire, destroying acres of timberland. He promptly forgot about timber and caught "silver fever." The bluish mud of the Comstock Lode, near Virginia City, would yield six million dollars in silver in 1862, not that Sam would have the luck to get any of it. He traveled to different mining districts and met some of the "nabobs," swaggering men who had gotten rich overnight. He wrote to Orion, "Twelve months, or twenty-four at furthest, will find all our earthly wishes satisfied, so far as money is concerned." Before long, however, Sam was shoveling nothing but sand in a quartz mine where the pay was ten dollars a week.

Broke, Sam was almost desperate enough to turn to writing. He had been doodling comical, descriptive letters for fun, sending them for publication to filler-hungry papers here and there, sometimes signing them with the pen name "Josh." When the editor of the *Territorial Enterprise*, Nevada Territory's biggest newspaper, wrote

DRINKING SLUMGULLION.

to Sam and offered him a position as reporter at twenty-five dollars a week, Sam hesitated, not ready to give up on the boom-or-bust world of the mining camps. Unlike other writers who claim that they were *born to write* or who boast that writing is *in their blood* or brag that they absolutely *must write or die*, Sam came to professional writing with pronounced reluctance. Did he really want to write for a living? After thinking about it, Sam decided to take the job. Penniless, he walked the one-hundred-and-twenty miles to Virginia City, which boasted nearly ten-thousand citizens, numerous saloons, breweries, jails, and whorehouses. It was a nearly lawless town, where it was said that the first twenty-six graves in the cemetery were "occupied by *murdered* men."

After his fruitless search for silver, Sam may have welcomed the familiar smell of printer's ink at the *Enterprise* office, but now, instead of being a typesetter, he was a roving reporter. He had always preferred a fantastical story to hard news and this was still true: he indulged in writing several fake-news hoaxes. The first and funniest was about the discovery of a petrified man who would be given a Christian burial just as soon as he could be blasted out

UNEXPECTED ELEVATION.

of the position in which he had spent three-hundred years; brashly thumbing his nose.

### On Your *Mark*, Get Set, Go!

February 3, 1863, came and went quietly, with little fanfare, but, on that date, a humorous travel letter, datelined Carson City, was published in the *Enterprise* with these prophetic opening words: "I feel very much as if I had just awakened from a long sleep." Twenty-seven-year-old Sam had written it, but he was trying out a new pen name: "Mark Twain." It was an awakening of sorts, to a name and an identity, though neither Sam nor the world would realize it for some time. For the rest of his life he would juggle his given name with his alias, but it was as Mark Twain that he would be claimed as the world's first modern-style celebrity. His pen seemed to fly across the page, and he began scripting editorials, satire, tongue-in-cheek sketches, travel letters, legislative reports.

Twain embarked on a pleasure trip to San Francisco where he boldly negotiated a deal with the city's paper, *Morning Call*; he would be its Nevada correspondent. Back in Virginia City, on the Fourth of July, a fire broke out in Twain's boarding house. He lost everything but the shirt on his back. Later that summer, Twain got a letter from his mother, who urged him to grow up and get a real job. Hurt, he wrote back:

> No paper in the United States can afford to pay me what my place on the "Enterprise" is worth. . . . Everybody knows me, & I feel like a prince wherever I go. . . . And I am proud to say I am the most conceited ass in the Territory.

In October, Twain proved just how much of an "ass" he could be; he composed a hoax titled "A Bloody Massacre near Carson." Borrowing the name of a real person, Twain reported that the man, distraught after being swindled in a dividend fraud, had slaughtered his wife and children. The public was outraged. To have a reporter pen such a grisly item and have the audacity to publish it as though it was a real news story was too much. Twain had crossed the line.

That December, Artemus Ward, America's favorite stand-up comic and traveling humorist, hit town. He was effeminate, funny, and sweet, the king of understatement, deadpan delivery, and the dramatic pause. A favorite of President Lincoln's, he and Twain hit it off immediately and, for the rest of Ward's short life, the two formed a mutual-admiration society. Watching him on stage and hearing the roar of the audience, Twain listened and learned.

Artemus Ward

Then, in May 1864, Twain took another serious misstep. He had been walking a fine line before, with his fantastical hoaxes, but now he composed a piece of fake news that backfired. He reported that funds collected by some Carson City women to benefit wounded Union soldiers, had, instead, been used to aid the Miscegenation Society. Miscegenation was no laughing matter in Civil War America. Evidently, the piece had been written as a drunken prank, but was accidentally picked up and published. Suddenly, Twain became reckless and irresponsible to the point of being suicidal. The day after the miscegenation hoax, he provoked a senseless fight with staff members of the *Union,* a rival paper, and, within days, challenged one of the reporters to a duel. For a week, the reporters postured and taunted each other. Tensions escalated as offensive words appeared in print: "fool!" "liar!" Only later would Twain downplay the whole thing, writing a comic piece entitled "How I Escaped Being Killed in a Duel." In reality, he left town.

His stint at the *Enterprise* was over. The West had been his escape valve once before; now, there was only a little bit of "west" left. He headed for San Francisco with Stephen E. Gillis, the news editor of the *Enterprise.* Restless but still alive, Twain tried to focus on his writing, working as a reporter for the *Morning Call* and submitting various articles to the *Golden Era* and to a new literary magazine, the *Californian,* edited by that rising star, Bret Harte. Before long, Twain's pen got him into trouble again, when he wrote about corruption on the San Francisco police force and, specifically, their mistreatment of Chinese immigrants. Stephen Gillis was in trouble, too, for getting into a barroom brawl.

The two writers headed, significantly, for Jackass Hill where Steve had two brothers, Jim and Billy, who shared a cabin with a man named Dick Stoker. The men spent nights drinking whiskey around the log fire, telling tall tales. Steve returned to San Francisco, but Sam and Jim headed for Angel's Camp in Calaveras County to pan for gold. They sought refuge from a cold rain in a dreary mining hotel, where Ben Coon, a river-pilot-turned-bartender, lolled by the fireside. One day, Coon told a story about a gambling man and his frog. Twain listened, and let it percolate like a strong cup of coffee. By February, he had had enough of cabin life in the wintertime. Returning to the little city by the bay, he settled into the writing life, pulling sketches and letters from his pen. At the urging of Artemus Ward, Twain worked on his story about the frog for possible publication in a book of stories being put together back East; but, by the time he sent the story off, he had missed the deadline.

The money Twain made from his writing was not enough to live on. He was almost penniless and wrote to his brother, "I have a religion – but you will call it blasphemy. It is that there is a God for the rich man but none for the poor." He was sick of the Wild West. His depression deepened as he grew more desperate. He wrote to Orion, "If I do not get out of debt in 3 months, – pistols or poison for one – exit *me.*" He would later reveal that he came very close to attempting suicide. His old colleagues at the *Call* publicly teased him in print, writing about "a melancholy-looking Arab, known as Marque Twein. . . . His favorite measure is a pint measure." Despite his obvious discouragement and depression, Sam was beginning to realize that he had a gift. In a letter to Orion and Mollie that fall, he wrote:

Steamship leaving San Francisco

*If I were to listen to that maxim of stern duty which says that to do right you must multiply the one or the two or the three talents which the Almighty trusts to your keeping, I would long ago have ceased to meddle with the things for which I was by nature unfitted & turned my attention to seriously scribbling to excite the laughter of God's creatures.*

He instructed his brother to throw the letter in the stove, writing prophetically, "I don't want any 'absurd literary remains' & 'unpublished letters of Mark Twain' published after I am planted."

Just days before his thirtieth birthday, always a significant date in a lifetime, "Jim Smiley and His Jumping Frog" by Mark Twain was published in New York's *Saturday Press.* It was an immediate and outrageously popular hit, quickly copied and widely reprinted. The Civil War was over and weary Americans were ready to laugh; here was the writer to help them do it.

Then came a new and life-changing turn of events; the California Steam Navigation Company began carrying pas-

sengers across the ocean to the Sandwich Islands (as the Hawaiian Islands were known at the time). Twain was not on the inaugural trip, but he was on the *Ajax* when it set sail in March 1866. One more time, he headed West. He spent four months on the green and lush islands, soaking up the whole watery world as if he had been parched from his days in the desert. He wrote letters for publication in Sacramento's *Union* describing the food, the people, their myths, and their music. He rode horseback through the jungles and mountains, and returned to Honolulu with saddle boils that left him bedridden, unable to sit.

While he was recovering, a tragic news scoop fell into his lap when a lifeboat washed ashore, south of Honolulu, carrying fifteen survivors of a shipwreck. The *Hornet* had caught fire off the coast of South America forty-three days earlier. The men were in bad shape, having drifted thousands of miles across the ocean with only ten days of food. Hearing the news, Twain arranged to be taken to the hospital on a stretcher, where he interviewed the survivors. After working on the story all night, he got it on the next boat leaving for

California. The story was his, exclusively, and caused a sensation when it was printed in the *Union* that July. It would, along with the tall tale about the frog, make Mark Twain famous.

## Exciting the Laughter of God's Creatures

In July, Twain sailed to California where he discovered that his reports from Hawai'i had earned him an avid readership. Realizing that this was his moment, he headed for Sacramento where he requested twenty dollars for each letter published and three-hundred dollars for the scoop about the shipwreck survivors. To his surprise, no one argued with him. Sam Clemens began to realize that Mark Twain was, perhaps, more marketable than he had imagined. He reworked his notes and turned them into a literary piece, "Forty-three Days in an Open Boat," which ran in the December issue of the prestigious *Harper's Monthly.*

Riding the wave of his success, a new idea occurred to him. He decided that he would give the lecture circuit a try. On October 2, 1866, a trembling Mark Twain took the stage in San Francisco before a packed house and told about his adventures on the Sandwich Islands. The next day, the newspapers proclaimed the lecture "a hit, a great hit." Suddenly, Twain was welcomed with open arms in towns and cities throughout California and Nevada. Old acquaintances who had harbored a grudge against the writer of hoaxes, now forgave and welcomed Twain-the-celebrity. By December, he had earned enough money to finance his return to the East Coast. He left the West as a roving correspondent for San Francisco's *Alta California,* a daily newspaper.

After a quick visit home to Missouri to see his mother, Twain returned to New York and booked the Great Hall at Cooper Union. He gave away hundreds of free tickets to his lecture and kept the packed house laughing for over an hour, which earned him rave reviews in the city newspapers. A few nights after this success, Twain, walking home at midnight, tried to help break up a street brawl and was arrested. He spent the night in jail, which was just enough time to observe the colorful characters for a piece in the *Alta,* where he wrote about "the dilapidated old hags, and battered and ragged bummers" and the "vile" policemen.

Twain now had the urge to travel East, and New York City wasn't East enough. The prestigious passenger list for the first pleasure cruise from America to Europe was being assembled. Initially billed as an "educational" excursion, the trip was organized by members of Brooklyn's Plymouth Church, whose famous preacher, Henry Ward Beecher, was popular in liberal circles. Though Beecher and a number of his parishioners ultimately remained ashore, the ship set sail with five dozen privileged, prosperous, and middle-aged passengers and Mark Twain, who had arranged to have his expenses paid by the *Alta.*

After an exciting send-off, the ship remaining anchored for two days at the tip of Brooklyn, while an ocean storm whipped up the waves. It was a rough ocean crossing, with almost everyone aboard experiencing extreme seasickness, except Mark Twain. On a trip lasting one-hundred-and-sixty-four days, the *Quaker City* carried its passengers to a variety of ports: Gibraltar, Tangier, France, Italy, Greece, Turkey, Russia, Lebanon, the Holy Land (Palestine), Egypt, and Bermuda. Along the way, Twain penned a series of letters for publication in the *Alta.*

As the ship crossed the stormy Atlantic, many of the voyagers spent their time in Bible study and prayer. They were a pious lot, but Twain participated in their activities when he could, though he was more at home with the "*Quaker City* night-hawks" who crowded into the bad-boy humorist's smoky cabin, drinking, swearing, and playing cards. Mary Fairbanks was an intellectual figure onboard, quickly gathering around her a circle of thinkers. She sent a letter home for publication in a Cleveland paper, writing:

*There is one table from which is sure to come a peal of contagious laughter, and all eyes are turned toward "Mark Twain," whose face is perfectly mirth provoking.*

Though Fairbanks was not yet forty at the time of the cruise, she was warm and self-assured, and so became a maternal figure for Twain. In his letters to her in the following years, he always addressed her as "Mother Fairbanks."

Included in Twain's *Quaker City* clique was Charley Langdon, a seventeen-year-old from a prosperous Elmira, New York, family. According to the legend Twain made of his life, it was while the ship was docked at the harbor in Smyrna, Turkey, that Charley showed him an ivory miniature, a portrait of his older sister Olivia. It was love at first sight for Twain who found the image "something more than a mere human likeness." Here was Livy. Here was love.

The treasure hunt was over.

# Yours, Dreamily, Mark Twain

. . . . . . . . . . .

Sam Clemens had fun with names, much like Huckleberry Finn would in his fiction, freely trying on this name or that, along with the appropriate style and disposition each name suggested. Pen names were popular at the time, and, when he was only seventeen and beginning to get published, Sam tried on quite a few:

✓ W. Epaminondas Adrastus Perkins
✓ Thomas Jefferson Snodgrass
✓ W. Epaminondas Adrastus Blab
✓ Sergeant Fathom
✓ Josh
✓ Rambler
✓ Grumbler
✓ John Snooks

It was when he was twenty-seven and writing for the *Territorial Enterprise* that he first used the pseudonym that would not only stick, but become an alternate persona that would stay with him well past his last breath. On February 3, 1863, Sam contributed a humorous letter, datelined Carson City, and signed it, "Yours, dreamily, Mark Twain."

Sam had heard "mark twain" as a nautical term during his days as a riverboat pilot. A boat's crew would measure the depth of the water by lowering a notched rod or rope and call out the number of fathoms. One fathom is a measurement of six feet. Entering a depth of twelve feet, they would call "mark twain," two fathoms. The mood of the pilot and the crew at this crucial juncture would depend on whether the boat was coming or going. If called as the boat was heading toward the shore, it meant that the boat was entering dangerously shallow waters. Caution was required or the boat could run aground, scrape the bottom, capsize. But when "mark twain" was called as the boat was leaving the shore, the pilot could begin to breathe easier. The boat was past the danger point and was approaching the place where it would be free sailing into the deeper waters of the rolling river.

This pseudonym would suit Sam Clemens, who spent a lifetime playing with the river of his imagination. As Twain, his writing could run shallow or deep, but his eyes were always open to the danger of the shore. Once, hearing a leadsman on a steamer call out "mark twain!" one of his daughters said to her father, "Don't you know that they are calling for you?"

Twain always claimed that he had not thought of this pen name himself, but had borrowed the alias from Isaiah Sellers, an old pilot: try as they might, however, researchers have failed to find any evidence of this earlier "Mark Twain." According to biographer Justin Kaplan, there is another theory; that the name might have been inspired by the Nevada saloon keepers who marked up two drinks on credit. "Twain" can also be read as a play on the author's lifelong fascination and obsession with duality.

It has been called the most recognized alias in world literature, but it wasn't always this way. When his piece about the shipwreck survivors appeared in *Harper's Monthly*, Twain was mortified that they got his name wrong:

> *I had not written the "Mark Twain" distinctly; it was a fresh name to Eastern printers, and they put it "Mike Swain" or "MacSwain."*

# The Celebrated Jumping Frog of Calaveras County

· · · · · · · · · · · ·

**Setting:** A gold-mining camp in California
**Period:** The Gold Rush era, 1850s

This first short story to win acclaim for Twain is framed as a visit to a mining camp where the story's refined narrator is ostensibly seeking information about a friend of a friend, one Leonidas W. Smiley. He meets a gabby old codger named Simon Wheeler, who does not know anyone with such a pretentious name as Leonidas, but he does know of an "enterprising vagabond" named Jim Smiley. Taking his time in a long drawl, Wheeler tells a tall tale about this Smiley, the "dangdest feller," who would place a bet on just about anything. "Why, if there was two birds setting on a fence, he would bet you which one would fly first."

Having exhausted both horses and dogs in his bets, Smiley caught a frog, named it Dan'l Webster after a famous politician, and "done nothing for three months but set in his backyard and learn that frog to jump." Smiley's frog became a plentiful source of prize money. Even so, said Wheeler, "You never see a frog so modest and straightfor'ard as he was, for all he was so gifted." One day, after Smiley boasted that his frog could leap farther than any other frog in all of Calaveras County, a stranger took him up on his forty-dollar bet.

Problem was, the stranger did not have a frog: eager for the challenge, Smiley offered to find a frog in a local swamp. While he was gone, the stranger forced little pellets of quail shot down Dan'l Webster's throat.

Smiley returned with a frog for the stranger, but, when the contest began, his own frog couldn't budge, let alone leap. The stranger won the bet and promptly skedaddled, stopping only long enough to say his famous line, "Well, I don't see no p'ints about that frog that's any better'n any other frog." Only then did Smiley examine his poor frog who, when he was turned upside down, belched out a double handful of quail shot pellets.

After a pause, Wheeler begins to tell another tall tale; this one, about a "yaller one-eyed cow that didn't have no tail." The narrator, feeling that he has been made a fool of by this long-winded Westerner, is not in the mood to hear another story, and so the story ends.

**The Story behind the Story**

In late 1864, Twain ran into some trouble in San Francisco and headed for a mining cabin on Jackass Hill belonging to Jim Gillis. It was a magical place, a men-only refuge with plenty of whiskey, a log fire, a few good books, and nights of sitting around the fireplace, telling stories. Later, at Angel's Camp, it was too cold and wet to pan for gold. Twain spent most of his time in a hotel, listening to the bartender, Ben Coon, tell stories, including his favorite, a long-winded account about an ill-fated frog. Twain jotted a few key words in his notebook. Later, back at Jackass Hill, he fiddled with the story, telling Jim Gillis's brother Billy, "If I can write that story the way Ben Coon told it, that frog will jump around the world." After three months, Twain returned to San Francisco and found an invitation from Artemus Ward in New York, who was putting together a book of stories about the Nevada Territory. By the time Twain finished the story to his satisfaction and sent it off, however, he had missed the deadline. As a favor to Twain, the story was forwarded to the failing *New York Saturday Press,* which published the story as "Jim Smiley and His Jumping Frog" in its November 18, 1865, issue.

The story hit post-Civil War America's funny bone. One newspaper reporter, noting that "one who signs himself 'Mark Twain' . . . is, we believe, quite a young man and has not written a great deal," nevertheless predicted, "he may one day rank among the brightest of our wits." James Russell Lowell pronounced the story "the finest piece of humorous writing yet produced in America." Twain was mystified and wrote to his mother, "To think that, after writing many an article a man might be excused for thinking tolerably good, those New York people should single out a villainous backwoods sketch to compliment me on!"

This story launched Twain's career as America's humorist. His yarn about the overworked amphibian leapt off the page and into the hearts of war-weary Americans who found the story a natural side-splitter. The story did something else; it redirected U.S. dependence on Old Europe for its literary taste and introduced a style unique to the American West, the written tall tale with its bawdy exaggerations, meant to mock the refinement of condescending visitors.

Ironically, this story about multiple deceptions met with deception and bad luck. Charles H. Webb, editor of the *Californian,* suggested that Twain pull together a volume of sketches, with the frog story as its lead. Twain took the stories to a New York publisher, G. W. Carleton, who rudely showed Twain the door. Twenty-one years later, Carleton sheepishly apologized to Twain: "I refused a book of yours and for this I stand without competitor as the prize ass of the nineteenth century." Confessing to years of revenge fantasies, Twain accepted the apology.

After the book was rejected, Webb published it himself and brought it out in 1867 with a blue-and-gold cover. Twain's first book, *The Celebrated Jumping Frog of Calaveras County, and Other Sketches,* sold at $1.25 a copy. Twain had mixed feelings. When he was courting Olivia Langdon, he wrote to her, begging, "*Don't* read a word in the Jumping Frog book, Livy – *don't.* I hate to hear that infamous volume mentioned. I would be glad to know that every copy of it was burned, & gone forever." He had reason to feel uneasy. Webb had tricked Twain, persuading the first-time author to surrender all rights, royalties, and copies of the book. After years of hindsight, Twain would call Webb a fraud, writing, "As a liar he was well enough and had some success but no distinction. . . ." Twain's book became a little like that poor old frog back in Calavaras County; a prize winner but unable to budge, due to a mean-spirited trick.

## Life Imitates Art

It had to happen, and it did. In 1928, when the city of Angels Camp, California wanted a special event to help celebrate its first paved streets, it instituted the Jumping Frog Jubilee, inspired by Twain's famous story. Fifteen thousand people attended to watch a parade and cheer the winner of the first official frog jump who set the record at three-feet-six-inches.

Today, the Jubilee attracts crowds of over forty thousand every May, with two thousand frog-athletes placed in contention. The world record jump of twenty-one feet, five-and-three-quarters inches (actually a three jump combined total) was made in 1986 by Rosie the Ribiter who has a commemorative bronze plaque on the downtown "Hop of Fame" alongside those of other champions: Ripple, Splashdown, Wet Bet.

In 1995, after animal-rights activists raised serious concerns about the frogs and their habitats, a "Frog Welfare Policy" was adopted, outlining the rules of humane treatment. The protection was long overdue: the last time a red-legged frog, like the one in Twain's story, was seen in Calaveras County was in 1979. Warren "Buck" King, manager of the jubilee and unofficial Frogtown mayor, said in a 2003 article in the *Los Angeles Times*, "I'll bet old Mark Twain is laughing up there right now. Problems with animal-rights groups. Problems with environmentalists. He's saying, 'Look what I started!'"

# Short Works of the 1870s

. . . . . . . . . . .

1870 **"A Ghost Story"** (Short story)
After P. T. Barnum made a plaster cast of the Cardiff Giant to exhibit in New York City, Twain riffed on the expanded hoax with this story, in which the giant's ghost is confused, haunting the New York exhibit instead of the original site outside of Albany.

1870 **"A Curious Dream"** (Sketch)
A man dreams that the dead of a neglected cemetery rise up, dragging their chipped headstones out-of-town, in search of people who care about their ancestors' graves.

1870 **"Political Economy"** (Short story)
A writer, repeatedly interrupted by a lightning-rod salesman, buys over a thousand rods. Days later, lightning strikes his house hundreds of times.

1870 **"Post-mortem Poetry"** (Sketch)
Anticipating the death-obsessed Emmeline Grangerford of *Huckleberry Finn,* Twain spoofed Philadelphia newspapers which attached maudlin rhymes to death notices.

1870 **"Goldsmith's Friend Abroad Again"** (Short story)
Ah Song Hi, a Chinese immigrant, sends optimistic letters home, until he is accused of a crime and experiences the deeply flawed American system of justice.

1870 **"About Smells"** (Essay)
After reading that the minister of a Brooklyn church complained about the bad smell of his working-class parishioners, Twain pondered the "fishy smells" of Christ's disciples and anticipated the smells one is likely to encounter in heaven.

1870 **"Running for Governor"** (Sketch)
Twain reports on a fictional run for governor and how the press tried to ruin him with unsubstantiated reports of misconduct.

1870 **"How I Edited an Agricultural Paper Once"** (Short story)
Though he has misgivings, the narrator agrees to fill in while the editor of an agricultural paper goes on vacation. Before long, readers are outraged by the misinformation being published: that turnips grow on trees, that the pumpkin is a berry of the orange family, that there is a molting season for cows. After he is fired, the narrator objects, claiming that newspaper editors have never been expected to know anything.

1870 **"The Story of the Good Little Boy"** (Short story)
Jacob Blivens believes that he will die young, like the good boys in his Sunday School books. He composes a death speech, but he dies trying to rescue an abused dog, never getting the chance to give his prepared speech.

1871 **"A Burlesque Autobiography"** (Sketch)
The thumbnail sketch of each forefather in the fictional Twain family is presented in the best possible light. Astute readers perceive the truth: that each ancestor was a criminal who came to a violent end.

1871 **"Sociable Jimmy"** (Sketch)
Twain, resting in his Illinois hotel room, met a ten-year-old black servant named Jimmy. Given a little encouragement, the child starting chatting about his observations of life. Twain sat back and listened carefully.

1873 **"A Memorable Midnight Experience"** (Sketch)
It was a dark and stormy night in London when Twain was given a tour of Westminster Abbey, burial ground for some of Britain's greats. Separated from the others, he scared himself silly.

1874 **"A Curious Pleasure Excursion"** (Science fiction sketch)
Twain has joined forces with P. T. Barnum to advertise a luxury cruise aboard a comet, for which complimentary tickets are being offered to a number of corrupt politicians.

1874 **"A True Story: Repeated Word for Word"** (Short story)
Mary Ann "Auntie" Cord, the cook at Quarry Farm, always seemed light-hearted until the evening Twain asked about her trouble-free life. With great restraint, she set Twain straight, telling of her years as a slave, of the day her husband and children were sold and her youngest son was ripped from her side, and of the remarkable day when she was reunited with that son, a grown man, serving as a Union soldier.

1875 **"The Curious Republic of Gondour"** (Sketch)
Gondour, a fictional democracy, suffered from a system of universal suffrage in which the vote of the uninformed was worth as much as the vote of an educated person. To remedy this, Gondour developed a new voting formula.

1875 **"An Encounter with an Interviewer"** (Sketch)
The narrator confounds a reporter by giving strange answers to his questions, including that he was born a twin but that one of the babies died and no one was sure which one.

1876 **"The Canvasser's Tale"** (Short story)
The narrator complains about all the useless items he has been pressured to buy from that day's stream of door-to-door salesmen; he even bought three echoes.

1876 **"The Facts Concerning the Recent Carnival of Crime in Connecticut"** (Short story)
The Twain-like narrator, anticipating a visit from his holier-than-thou aunt, is startled when his conscience walks through the door in the form of an imp covered in green mold. The gremlin reels off the narrator's offenses and explains that healthy consciences grow tall and strong whereas neglected ones shrivel. When the aunt arrives, she badgers the narrator about his smoking. Before long, the narrator orders her out the door and throws his conscience into the fire. By story's end, there are dead tramps in his basement.

1876 **"Punch, Brothers, Punch!"** (Sketch)
An addictive sing-song jingle is getting on Mark's nerves:

> *Conductor, when you receive a fare,*
> *Punch in the presence of the passenjare!*
> *A blue trip slip for an eight-cent fare,*
> *A buff trip slip for a six-cent fare,*
> *A pink trip slip for a three-cent fare,*
> *Punch in the presence of the passenjare!*
> *Punch, brothers, punch! Punch with care.*
> *Punch in the presence of the passenjare!*

The jingle nearly drives Mark mad until he unloads it on his minister friend, who is nearly driven mad himself until he passes it on to unwitting students at a university.

1876 **"1601"** (Parody)
Subtitled "Conversation as It Was by the Social Fireside in the Time of the Tudors," this bit of bawdy prose was meant for the private consumption of

Twain's friend and pastor, Joe Twichell. In it, Queen Elizabeth, Shakespeare, and others converse in high tones about low subjects: flatulence, masturbation, sex.

1877 **"The Invalid's Story"** (Short story)
The narrator must escort the corpse of a friend on a train during a snowstorm. Oddly, the coffin is switched with a box of rifles and a package of ripe Limburger cheese is left on top of it. When the doors of the car close, a foul odor fills the air. By the end of the journey, imagination has done its work: both the narrator and the expressman are riding outside the train, "frozen and insensible." The narrator becomes an invalid.

1877 **"The Loves of Alonzo Fitz Clarence and Rosannah Ethelton"** (Novella)
Alonzo is talking with his aunt via transcontinental phone and hears Rosannah in the background singing a hymn. The two begin to talk and are soon in love. A jealous rival impersonates Alonzo, offending Rosannah by asking her to sing something other than the hymn. Hurt, Rosannah calls off the wedding and disappears. Only later, when Alonzo is in a madhouse, are the two reunited, again by phone. All is explained, and the two get married. When Twain wrote this story, long-distance telephoning was not yet possible.

1877 **"Some Rambling Notes on an Idle Excursion"** (Sketch)
This is a paean to that little piece of heaven called Bermuda, replete with anecdotes about the island's many cats and bits of gossip Twain overheard there.

1878 **"The Great Revolution in Pitcairn"** (Sketch)
Only four months after an American arrives at an idyllic, isolated island, he has created discord, convinced the population to proclaim him emperor, established a military, and levied taxes to pay for it. The people revolt and go back to their peaceful ways.

1878 **"The Stolen White Elephant"** (Short story)
After settling a border dispute, the king of Siam gives the queen of England a gift, a sacred white elephant, but it is stolen en route. In this burlesque of detective fiction, Inspector Blunt fumbles the clues until he actually trips over the body of the dead elephant. He is subsequently hailed a hero.

# The Family Man

· · · · · · · · · · ·

## (1868–80)

Having returned from his *Quaker City* tour, Twain suddenly knew desire: "I want a good wife – I want a couple of them if they are particularly good," he wrote. First, however, he headed for Washington where he worked as a private secretary for a senator. Twain lasted two months and then quit his job saying, "There are lots of folks in Washington who need vilifying." By Christmas, he was back in New York City, reminiscing with the *Quaker City* nighthawks.

A week later, on New Year's Eve, he called on fellow-nighthawk Charley Langdon, who was staying at the fashionable St. Nicholas Hotel with his parents and beautiful sister, Olivia. Twain managed to avoid anything that would offend and was invited to dinner with Charley's respectable family, and joined them later to hear Charles Dickens read from *David Copperfield*. Twain was not impressed with Dickens, but was enchanted by Livy.

Smitten, he nevertheless turned his mind to writing a book on his recent trip; it would highlight the follies of his gullible and goofy fellow travelers as they *ooohed* and *aaaahed* their way across Europe and the Holy Land. Suddenly wild with writing, Twain stripped down to his pants and suspenders, paced, smoked, and rummaged through the newspapers in which his travel letters had been published. But there was trouble brewing out West; the editors at the *Alta*, hearing that Twain was writing a book based on letters they had published, preempted his plan and announced that they would bring out a book of their own.

To smooth some feathers, Twain made the sea voyage West, sailing south to Panama, then north to San Francisco. He managed to work out a deal with the newspaper. Greeted as a celebrity, he took to the stage again, regaling audiences with tales of his trip abroad. The papers were less than kind, and the clergy were offended by his irreligious comments on the Holy Land. He took the criticisms to heart and cleaned up his act. Returning to his manuscript, he lugged his messy sheaf of pages over to Bret Harte's office and begged him to take a look. Harte obliged. Having calmed several storms and finished his rough draft, Twain sailed back East. It would take a few more months to come up with the title *The Innocents Abroad*, but the book that would push Twain to worldwide fame was almost ready.

Just days after his return to New York, Twain accepted an invitation to visit the Langdons. Elmira's most genteel family opened its arms to the cigar-smoking, slow-talking, red-haired Sam Clemens. Jervis Langdon, generous and jovial, was a wealthy man with a conscience. An outspoken abolitionist, he had made his home a stop on the Underground Railroad and secretly provided shelter to runaway slaves, including Frederick Douglass. Risking ostracism, the Langdons had been instrumental in founding a socially progressive congregation, an alternative to Elmira's pro-slavery Presbyterian church. Jervis owned coal deposits that were in great demand during the Civil War; by war's end, he had a fortune.

The children of this prosperous family included Susan (adopted in 1840 at age four) who had married Theodore Crane in 1858; Olivia (the little surprise born in 1845); and Charles (born in 1849). It was a happy household, welcoming and gracious. Charley and Sam entertained everyone with stories from their recent trip.

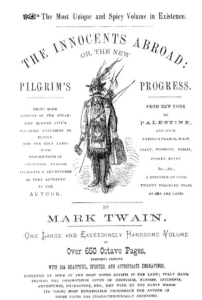

At twenty-two, shy and beautiful Livy was a child of luxury, an intellectual, well-schooled in Greek and Latin. She had recovered from a fall on the ice at age sixteen but remained fragile. Twain's courtship of Livy was a work of art. It took over one-hundred-and-eighty-four love letters from America's most gifted writer to persuade her to give him a chance. Livy saved each letter, but played hard-to-get, demurely refusing three marriage proposals. Twain focused on improving himself so that Livy, who considered herself to be deeply religious, might learn to love him. He made a new best friend, the Reverend Joe Twichell, with whom he now prayed and discussed theology. He read the Bible and quoted from it liberally in his letters.

These efforts eventually paid off. Taking a break from the lecture circuit and his popular talk "American Vandals Abroad," Twain visited the Langdons at Thanksgiving and proposed again. This time, Livy consented, but her father insisted that the engagement be kept a secret until he could look into the relentless suitor's background. Twain wrote to a friend, "I am so happy I want to scalp somebody." He wasn't worried, though he should have been. When his references finally responded, each one was worse than the last. Jervis Langdon took pity on his daughter's suitor, however, and gave Livy and Sam his blessing.

Fortuna's wheel was turning in Twain's favor. In July 1869, *The Innocents Abroad* came out and was sold, not in bookstores, but by the subscription system. Twain was billed as the "People's Author" and wrote to a friend, "My books are water; those of the great geniuses, wine. Everybody drinks water." He was now part owner of the Buffalo *Express*, thanks to a gift from his future father-in-law, who clearly hoped this would help the redheaded roamer settle down.

Livy and Sam were married at an evening service on February 2, 1870, in the parlor of the Langdon mansion in Elmira. The next day, Twain and his new bride, her family, and a number of guests boarded a private railroad car and headed for Buffalo, where Jervis had bought the newlyweds an elegantly furnished brick house. For a while, Twain would consider himself the luckiest man on earth, jokingly referring to himself as "Little Sammy in Fairyland." He was married to "the only sweetheart I ever loved." Livy was to him a woman-child. He would insist that she "sivilize" him and then resist her efforts. She was also his "comrade," mentor, muse, editor, adviser. He called her his "precious little philosopher" and "little saint" and "human angel." She called him "Youth."

Within three months of their wedding, Livy was pregnant. The couple's mutual happiness seemed complete, until Fortuna gave the wheel a downward spin. The new

book Twain was writing about his experiences out West would someday be titled *Roughing It*. Coincidentally, that is just what Sam and Livy found themselves doing, roughing it through a period of extreme emotional challenges. In August, Livy's beloved father became sick with stomach cancer and died a painful death. In September, Livy's childhood friend, Emma Nye, came to visit, intending to comfort Livy and help her cope with the dual stresses of pregnancy and grief. Instead, Emma contracted typhoid fever and died in the Clemens' home. Langdon Clemens, born prematurely in November, weighed only four-and-a-half pounds at birth; against the odds, he lived and was tended by a wet nurse. Twain struggled through all the distractions to write his book.

The wheel of fate was still on a downward spin, and the new year didn't improve the odds. Livy, never healthy to begin with, contracted typhoid fever. The baby, too, was sickly and in need of constant care. In March, 1871, Twain threw in the towel. Buffalo seemed to be a cursed place for them, cold and chaotic. He sold off his part of the *Express* as well as the grand house (both sold, hurriedly, at a loss) and moved his sick wife and son back to Elmira, where Livy and the baby improved, and Twain began writing again.

On a visit to Hartford, Connecticut, to meet with his publisher, Twain was invited to rent a Victorian Gothic mansion at Nook Farm, a literary and intellectual community, located on one-hundred-and-forty acres in the western part of the city. By October, Hartford was home to Sam, baby Langdon, and Livy, who was pregnant again. Twain barely had time to help Livy set up house; he embarked on a lecture tour throughout the East and Midwest that left his new wife lonely and distressed.

Briefly, the wheel of fortune seemed to take an upward spin. *Roughing It* was published and became an overnight success. In March 1872, Livy gave birth to Olivia Susan Clemens (Susy) in Elmira. Like Langdon, the baby was tiny at five pounds, but healthy. Their happiness was short-lived. Within months, Langdon developed diphtheria and, shortly after the return to Hartford, died in Livy's arms. Twain blamed himself for his son's death, while Livy sank into a deep depression, saying that her pathway in life "was to be from this time forth lined with graves."

That fall, Twain left for England to meet with publishers in an effort to protect his work from unauthorized sales, but returned home for the holidays. Twain and his friend Charles Dudley Warner, on a dare from their wives, decided to collaborate on a novel; *The Gilded Age* was published the following December. This shared effort at writing book-length fiction, gave Twain the

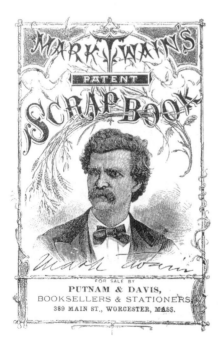

courage to tackle the next novel on his own. That same year, he patented an invention; a self-pasting scrapbook. Each page had a strip of glue which, when moistened, would hold a photograph or news clipping. Four years after securing the patent, he would sell twenty-five thousand scrapbooks.

Meanwhile, he and Livy had decided to buy a lot at Nook Farm. Livy had been sketching ideas for her dream house, and she presented these to Edward Tuckerman Potter, an architect who was not afraid to try something different. The Clemenses instructed him to build a house unlike any other in Hartford. While the house was being built, Twain returned to England, this time with Livy, baby Susy, and several friends and assistants. He and Livy entertained visitors in their hotel suite and toured the sights in England, Scotland, and Ireland before heading to Paris. After four months, they had spent ten-thousand dollars. Livy was homesick; she was also pregnant again. Twain accompanied his wife and daughter to temporary lodgings in Hartford, observed that the new mansion was coming along, then returned to England to do some research. He also delivered more lectures, his true bread and butter.

In 1874, back in the States and happy, he declared himself "the busiest white man in America" and claimed to be writing two novels at once. While the finishing touches were being put on the Hartford house, he moved his little family to Quarry Farm outside of Elmira. It was the first of many summers Twain would spend in this little piece of paradise. Livy's sister, Sue, had inherited the farm at Jervis's death and had a hilltop gazebo built, where Twain could spend his days writing. It was a productive summer. First, Livy (assisted by a female physician) gave birth to Clara, who weighed in at almost eight pounds; Twain dubbed her "the Great American Giantess." Daily, in his breezy studio far above the coos and cries of a newborn, Twain worked on *The Adventures of Tom Sawyer*, revisiting his boyhood days in Hannibal. After writing all day at a furious pace, sometimes fifty pages at a stretch, Twain spent the evening with his family. Sue and her husband Theodore Crane were progressive and intellectual; the two couples enjoyed each other's company. It was a good summer until the words stopped. "It was plain that I had worked myself out, pumped myself dry," he wrote to a friend.

In September, the Clemens family moved into their new house on Farmington Avenue in Hartford. The house was everything they had hoped it would be: one of a kind, a source of curiosity in the city, and comfortable; the seven bathrooms even had flush toilets. The remarkable house was, as biographer Justin Kaplan described it, "part steamboat, part medieval stronghold, and part cuckoo clock." It was a three-story castle with turrets, balconies, a long porch, and an octagonal perch that Twain would call his "texas deck."

The dining room would see an endless parade of visitors, but the true gem of the first floor was the library, a long book-lined room with a glass-enclosed garden at the far end, filled with sunlight, plants, and a gurgling fountain. The second floor was devoted to a schoolroom for the children and to bedrooms. Susy had her own room; Clara was destined to share the nursery with Jean who would be born in 1880. The master bedroom would eventually feature a bed with angels adorning the heavy, carved oak headboard. Livy and Sam loved the angels so much, they reversed direction and slept so that they could admire them; the girls, too, as they grew, would be enchanted by

Credit: www.twainquotes.com, courtesy Barbara Schmidt

the angels, often dressing them in doll's clothes. The third floor was reserved for the author's study, an airy room with a small desk at one end and an oversized billiards table taking up the rest. Here, Twain would spend his days smoking and writing, and his evenings smoking, drinking, and playing billiards with friends. It took seven servants to run the household. George Griffin, once a slave, showed up to wash the windows one day in the late 1870s and stayed with the family until 1891, serving as their intelligent, protective, and opinionated butler. Livy once tried to fire him, but he refused to go.

Although there would be long absences for lecture tours, Mark Twain now entered a seventeen-year stretch as the pillar of a New England community, churchgoer,

family man, and celebrated author. Wherever he found himself, he was the center of his universe; others would be drawn to that vibrant and vibrating center, or repelled, but there was no mistaking it.

No one in the Nook Farm community locked their doors or needed to, except occasionally when Twain's neighbor, Harriet Beecher Stowe, wandered through their houses uninvited. Creativity and industry were in the air in Hartford. Twain was accepted into the Monday Evening Club, an invitation-only discussion group for the intellectual men of the city. Hartford was a stimulating place for a writer, but the Farmington Avenue house generated its own atmosphere of creative hijinks. The girls both demanded and provided entertainment in the Clemens' household. Often, before going to bed, the girls begged their father to make up a story using the items on the library mantelpiece, in order. Dark-eyed Susy, the oldest, was moody and creative. When she was thirteen, "the busiest bee in the household hive," she wrote a biography of her father. Delighted, he included whole passages from it in his own writing.

For a time, Hartford was the perfect home base, but something happened the week before Christmas, 1877, that prompt-

ed Twain to want to get out of town. He was an invited guest at the seventieth birthday party for esteemed New England poet John Greenleaf Whittier at a ritzy hotel in Boston. Twain delivered what was intended to be a humorous speech, poking fun at the literary giants in attendance that night. He later remembered that, not only did no one laugh, no one smiled. "The expression of interest in the faces turned to a sort of black frost." Within days, he wrote letters of apology to the key figures, but remained haunted by this public humiliation. Several days after Christmas he wrote to a friend, "Ah, well, I am a great & sublime fool. But then, I am God's fool, & all His works must be contemplated with respect."

Suddenly, he longed for anonymity. He wrote to Mother Fairbanks, "I want to find a German village where nobody knows my name or speaks any English." He packed up Livy and the girls and set sail for Germany. Now, he craved order, and this country was nothing if not orderly. "What a paradise," he wrote. By May, Twain had begun jotting sketches that would become the basis for *A Tramp Abroad*. He sent for his friend and pastor, Joe Twichell, paying all expenses. With Livy and the girls secure in Baden-Baden, Sam and Joe toured Germany and Switzerland.

After Twichell returned to the States, Twain and his family toured Geneva, Venice, Florence, and Rome before settling into Munich for the winter. In February 1879, he moved the family to Paris. It had seemed like a good idea, but the city was noisy and the weather was rainy. Twain developed rheumatism and dysentery and spent five weeks in bed. Despite setbacks, by the end of May Twain had written over two-thousand pages of *A Tramp Abroad*. After more touring, the family summered in England. Like Livy, Twain was finally homesick, yearning for "fried chicken, corn bread, *real* butter . . . *good* roast beef with *taste* to it." It was time to go home.

He arrived in New York City at the beginning of September, with his wife, two children, twenty-two freight boxes, and twelve trunks. This did not count the carved oak bed from Venice and other furniture that had been shipped ahead. Livy set about hiring servants, opening the house, decorating, renovating, and hosting dinner parties, while Twain labored over the *Tramp Abroad* manuscript.

Bogged down, he was happy-then-hesitant-then-happy-again for an excuse to go to Chicago where Ulysses S. Grant was being honored. Twain, the fifteenth and final after-dinner speaker, didn't stand to speak until 2:00 A.M., but his speech rocked the house. There was one other speech of note that season, at a birthday breakfast honoring Oliver Wendell Holmes on his seventieth birthday. It had been almost two years since Twain had bombed at Whittier's birthday celebration. He redeemed himself with an appropriately humorous and elegant speech. America's literary lions quietly nodded their approval. Mark Twain was back.

# The Gilded Age:
# A Tale of To-day

· · · · · · · · · · ·

**Setting: Tennessee, Missouri**
**Period: Late 1840s through mid-1870s**

How better to work through resentment toward your father than by making him a character in your first novel? Like John Clemens, Si Hawkins will torment his children with an inheritance of Tennessee Land, and with it, the curse of wealth, always just out of reach. He will be dead when the land is finally sold for taxes.

As the story opens, Si Hawkins, known as "Squire" in impoverished Obedstown,

Tennessee, is lured to Missouri by Colonel Sellers, an old friend. Hawkins packs up his wife; two children, Emily and Washington; two slaves; and his dogs. Along the way, the kind-hearted Hawkins adopts a boy, Clay, whose mother has just died; and a girl, Laura, who has survived a fiery steamboat accident and is presumed orphaned. The hearty, optimistic dreamer, Colonel Sellers, meets the growing family in a forlorn backwoods settlement in Missouri.

Within mere sentences, ten years have passed. Laura Hawkins, a name borrowed from Twain's childhood sweetheart, has become a budding beauty. Si Hawkins and Sellers have made and lost fortunes several times over. On his deathbed, Hawkins admonishes his children "Never lose sight of the Tennessee Land!" Before long, papers are discovered revealing that beautiful Laura was adopted. She is surprised at the news and shocked to learn that her natural father survived the steamboat accident, but has never been told about her. The Hawkins family moves to Hawkeye near the ever-optimistic and bombastic Colonel Sellers who, penniless, is able to feed his family little more than turnips and water.

Two graduates of Yale enter the story: Philip Sterling and Harry Brierly. They have decided to head for Missouri to make their fortune. On the way, they meet Colonel Sellers, who is full of big talk and get-rich-quick schemes. While Philip writes affectionate letters to Ruth Bolton, a Philadelphia Quaker girl who plans to study medicine, Harry is increasingly involved in Sellers's schemes.

A few more years pass. The War Between the States is over. Laura had left home, fallen in love with a Confederate colonel named Selby, and married him. When she learned that her "husband" was already married, however, she returned home to Hawkeye with a broken heart, telling only her mother and brother about the sham marriage. Harry Brierly is still in town, working on a petition for Congress, and they flirt, but Laura dreams of going to Washington, D.C.

Senator Dilworthy visits Missouri, meets the Hawkins family, and invites Washington and Laura to visit him in the capital. The scenes alternate between Missouri and Washington, D.C., where Washington Hawkins, thrilled with political intrigue, becomes Dilworthy's secretary, and gets tangled up in working on get-rich-quick schemes and the petition to Congress with Colonel Sellers and Brierly. Philip Sterling, a hard worker, grows increasingly wary of the river schemes and turns to mining a vein of coal running through Pennsylvania land belonging to his sweetheart's father. For Sellers, Hawkins, and Brierly, everything unravels after a work stoppage, loss of funders, and bad news about the railroad.

Laura finally makes it to D.C. where she soon makes a stir in high society. Soon, the town is buzzing about the "landed heiress" from a powerful Western family. A rising star, Laura charms the members of Congress and engages in sparkling conversation, hoping to influence votes primarily for the bill concerning the Tennessee land. One day, however, her old heartbreaker, Selby, walks into a reception and, seeing him, Laura makes a quick exit, telling her bewildered brother, "The scoundrel lives, and dares to come here. I ought to kill him."

Meanwhile, Harry Brierly, still wheeling and dealing with Sellers, falls in love with Laura who engages in blackmail for passage of her pet bill. Philip Sterling hurries to Washington to warn Harry that this femme fatale is bad news, but he is too late. Shortly after the House of Representatives passes the bill, it is discovered that Laura has persuaded Harry to accompany her on a trip to New York in hot pursuit of Selby. Philip's worst fears are confirmed when he sees a newspaper headline: SHOCKING MURDER!!! TRAGEDY IN HIGH LIFE!! A BEAUTIFUL WOMAN SHOOTS A DISTINGUISHED CONFEDERATE SOLDIER.

Harry, present when Laura shot the Colonel, has been arrested with her, but Philip gets him out of jail and away from the sensational headlines to Pennsylvania to work on the coal-mining operation. Laura has the support of friends and family and the aid of excellent defense lawyers; the newspapers, too, have come around to a sympathetic stance on the brazen beauty behind bars.

While Harry is repeatedly called back to New York for the on-again-off-again trial, Philip continues to work on his coal mine. In Washington, Senator Dilworthy and Washington Hawkins work hard for passage of their bill in Congress. On the day that Laura is found not guilty, Congress votes down the bill, and Senator Dilworthy learns that he has lost his bid for reelection due to charges of bribery. Laura is supposed to be sent to the State Hospital for Insane Criminals, but is freed instead and goes on the lecture circuit, where she is inexplicably laughed off the stage on the night of her first lecture. The next morning, she is found in her room, dead of heart failure.

The book, nonetheless, ends on a happy note. Philip Sterling, who has almost given up hope of finding coal, finds it, and he and Ruth profess their love for each other. The two begin to make plans for the future, grateful that they are not loveless and lonely.

### The Story behind the Story

One evening, in early 1873, Sam and Livy entertained their friends Susan and Charles Dudley Warner. When the two men began teasing their wives about the novels they read, Susan and Livy challenged their husbands to write a better one. The men accepted the challenge and began to collaborate on a novel, each writing a set of interlaced chapters. According to Twain biographer Ron Powers: "The two would read their work to the wives each week, and challenge them to guess which part was written by which husband."

What is most significant about this novel, part epic saga, part political satire, is the title; one that named the era it described. It reveals the American Dream as one that squeezes the life out of the dreamers. The death-grip of capitalism is played out in Washington, with its greed, corruption, and sexual intrigue; then, and, sadly, now.

# A Little Bit of Porn
# for the Pastor

· · · · · · · · · · ·

In 1876, Twain was immersed in research which would inform both *The Prince and the Pauper* and *A Connecticut Yankee in King Arthur's Court*. Steeped in the history of Britain, from the days of legendary King Arthur to the heady days of Shakespeare, Twain was shocked to learn that bawdy puns had not been reserved only for the stage, but were common in the conversations of the people. Delighted, Twain practiced the rhythms and tone of indelicate dialogue in the form of a letter addressed to his best friend, the Reverend Joseph Twichell.

Twain had met Twichell in 1868, while he was still courting Livy. Smart, handsome, and virile, Joe Twichell had served as a Civil War chaplain. He was assigned to the fierce New York Zouaves, a unit modeled on the legendary French colonial troops known as dashing daredevils. Initially shocked by the coarseness of the Zouaves, Twichell learned to love these boys, who fought courageously for the Union.

After the war, Twichell was assigned the pastorship at the upscale Asylum Hill Congregational Church in Hartford. At a reception in October, 1868, he overheard Mark Twain make a wisecrack about the "Church of the Holy *Speculators.*" The two were introduced moments later, and a life-long friendship began. Twichell was a pastor Twain could respect, one who enjoyed the challenges of a questioning mind. The two regularly hiked ten miles on Saturday mornings and discussed religion and ethics. The pastor appreciated his parishioner who never ceased to wrestle with his faith while relentlessly mocking organized religion. A companion at the big junctures in Twain's life, Twichell officiated at Twain's wedding, was his traveling companion in Bermuda and Europe, (he's thinly disguised as Mr. Harris in *A Tramp Abroad*), presided at Clara's wedding, and officiated at the funerals of Susy, Livy, Jean, and of Twain, himself.

But in 1876, Joe Twichell was a young pastor in well-manicured Hartford. Twain, needing to "practice my archaics," wrote a bit of lurid dialogue imaged from an Elizabethan point of view. In the sketch, which Twain titled "1601: Conversation as

It Was by the Social Fireside, in the Time of the Tudors," Queen Elizabeth, entertaining friends in her royal parlor, asks who is the one who did "breake wind?" After some coarse talk about the "thunderguft," Sir Walter Raleigh confesses to the indiscretion, then produces a repeat fart. From this crude set-up, the sketch turns more sexually explicit. Twain put the whole thing in an envelope and sent it off to the Reverend. That fall, when the humorist and his pastor resumed their Saturday morning hikes, they read aloud from the letter and laughed themselves silly.

Twichell, it seems, never could keep a secret, not a great trait in a pastor; he showed the letter to a friend, who enjoyed it so much that he dropped it in the aisle of a smoking car just to watch it being passed from one hand to another. That same friend copied the pages, and sent one set to a rabbi in Albany, another to a friend in Japan. And this is how the letter, originally unsigned by Twain, became an underground classic. One fan told Twain, "Your *Innocents Abroad* will presently be forgotten, but this will survive."

# The Adventures of Tom Sawyer

. . . . . . . . . . .

Setting: St. Petersburg, Missouri, and
environs
Period: Before the Civil War, ca. 1834

"Tom!" This is the book that famously opens with a one-word exclamation, naming the boy who will fill our universe for pages to come.

Life is a game to Tom Sawyer, and we know this from the opening paragraph. Aunt Polly is calling for her dead sister's son, now in her charge, but he is a slippery kid, always just out of reach. Tom, a prankster "with his mouth full of harmony and his soul full of gratitude," lives in a world of rules, all meant to be broken. He tries the patience of everyone around him, including his younger half-brother Sid and his cousin Mary.

When Aunt Polly gives him the chore of whitewashing the fence one day, life suddenly seems hollow and "existence but a burden" to Tom, but as the neighborhood boys begin to file by, choreless, he slyly pretends that the task of whitewashing is the greatest joy of his life. Suddenly, all the boys beg to take a turn and are willing to pay Tom for the privilege with whatever they have to barter. Feigning reluctance, Tom gives up the brush and sits in the shade, looking over his prizes: an apple, a kite, a dead rat and a string to swing it with, marbles, a key, chalk, a tin soldier, firecrackers, a one-eyed kitten, a brass doorknob. With his chore so cleverly completed, Tom is free to play, but just then he spots an angel, Becky Thatcher, a "lovely, little blue-eyed creature with yellow hair plaited into two long tails." Fickle Tom is immediately over Amy Lawrence, his old girlfriend.

His heart, now and forever, belongs to Becky.

The next day, Sunday school is unusually eventful, due to the arrival of the impressive Thatcher family. Everyone shows off for the judge, especially Tom, who has enough loot, accrued the day before, to illicitly trade for the coveted tickets rewarded for memorizing Scripture. Tom beams as a Bible is presented, but when the judge asks him to name two of the twelve disciples, he blurts out his best, albeit wildly wrong, guess: David and Goliath. Later, he sulks through the church service, famously distracting himself with the antics of a pinch bug.

The next morning, though he tries desperately to find reasons not to go, Tom is sent to school. On the way, he meets Huckleberry Finn in his "gaudy outcast condition," swinging a dead cat. He is the son of the town drunkard; feared by mothers, admired by boys. Tom and Huck discuss ways to cure warts. The best way, according to Huck, is to take a dead cat to the grave of a wicked person, and, at midnight, chant, "Devil follow corpse, cat follow devil, warts follow cat, I'm done with ye!" The boys agree to meet later that night and try the dead-cat cure.

All this negotiating has made Tom late for school. As punishment, he is whipped and sent to sit with the girls, right next to Becky. By that afternoon, Tom and Becky have confessed their undying love for each other, until Tom lets it slip that he has been engaged before. When Becky begins to cry, Tom runs away to the woods behind the Widow Douglas's mansion, where he fantasizes how nice it would be to "die temporarily" or become a soldier or a pirate, or join the Indians or the circus.

That night, Tom hears the signal from Huck, a long "meow," and slips out of the house. Huck has brought the dead cat and, the two boys make their way to the graveyard. No sooner do they get there, than three gravediggers arrive: an old drunk named Muff Potter; Injun Joe, known to the boys as "that murderin' half-breed;" and young Dr. Robinson. Tom and Huck watch in the moonlight as the three men extricate a corpse and wrap it in a blanket. Suddenly, Injun Joe, who has been nursing a five-year grudge, turns and threatens the doctor, and, in moments, all three men are going at it. The doctor hits Potter on the head with a gravestone, then Injun Joe picks up Potter's knife and stabs Robinson in the chest. The bleeding doctor falls on top of Potter and dies. Before Potter regains consciousness, Joe plants the bloody knife in the drunk's right hand. When Potter wakes up, Joe is murmuring "What did you do it for?"

Muff Potter is too drunk and disoriented to remember what really happened, but Tom and Huck, hiding nearby, know everything. In horror, the two boys run out of the graveyard to the old tannery where Tom writes out an agreement on a pine shingle: HUCK FINN AND TOM SAWYER SWEARS THEY WILL KEEP MUM ABOUT THIS AND THEY WISH THEY MAY DROP DOWN DEAD IN THEIR TRACKS IF THEY EVER TELL AND ROT. After Tom shows Huck how to form an H and an F, they sign their initials in blood.

The whole town comes alive with gossip about the open-and-shut case against Potter, but Tom is wracked with guilt. He sees the murder in his nightmares and mutters in his sleep, "it's blood, it's blood." Aunt Polly, concerned about Tom, tries to cure what ails him with a variety of treatments, including a new medicine called simply the "Painkiller," which is "fire in liquid form." Tom pours a spoonful of

Painkiller into the mouth of Peter the cat, who goes berserk, leaping and yeowling. Aunt Polly is dismayed at Tom's cruelty, but when he says, "I done it out of pity – because he hadn't any aunt," she feels remorse for her own lack of pity.

At school, Becky Thatcher dismisses Tom as a show off, and he decides that he will turn to a life of crime. Tom and his buddies Joe Harper and Huck Finn agree to run away and become pirates. That night, the boys climb aboard a raft, with Tom in command, barking orders. Minutes later, they reach Jackson's Island. For the next few days, the boys live as they imagine pirates would. When their raft comes unmoored and floats away, they don't care: they are planning to live out their days on Jackson's Island, free and happy, with no one to tell them what to do. By the second afternoon, however, an "undefined longing" begins to creep into the stillness. The boys are already homesick, though none will admit to this.

The three pirate-boys are jarred from their lonely revery by a loud boom in the distance. It is not thunder, but the sound of a cannon, used to make a drowned body rise to the surface of the water. They realize that the hunt is probably for them. Far from feeling remorse, the boys are triumphant; they are the center of attention in abstention, heroes, missed and mourned.

That night, Tom slips out of camp and surreptitiously returns to his aunt's house. Peeking through the window, he sees Aunt Polly, Sid, cousin Mary, and Joe Harper's mother deep in conversation. He slips into the house and eavesdrops, listening to the weeping women discuss plans for the boys' funeral. Touched by Aunt Polly's grief, Tom almost leaves a message, but at the last minute changes his mind. Returning to Jackson's Island, he must use

every ploy to keep his friends from giving up the pirate's life. Reassured that Tom has a big plan, they agree to stay the night, smoking and bragging through an all-out thunderstorm.

The next morning, the church bells toll as the villagers gather for the funeral where the lost boys are remembered fondly, their pranks turned into noble episodes. Just as the entire assembly succumbs to anguished sobs, the minister stops, mid-sentence, transfixed at the sight of the three dead boys marching up the church aisle.

By Monday, the mood has shifted from gratitude that the boys are miraculously alive, to resentment that the boys could be so cruel to their loved ones. Tom, ever the master of spin control, tells Aunt Polly that he almost left a note of reassurance for her. The tormented aunt looks through Tom's pockets and is relieved when she finds a scrap of sycamore with Tom's undelivered message: WE AIN'T DEAD – WE ARE ONLY OFF BEING PIRATES.

At school, Tom has returned with a hero's swagger, but, after a series of misguided moves designed to get Becky's attention, watches his sweetheart flirt with his rival, a "St. Louis smarty." The tables turn again, a few times, but the outcome is inevitable; by the time school is out, Tom has gotten an undeserved punishment and taken a second whipping to spare Becky who coos, "Tom, how could you be so noble!" All that is left to do is play a memorable trick on the schoolmaster on Examination Day.

Summer vacation wavers between being disappointing and disastrous. It only becomes lively when Muff Potter's murder trial gets underway. Tom is crazy with remorse and guilt; Huck Finn is bothered too, but both boys have sworn to keep their mouths shut, believing that to tell the truth would mean certain death at the hands of the vengeful Injun Joe. They visit Muff Potter in his unguarded jail cell on the outskirts of town, bringing him tobacco and matches, and wait, in vain, for angels and fairies to work some magic and right this wrong.

When the trial begins, all of the circumstantial evidence points neatly to Potter's guilt. His lawyer does not bother to cross-examine the prosecutor's witnesses, but, at the last moment, to everyone's amazement, the defense calls Thomas Sawyer to the stand. He swears that he was in the graveyard and witnessed Injun Joe, not Muff Potter, grab the knife. Even before he finishes his sentence, Injun Joe jumps out of the courthouse window and disappears.

Though Injun Joe lurks through his nightmares, Tom is now hailed as a hero. Huck, still sore that his pal didn't keep "mum" as he had promised, nevertheless agrees to go along to dig for buried treasure. After futilely poking around

the grounds of a haunted house, the boys enter, prop their pick and shovel in a corner, and climb to the second floor. Almost immediately, they hear two men enter the house. Peering through holes in the floor, they see that one is an unkempt stranger and the other is a Spaniard with long white hair who has presented himself in town as a deaf mute. When the "mute" suddenly begins to talk, the boys recognize his voice; it is Injun Joe.

The boys eavesdrop, while the outlaws plan a crime of revenge and dig a hole in which to temporarily stash some silver coins. Seeing this, Tom and Huck are elated, but when Injun Joe and his partner unearth a box full of gold coins worth thousands, the boys can hardly contain their excitement. Suddenly, Injun Joe spots the pick and shovel; putting two and two together, he concludes that someone must be hiding in the house. The boys freeze as the villain begins climbing the stairs, but, when the rotten wood gives way beneath him, Injun Joe and his pal decide to leave and hide the treasure in "den Number Two." The boys try to make sense of what they have heard and decide that "den Number Two" must be a hotel room. Using a process of elimination, the boys stake out the Temperance Tavern, where Tom finds barrels of illegal hootch next to Injun Joe, asleep on the floor, drunk in room number 2.

In the middle of this adventure, Becky invites her school chums to a picnic. That Saturday morning, chaperones accompany the children on a trip down the river. After playing in the warm summer air, the children explore McDougal's Cave, famous as a labyrinth of corridors, filled with stalactites, stalagmites, waterfalls, and pools. Tom and Becky soon tire of playing with the others. They wander down one path, then another, farther and farther into the cave, marking the walls with the smoke of their candles as they go. When bats swoop down at them, the children run deeper into the darkness of the unexplored avenues, until the two gradually realize that they are lost. What was once fun is now terrifying. Exhausted and hungry, their shouts for help go unheard. Soon, their candles burn down; they are left in utter darkness.

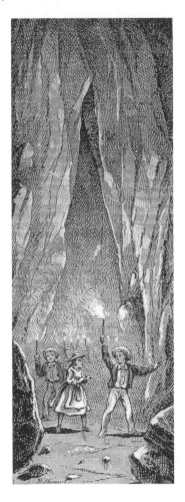

While Becky rests, Tom takes some kite string from his pocket, ties it to a stalagmite, and begins to feel his way in the dark, unwinding the string as he goes. At the end of a corridor he stretches to feel around a corner. Out of the darkness, not twenty yards away, a candle appears and illuminates a hand. Tom gives a loud shout; they have been found! The instant of relief vanishes when Tom realizes that it is the hand of Injun Joe. Tom is instantly paralyzed, but Injun Joe is not; he turns and runs, not realizing that the explorer in the darkness is young Sawyer. Tom does not tell Becky about who is lurking nearby. Weak with hunger, she prepares for death, but Tom begins unwinding his kite string again, determined to find a way out.

Meanwhile, back in town, Huck, not invited to the children's picnic, has been guarding the Temperance Tavern, just as he promised. At eleven o'clock, Injun Joe and his sidekick brush by carrying the treasure. Huck, walking catlike in his bare feet, follows them to Cardiff Hill and the mansion of Widow Douglas, "fair, smart, and forty." The evil plot is made clear: Injun Joe plans to commit a crime of revenge against the Widow in order to get back at her late husband, a justice of the peace, who once had him publicly horsewhipped for vagrancy. The bitter outlaw whispers, "I'll take it out on her." Huck sprints silently to the home of the Welshman and his sons and tells them that the Widow is in danger. The men grab their guns and round up a posse to guard the mansion where the unsuspecting Widow is in bed, curled up with a good book.

The next morning, over breakfast at the Welshman's home, Huck learns that the sheriff is searching the woods. When Huck identifies one of the villains as Injun Joe, disguised as a deaf-mute Spaniard, the listeners realize how serious the situation really is. Word spreads, and visitors, including the grateful Widow Douglas, come knocking at the door to hear the remarkable story. The Welshman gives all the details but one; he has promised not to reveal Huck's heroic role. After everyone else goes off to Sunday worship, Huck crawls into the bed, delirious with fever.

At church, Aunt Polly and Mrs. Thatcher compare notes and realize that their children did not return with the others. Suddenly, everyone is talking, not about the villains, but about the two lost children. A search party is sent out, but, apart from finding a bit of ribbon and the names BECKY & TOM written in candle smoke, there is no sign of the missing pair. By Tuesday evening, everyone is despondent; Aunt Polly's gray hair has turned white, and Mrs. Thatcher is delirious, repeatedly calling out Becky's name. The Widow, meanwhile, tends poor, bedridden Huck, but keeps the bad news from him.

It seems like a miracle when, late on Tuesday night, everyone is awakened by pealing bells and the shout, "They've been found!" After three days and three nights of hunger and fear, Tom had spotted a speck of daylight coming from a small hole in the cave near the Mississippi River, coaxed Becky out of the cave, and flagged down a passing skiff.

While Becky is put to bed to recover, Tom lies on a sofa and entertains half the town, embellishing the adventure and basking in the attention. After a fortnight, he is allowed to visit Huck, but stops on his way to see how Becky is coming along and learns that Judge Thatcher has sealed the entrance to the cave. Tom turns ghostly white and says, "Oh, Judge, Injun Joe's in the cave!" Once again, Tom, the Judge, and half the town set out for the cave, where they make a gruesome discovery: opening the iron door, they find Injun Joe, dead of starvation. Tom is moved to pity by evidence of the villain's last struggle.

Both recovered, Tom and Huck return to the task of finding the missing treasure. Tom has figured out that "den Number Two" must be in the cave; the boys return and explore the darkness with their candles. Eventually, they discover a cross drawn in candle smoke, and, though they fear Injun Joe's ghost, poke around until they find the treasure. Tom and Huck remove the heavy coins from the cave in bags. They plan to hide the treasure in the Widow's woodshed, but are intercepted by the Welshman who insists that they come to the Widow's mansion. There, Aunt Polly and important townspeople are waiting for them, and Huck Finn is greeted as a guest of honor; the Widow, having learned that he risked his life for her, intends to give him a home, an education, and, someday, a start in business.

Just then, Tom blurts out the news that Huck will not need all that help, because he is rich. He runs out and returns with a bag of the treasure as proof. All assembled are astonished at the sight of the gold, over twelve thousand dollars when counted, more than anyone has ever seen in one place. The judge and the Widow vow to protect it and help the boys handle it.

The story ends with Huck on the run, after three weeks with the Widow, unable to endure "the bars and shackles of civilization." Smoking behind the abandoned slaughterhouse, Huck offers Tom his share of the treasure, saying, "Being rich ain't what it's cracked up to be. It's just worry and worry, and sweat and sweat, and a-wishing you was dead all the time." Tom is sympathetic, but talks Huck into giving it another try, promising that, if he'll become respectable, he will be able to join Tom's gang of robbers. This is where we leave the two boys, for now.

**The Story behind the Story**

During the summer of 1874, boyhood memories washed over Twain. Each day, in his hilltop studio overlooking Elmira, he was transported back to his barefoot days in sunny, grubby Hannibal. Inspired to write *Tom Sawyer*, he scribbled an outline at the top of the first page as a guide. To those who know the novel, the outline comes as something of a shock: almost nothing here is recognizable.

*1. Boyhood & youth; 2 Y & early Manh; 3 the Battle of Life in many lands; 4 (age 37 to 40,) return & meet grown babies & toothless old drivelers who were the grandees of his boyhood. The Adored Unknown a faded old maid & full of rasping, puritanical vinegar piety.*

Outline be damned! The words tumbled effortlessly, as Twain wandered through recollections of childhood; Hannibal became St. Petersburg, and Glasscock's Island reappeared through the mist as Jackson's Island. Mother morphed into Aunt Polly; brother Henry lent his goodness and obedience to Sid. Poor, good-hearted Tom Blankenship was resurrected as Huckleberry Finn. Playmate Will Bowen inspired the character of Joe Harper. Anna Laura Hawkins, the sweetheart across the street, lived again as the little blue-eyed blond we know as Becky Thatcher. Hannibal's "Indian Joe" Douglas, a hardworking man, was nothing like the fictional "Injun Joe." Until his dying day at the age of one-hundred-and-two, Douglas denied that he was the model for Twain's murderer, but the people of Hannibal engraved his headstone with INJUN JOE in giant letters.

That summer of 1874, Mark Twain wrote four hundred pages at a rapid pace, pen flying; but, in September, the writing came to an abrupt stop. As if he had heard Hucky's secret "meow," Tom Sawyer skipped right off the page and "died temporarily," as he was wont to do. The following summer, Twain returned to the manuscript. He had been advised to let Tom grow up, but, back in his Quarry Farm study, Twain decided not to make the boy age against his will. With that decision, the adventures began to tumble forth again; still full of vim and vinegar, Tom returned, smirked through his own funeral, enjoyed a little romance and some real danger, and finished with a few gold coins jingling in his pockets. On the fifth of July, Twain completed the book. After months of revisions, *The Adventures of Tom Sawyer* was published in 1876, as the United States celebrated its centennial.

# Billiards (*Good*),
# Bicycles (*Bad*)

. . . . . . . . . . .

Bicycles were all the rage in 1884 when Mark Twain and Joe Twichell studied the art of staying upright. It wasn't pretty. Twain and Twichell wobbled and fell, time and again. In his humorous essay, "Taming the Bicycle," Twain wrote, "Although I was wholly inexperienced, I dismounted in the best time on record." He knew how silly a grown man could look on a wavering bicycle and used this knowledge to good effect in *A Connecticut Yankee in King Arthur's Court,* when five hundred knights arrived on bikes to rescue the king.

The "Noble Game of Billiards" was much more to Twain's liking. He may have first begun playing the game on his off-hours, while piloting steamboats up and down the Mississippi River. He played billiards with the boys in Nevada during his gold-rush and silver-mining days and wrote about playing in a "perishing saloon" at Jackass Gulch.

*The balls were chipped, the cloth was darned and patched, the table's surface was undulating and the cues were headless and had the curve of a parenthesis – but the forlorn remnant of marooned miners played games there and those games were more entertaining to look at than a circus and a grand opera combined.*

Twain told a story about a time, in Virginia City, when he was challenged to a game played for money by a stranger who volunteered to play left-handed. Twain accepted the challenge but lost badly, saying, "all I got was the opportunity to chalk my cue." He then turned to the stranger and said, "If you can play like that with your left hand, I'd like to see you play with your right," to which the man replied, "I can't. I'm left-handed."

In Hartford, a billiards table dominated Twain's top-floor study, while the writing desk was pushed up against the far wall as if secondary to the game. Susy wrote of her father, "Papa's favorite game is billiards, and when he is tired and wishes to rest himself he stays up all night and plays billiards." Years later, after Susy's untimely death, the game was his solace.

In 1906, Emilie Hart Rogers, the wife of Henry Huttleston Rogers (one of the wealthiest industrialists in America and Twain's rescuer and business advisor), gave the aging author a new billiards table as a Christmas present. In his letter of thanks, Twain wrote that the table was good medicine: "It is driving out the heartburn in a most promising way. I have a billiardist on the premises, and I walk not less than ten miles every day with the cue in my hand." The "billiardist" to whom Twain referred was Albert Bigelow Paine, who had just moved in to organize Twain's autobiographical writings. Paine would later write:

Illustration by John O'Brien

*The morning dictations became a secondary interest. Like a boy, he was looking forward to the afternoon of play, and it seemed never to come quickly enough to suit him. . . . He was willing to be beaten, but not too often. We kept a record of the games, and he went to bed happier if the tally-sheet showed a balance in his favor.*

On his seventy-first birthday, Twain played billiards with Paine the whole day and invented a variation, with rules that changed by the minute. In a speech, he once quipped, "The game of billiards has destroyed my naturally sweet disposition."

# Writing in Bed

. . . . . . . . . . .

## Where Twain Wrote and How

"THE TALE OF JOAN WAS BEGUN IN THE ANCIENT GARDEN OF VIVIANI."

Mark Twain's life was one steeped in storytelling. The young Sam Clemens spent hours listening to stories told by his lively, imaginative mother. On long, steamy summer evenings, he lingered at the slave quarters on his uncle's farm and listened to Uncle Dan'l's ghost stories and to Aunt Hannah, who talked of witches. Little Sammy soaked it all in until he could mimic adults' rhythm and timing, their long pauses and colorful expressions. He took in the textures, the undertones, the frame, the whole scene. He was in training to be a writer; he just didn't know it. Bathed in the oral tradition, he consciously immersed himself in the written word. He played hooky from school, more often than not, to find the quiet he needed to read. He learned what made a good story and how to transfer it to the page. Twain biographer Ron Powers wrote:

> For Sammy Clemens, reading became metanoiac, life changing. Words became objects of almost physical beauty to him, tooled and precise and as distinct from one another as snowflakes, each with its unique function and value in the universe.

## A Hunger for Words

Twain collected words the way some people collect stamps or coins, not only in English, but in other languages as well. While still a boy in Hannibal, he and a friend took German lessons from a shoemaker. As an adult, he became comfortable with the language, reading German newspapers and translating a book of children's verse. He wrote two contrasting essays: "Beauties of the German Language" and "The Awful German Language" and poked fun at the language throughout many of his writings. In *A Connecticut Yankee in King Arthur's Court,* Hank listens to a woman ramble on and on, and eventually realizes that he is "standing in the awful presence of the Mother of the German Language." In spite of his ribbing, German was a language that Twain loved. His own children became proficient in it, and he had inscribed on Livy's grave marker the German words, GOTT SEI DIR GNÄDIG, O MEINE WONNE! ("God be gracious to you, Oh my bliss!") Twain played with the languages he encountered on his travels and came to the conclusion that a gifted person could learn English "in 30 hours, French in 30 days, and German in 30 years." He had no use for the language of Hawai'i because "there isn't anything in it to swear with."

As a young man setting out in the world, his first steady employment was in print shops where he spent many dreary hours picking up tiny metal letters and placing them on trays, s-l-o-w-l-y forming word after word, phrase after phrase, sentence after sentence. After that, he scorned long words, favoring the ones with fewest letters.

> I never write metropolis for seven cents because I can get the same price for city. I never write policeman because I can get the same money for cop.

Though he did not care how words were spelled, Twain cared passionately that the right word be used in the right place:

> Whenever we come upon one of those intensely right words in a book or a newspaper the resulting effect is physical as well as spiritual . . .

63

When he was almost twenty, Twain began keeping a notebook, a habit that was reinforced when, as an apprentice steamboat pilot on the Mississippi, he was instructed to maintain a journal about the river. It would remain a lifelong discipline; he would fill almost fifty notebooks over time, with lists of new words, overheard bits of conversation, anecdotes and observations, ideas for books and stories to be written, maxims, musical notations, estimations of profits, lists of things to do, regrets.

Throughout his life, casual swearing (as opposed to angry swearing) was part of Twain's charm in person, but a detriment to his writing. Katy Leary, who worked for the Clemens family in Hartford, said that Twain's swearing was more amusing than offensive, claiming "he swore like an angel." In his writing, Twain sometimes tried to tone down his more colorful expressions in order to be palatable to the masses, and, increasingly, as bitterness lapped at the edges of everything he wrote, he would struggle with self-censorship. After finishing *A Connecticut Yankee*, he wrote to a friend,

*Well, my book is written – let it go. But if it were only to write over again there wouldn't be so many things left out. They burn in me; and they keep multiplying; but now they can't ever be said. And besides, they would require a library – and a pen warmed up in hell.*

George Bernard Shaw recognized the dilemma, writing, "Mark Twain and I are in very much the same position. We have to put things in such a way as to make people who would otherwise hang us, believe that we are joking." Twain kept the warmth and humor in his writing, edited

out as much of the hell and damnation as he could, and was ruthless with fluff and flowers, warning, "When you catch an adjective, kill it."

## How He Wrote

A journalist who visited Twain where he was holed-up in a city apartment, writing *The Innocents Abroad,* reported that the author's workspace was one of chaos: there were torn-up newspapers everywhere and the air was foul with tobacco smoke. It was not a pretty sight. In his autobiographical writings, Twain described the rush of words as he wrote this first book:

*I worked every night from eleven or twelve until broad daylight in the morning, and as I did 200,000 words in the sixty days, the average was more than 3,000 words a day. . . .*

We have a much calmer, more pastoral vision of Twain-the-writer less than a decade later, during the summer of 1874. Each morning, he would enjoy a breakfast of steak and coffee, then cross the field and walk up the path to his octagonal gazebo at Quarry Farm, a studio that resembled the pilothouse of a steamboat. Weighing down his papers with bricks, he opened the windows to help lift the fog of the forty cigars he smoked every day at his round writing table. He worked without stopping for lunch and so gave himself to his "hymn to boyhood," *The Adventures of Tom Sawyer.* Twain wrote and edited his work simultaneously, jotting revisions in the margins of his manuscript. He let intuition shape the book, with one episode leading haphazardly to the next. After writing his usual fifty pages a day, with seventy to eighty words on a page, he would read aloud to his family and friends. The words tumbled along, until the day they stopped.

That fall, he visited Boston where he saw a "type-machine" in a store window. After observing a demonstration, Twain shelled out one-hundred-and-twenty-five dollars, a considerable amount at the time, and returned to Hartford with his new toy. He practiced typing the first line of "Casabianca," THE BOY STOOD ON THE BURNING DECK, over and over until he could type twelve words a minute. Discouraged, he put it aside. Later, he hired two assistants to type *Life on the Mississippi* from the handwritten manuscript before sending it to the publisher, boasting that he was "the first person in the world to apply the type-machine to literature." As far as anyone knows, he was right.

In 1882, he began *Adventures of Huckleberry Finn* at Quarry Farm, and wrote,

*Why, it's like old times to step straight into the study, damp from the breakfast table, & sail right in & sail right on, the whole day long, without thought of running short of stuff or words. I wrote 4000 words today. . . . And when I get fagged out, I lie abed a couple of days & read & smoke, and then go at it again for 6 or 7 days.*

As always, he depended on Livy to weed out anything too extreme for the readers. Daughter Susy would remember watching her mother look over a manuscript, turning down the corners of the certain pages "which meant that some delightfully terrible part must be scratched out."

Finishing a book could be brutal. When he completed *Personal Recollections of Joan of Arc*, Twain compared it to the shock of entering a hospital room where a loved one has died.

*He steps into his study at the hour established by the habit of months – and he gets that little shock. All the litter and the confusion are gone. . . . The housemaid, forbidden the place for five months, has been there, and tidied up, and scoured it clean, and made it repellent and awful.*

## Twain's Pain

In 1891, the rheumatism in Twain's writing hand became so debilitating, that he tried to learn how to write with his left hand. Working on a novel, he experimented with the phonograph, filling four-dozen wax cylinders with dictation, long since lost. He found the process vexing: "I not only curse and swear all the time I am dictating, but am impatient and dissatisfied because God has given me only one tongue to curse and swear with."

Shortly after Susy's death, Twain immersed himself in writing *Following the Equator*. He wrote to a friend: "I do it without purpose & ambition; merely for the love of it." Twain found some solace in writing again after Livy died in 1904. A year later, Isabel Lyon, his devoted personal secretary, wrote, "Hours and hours and hours he sits writing with a wonderful light in his eyes." The words saved Mark Twain, time and again, as he dictated his life's story. In January 1906, when star-struck Albert Bigelow Paine stopped by Twain's Fifth Avenue apartment in New York City, he was ushered into the author's bedroom, where Twain was smoking in a bed strewn with papers and books. Bed, as it turned out, had become one of his favorite places to write.

The words kept coming until the summer of 1908, when he discharged his stenographer. Twain made one last notation in his journal – "Talk."

# Short Works of the 1880s

. . . . . . . . . . .

1880    "The Awful German Language" (Essay)
Twain makes fun of the peculiarities of the German language in this comic essay, originally published as an appendix to *A Tramp Abroad*. He complains that it has ten parts of speech, "all troublesome," and ridicules the length of the words, quoting from his notebook, "July 1 – In the hospital, yesterday, a word of thirteen syllables was successfully removed from a patient."

1880    "Edward Mills and George Benton: A Tale" (Short story)
This is a bitter little story of orphaned cousins. Adopted by a childless couple, one matures into a hardworking and fairminded adult; the other must be bailed out, time and again. Both come to a sorry end, but public sympathy lies with the troublesome cousin.

1881    "A Curious Experience" (Short story)
Reminiscing about his days in the Civil War, a major tells Twain about the time a scruffy kid showed up at a Union fort in Connecticut. Suspected of being a Rebel spy, the boy named names during interrogation. Only later did the major learn the truth; the boy was from a good but boring home, desperate for adventure.

1883    "1002d Arabian Night" (Short story)
In this burlesque, Twain offers a new ending to the tale of Scherezade, who postponed her execution by distracting the sultan with stories. Here, Scherezade begins a new story, about two children whose gender identities are switched at birth.

1884    "Taming the Bicycle" (Essay)
For eight days, Mark Twain and his friend Joe Twichell took lessons in bicycle riding, mastering only the speedy and inelegant dismount.

1885    "The Private History of a Campaign that Failed" (Story)
In this comic but damning look at the foolishness of war, Twain embellishes his own experience as a Confederate soldier in the Civil War, describing a

ragtag troop of Hannibal boys who practice their horsemanship by taking frequent rides to see their girlfriends and retreating every chance they get.

1886    "Luck" (Short story)

The luck referred to in the title belongs entirely to Lord Arthur Scoresby, honored as a military hero. In reality, he is a fool whose every blunder has a good result.

1887    "English as She Is Taught" (Essay)

This is a compilation (with commentary) of student bloopers, such as: "*Equestrian,* one who asks questions."

c. 1889   "A Majestic Literary Fossil" (Essay)

Twain maintains that his boyhood doctors would have been in agreement with a physician in ancient Greece, so little advancement had been made. A spurt in new medical information in the subsequent fifty years, however, has been heartening.

# Publish or Perish

· · · · · · · · · · ·

## Marketing the "People's Author"

"How much bucksheesh?" That was Twain's only question after his first book, *The Celebrated Jumping Frog of Calaveras County and Other Sketches,* was published with a gold frog on the outside and lots of printing errors on the inside. When *Frog* sold poorly, Twain feigned nonchalance, but privately he dismissed writing as a poor money-making scheme. His attitude changed when he met Albert Deane Richardson in New York City. A Civil War veteran, Richardson had written a book about his time in a Confederate prison. Published by a subscription company, the book had sold one hundred thousand copies.

Subscription publishing relied on traveling salesmen who ventured into rural areas. They pushed one title at a time, in advance of the actual publication, carrying enticing prospectuses to show off the ornate title pages, dense tables of contents, lists of illustrations, and samples of the text. Customers could personalize the books by choosing from an array of cover swatches. People who purchased subscription books primarily wanted impressive covers and bulk. If they had to shell out $3.50, they expected something to show for it.

Before the Civil War, most books sold by subscription publishers were Bibles and hefty how-to books on legal matters or medical remedies. After the war, however, with unemployed vets looking for work, the publishing companies branched out, promoting books about the war (like Richardson's) as well as biographies and travel books. The salesmen worked on commission, making as much as fifty percent of the book's cover price.

After his excursion aboard the *Quaker City,* Twain was intrigued by the possibility of writing a book that would make money. Visiting Hartford, a major publishing center, Twain was awed by the wide, tree-lined streets, the air of prosperity, and the utter devotion to capitalism. After meeting with Elisha Bliss, secretary of the American Publishing Company, he signed a contract to write a book about his recent trip and agreed to write six hundred pages. According to Twain biographer Justin Kaplan, the subscription publishing system, "conditioned him to think of his writing as a measurable commodity, like eggs and corn." He wrote to fill the pages, padding his books with wordy, meandering observations. Until the early 1880s, the American Publishing Company published Twain's major works, including:

- *The Innocents Abroad* (1869)
- *Roughing It* (1872)
- *The Gilded Age* (1873) – the first novel published by a subscription house
- *Sketches, New and Old* (1875)
- *The Adventures of Tom Sawyer* (1876)
- *A Tramp Abroad* (1880)

The relationship between publisher and author began to sour with the delayed publication *Tom Sawyer*. At the same time, Twain grew to trust Andrew Chatto, a partner in the British publishing firm of Chatto & Windus. According to Twain scholar R. Kent Rasmussen, "Chatto became a close personal friend, earning the distinction of being the only publisher that Mark Twain never turned against." As a result, Chatto & Windus published most of Twain's work.

For U.S. editions, Twain turned to James Ripley Osgood, a man with an eye for good writing. Authors valued his literary sense, but found his business sense lacking. Twain shared this perspective after James R. Osgood and Company published his works, including:

- *A True Story, and the Recent Carnival of Crime* (1877)
- *The Prince and the Pauper* (1881)
- *Life on the Mississippi* (1883)

Twain decided he could do better with his own company, so he founded one. Charles Webster was Twain's nephew by virtue of his marriage to Annie Moffett, daughter of Twain's sister Pamela. In May, 1884, Twain named Webster as manager, and the Charles L. Webster & Company began bringing out books, including:

- *Adventures of Huckleberry Finn* (1885)
- *Personal Memoirs of U. S. Grant* (1886)

Grant, who had served as Commander of the Union Army and the eighteenth president of the U.S., died shortly after the publication of his book. His *Memoirs* sold very well, earning his widow several hefty royalty checks, with money left over to cover publication of Twain's works:

- *Mark Twain's Library of Humor* (1888)
- *A Connecticut Yankee in King Arthur's Court* (1889)
- *The American Claimant* (1892)

- *The £1,000,000 Bank-Note and Other New Stories* (1893)
- *Tom Sawyer Abroad* (1894)

Bad luck and a series of poor decisions undermined the initial success of the company. Twain blamed his nephew for each bad break, but Webster's departure failed to save the company, which declared bankruptcy in 1894. Hat in hand, Twain limped back to the American Publishing Company, which brought out two more of his books:

- *Pudd'nhead Wilson and Those Extraordinary Twins* (1894)
- *Following the Equator* (1897)

By this time, the world had changed: few people were buying books on the subscription marketing system. Mark Twain turned to the solid Harper and Brothers, founded in 1817, which, for the rest of Twain's life, would publish his writings, including:

- *Tom Sawyer Abroad; Tom Sawyer, Detective and Other Stories* (1896)
- *Personal Recollections of Joan of Arc* (1896)
- *The Man That Corrupted Hadleyburg and Other Stories and Essays* (1900)
- *Extracts from Adam's Diary* (1904)
- *Eve's Diary* (1906)
- *Extract from Captain Stormfield's Visit to Heaven* (1909)

After Twain's death in 1910, Harper published his posthumous writings, including:

- *What Is Man? And Other Essays* (1917)
- *Mark Twain's Autobiography,* edited by Albert Bigelow Paine (1924)
- *The Autobiography of Mark Twain,* edited by Charles Neider (1959)
- *Letters from the Earth* (1962)

# The Prince and the Pauper

· · · · · · · · · · ·

Setting: London and surroundings
Period: 1547

This is the story of two boys, born on the same day, in 16th-century London. From the day they are born, their lives are almost polar opposites. The first boy is Edward Tudor, the only son of the king. At news of his birth, a holiday is proclaimed, and all of London is turned into a party. Colorful banners wave from the rooftops, and there is dancing in the streets. Baby Edward is wrapped in silks and satins, fussed over, and adored.

The other baby is born in a dark corner ofo the city called Offal Court, not far from London Bridge. There is no rejoicing at Tom Canty's birth: he will be just one more mouth to feed in the cramped, rented room he will share with his cruel father, frightened mother, twin sisters, and ill-tempered grandmother. Tom's father, John Canty, an alcoholic, makes his living as a thief, prowling the dark, crime-ridden streets. From an early age, Tom spends his

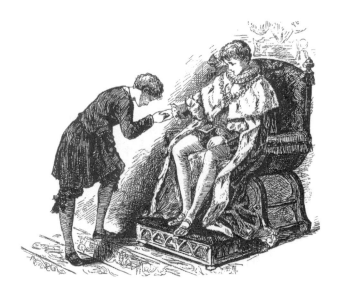

days begging and his nights dodging his father's fists. He survives on scraps and sleeps on a bit of blanket tossed over dirty straw on the floor. His only friend, old Father Andrew, has secretly taught Tom to read and write, and entertains the boy with tales of kings and castles.

One day, when he is fourteen, Tom finds himself in front of the palace. Hoping to catch sight of the real prince, he presses his face against the gate, but is caught by the guards and rudely tossed back into the crowd. Prince Edward happens to witness this and, on a whim, orders the beggar boy to be brought into the palace. Within minutes, the unthinkable has happened: the Prince of Poverty is standing face-to-face with the Prince of Limitless Plenty. Mutually fascinated, they swap clothes just for the fun of it, and only then do they realize the truth: they could be twins. As they stare at each other, the prince is outraged to see a bruise on Tom's hand caused by the rough treatment of the palace guard. The little prince hurriedly hides "an article of national importance,"

then flies off to reprimand the offending guard. To his horror, he is mistaken for the pauper and tossed unceremoniously into the street.

Now separated, the boys must fend for themselves in each other's worlds. Prince Edward embarks on a journey through a nightmare world of poverty, violence, hunger, and fear, experiencing, firsthand, the harsh reality of daily life for the masses. No one will believe that he is the Prince of Wales because, though he has the education, bearing, and speech of a prince, he is dressed in rags. Evicted from the castle, the prince runs to Christ's Hospital, established by his father as a refuge for poor children. The boys there laugh when he identifies himself and call out the dogs. Next, he limps to Offal Court hoping that the pauper's family will help him. Instead, the belligerent John Canty dubs him "Tom o Bedlam" and begins to beat the bewildered prince. One aged hand reaches out from the crowd to protect the child, and, in a blind rage, Canty turns and strikes the would-be helper with a violent blow to the head. The next morning, Canty learns that the man he clubbed was Father Andrew, who is now on his deathbed. In a matter of minutes, the family is on the run.

In the chaos, the prince breaks free from Canty, determined to resume his rightful place. When he proclaims his identity at the gates of Guildhall, however, he is mocked by the crowd. Only one man steps forward to commend the boy's spirit and courage; Miles Hendon, tall and muscular, his beautiful clothes in tatters and his sword rusting in its sheath. Miles vows to protect the boy. Just then, the crowd is dispersed by horsemen who are carrying an urgent message: the king is dead. The little prince shudders at the shocking news, repeated on a thousand lips, that his father has died. Miles guides the grieving boy to lodgings on London Bridge.

Meanwhile, Tom, the pauper, has also gotten off to a rough start. Hoping to avoid trouble, he has hastily confessed his true identity, inspiring the rumor, "The prince hath gone mad!" He is brought before the bedridden king, who tests Tom and is delighted when he shows a little knowledge of Latin. When Tom professes not to know French, however, the bewildered king commands those assembled:

*List ye all! This my son is mad; but it is not permanent. Overstudy hath done this, and somewhat too much of confinement. Away with his books and teachers! See ye to it. Pleasure him with sports, beguile him in wholesome ways, so that his health come again.*

Then, to Tom's dismay, the king orders the execution of the Duke of Norfolk, imprisoned in the Tower of London, so that the prince can inherit the throne without interference.

Tom does his best to fake familiarity with royal rituals, and members of the court graciously overlook his odd behavior. It is a different matter when he claims ignorance of the Great Seal. King Henry VIII, near death, wishes to address Parliament, put his hand on the seal, and finalize the command to execute the Duke of Norfolk, but Tom, pressured to "remember" where he hid it, is alarmingly blank.

During a sumptuous celebration at Guildhall, the stark announcement is made: "The king is dead!" At once, all assembled kneel, stretching their hands toward the pauper and shouting in one voice, "Long live the king!" Knowing he cannot dissuade the erring believers, Tom decides to use his new powers for good and issues his first proclamation as the supposed king:

*Then shall the king's law be law of mercy, from this day, and never more be law of blood! Up from thy knees and away! To the Tower and say the king decrees the Duke of Norfolk shall not die!*

Meanwhile, back on London Bridge, the prince has interrogated Miles Hendon and learned his rescuer's sad story: one about betrayal by a younger brother, Hugh; an ill-fated love with the wrong woman, Edith; and banishment by his naive father to three years military service. There, the multiply wronged Miles was taken captive and locked in a dungeon for seven years. Now free, he is on his way to confront Hugh, restore his good name, and receive his father's blessing. The prince (now king) is outraged by the misfortune Miles has suffered and feels indebted to his rescuer. He asks Miles to name his reward. Kneeling, Miles plays along, and, after citing a precedent, asks "that I and my heirs, forever, may sit in the presence of the majesty of England." The petition is promptly granted.

Miles hurries out to buy clothes for the fragile child who, he believes, lives in a "Kingdom of Dreams and Shadows." When he returns from his errand, Miles is shocked to discover that the boy is gone, having been lured to the bridge on the Southwark side. From the bridge, the boy was led to an abandoned barn where he was met by none other than John Canty, still on the run; in disguise, Canty has changed his name to John Hobbs. He gives the king, who he still supposes is his mad son Tom, an alias, too: Jack.

The young king, allowed to rest, cries for his late, dead father. When he wakes up, he finds the barn inhabited by a gang of loud and dirty outcasts and their chief, the Ruffler. Some have spent the day pretending to be blind or lame, but, here in the barn, they discard their eye patches and cast aside their crutches. The young king is moved to pity by the stories of hardship he overhears. Canty/Hobbs explains that the child believes he is the king of England; the vagabonds laugh and dub the king "Foo-foo the First, king of the Mooncalves."

The king is forced to travel with the tramps as they terrorize the countryside, but he refuses to act as decoy for pickpockets. During a moment of chaos, he breaks free from the thieves and wanders the land, begging for food and shelter; still dressed in rags, he is turned away with curses. One night, he finds shelter with a demented holy hermit, who restrains him and lifts a knife over his head. Both Miles Hendon and Canty/Hobbs show up, but, to the tethered king's dismay, Miles is persuaded to leave; the king is forcibly reunited with the outlaws.

One day, he is falsely accused of theft, arrested, and hauled into court. Just then, Miles Hendon reappears to save the day. The king and Miles head for the Hendon estate where Miles anticipates a joyful reunion with his father. Instead, he learns devastating news, that his father and brother Arthur are dead, and all but five of the servants are gone. Both Hugh and Lady Edith pretend not to recognize him: Miles is set up as an imposter. Then, he learns more crushing news: wretched Hugh has married Edith. Miles and the king are put under armed guard.

Lady Edith warns them that their lives are in danger but, before they can respond to her warning, the king and Miles are thrown into an overcrowded, soiled prison cell. People are paraded past the cell and asked if they recognize Miles. All deny him except one aged servant, Blake Andrews, who, after making his denial, whispers to Miles, "God be thanked, thou'rt come again, my master." He manages to smuggle in bits of food and information about what happened during Miles's absence from the estate. Andrews also brings the news that Henry VIII is to be buried at Windsor in two days and the new king crowned at Westminster four days later.

When Miles is tried and sentenced to sit two hours in the pillory, the king confronts the officer in charge and is seized and sentenced to be whipped. From the stocks, Miles insists on taking the whipping himself. The king vows to remember this sacrifice on his behalf and whispers, "Kings cannot ennoble thee, thou good, great soul, for One who is higher than kings hath done that for thee; but a king can confirm thy nobility to men." The king dubs Miles an earl.

When Miles is freed from the stocks, he is ordered to leave the region. He and the king head toward London, each with a separate goal: the king has written a paper in three languages to be delivered to his uncle, sure that his scholarship will be recognized. Miles wants to petition the new king, who is said to be a champion of the wronged. When they reach London Bridge, however, they are separated.

Back at the palace, Tom the pauper, now addressed as king, puts up with being dressed each morning by fourteen servants. In an attempt to lessen the impact of the rumors about the king's madness, a state dinner is planned. The public needs to see that the new king is competent. Tom is careful not to hurry or to do one blessed thing for himself and so passes as royalty. If only he could find the Great Seal everyone is fussing about.

Coronation Day is a glorious day for the mock king who is paraded past adoring throngs. Full of pride, he suddenly sees his mother: at the same moment, she recognizes a gesture unique to young Tom Canty, and sees, not the king, but her son. She throws herself as his feet, but Tom denies her, saying, "I do not know you, woman!" Now, though the crowds cheer for him, Tom can hear nothing but these words. Despondent, he is clothed in a gold robe and welcomed into Westminster Abbey for the solemn ceremony. Just as the Archbishop of Canterbury lifts the crown from its cushion, a voice of authority calls out, "I forbid you to set the crown of England upon that forfeited head. I am the king!" It is the ill-shod Edward VI, making his brave way down the center aisle. Guards rush to seize the intruder, but Tom cries out, "He is the king!"

There is great turmoil as both boys speak the same truth. Proof is needed that the new boy is who he says he is, and a test is devised: he is asked to tell where he hid the Great Seal. Edward is quick to answer, describing precisely where he left it. Lord St. John is sent to find it, but returns with the news that the seal is not there. Edward is about to be cast out of the Abbey once again, when he ponders aloud, wondering where the "massy golden disk" could be. Hearing the description, Tom finally knows what the Great Seal is and where Edward hid it. He prompts Edward's memory, until, at last, the king remembers. He excitedly orders St. John to return to the palace and look "in an arm-piece of the Milanese armor that hangs on the wall." Soon, St. John triumphantly returns, holding the Great Seal over his head. Tom sheepishly explains that no one had ever described it before; he has been using it to crack nuts.

The story ends happily, with Edward on the throne, doling out both justice and retribution. Searching for "the little lunatic," Miles is astonished to find his young friend reigning on the throne. As for Tom Canty, he is reunited with his mother and sisters, whom the king rewards for their kindness. Tom, granted the title of King's Ward, is given a position at Christ's Hospital and permitted to wear a royal costume, by which he will be known for the rest of his long and happy life.

## Story behind the Story

In developing this story, Mark Twain was inspired by a book for children authored by Charlotte M. Yonge, *The Little Duke,* and a story in which a prince is disguised as a blind beggar. Twain made it a double swap, then added humor and social commentary to the adventure. He based his story on a real king. When Henry VIII died in 1547, his only legitimate son, nine-year-old Edward VI, was crowned king as England's first Protestant ruler. Bright and well educated but sickly, he was only fifteen when he died and was buried in Westminster Abbey.

Twain began writing the story in the summer of 1877. Then, he put the manuscript aside to mature, happily returning to it three years later, after the tedium of writing *A Tramp Abroad.*

# Adventures of Huckleberry Finn

. . . . . . . . . . . .

Setting: Mississippi River and towns
along the shore
Period: Pre-Civil War, ca. 1835

We begin with Huck. This is his story, written, significantly, in his own voice. We have met him before in an earlier book, as he famously tells us in the opening lines.

*You don't know about me, without
you have a read a book by the name*
*of "The Adventures of Tom Sawyer,"*
*but that ain't no matter. That book*
*was made by Mr. Mark Twain, and*
*he told the truth, mainly.*

Huck reminds us of the fortune he and Tom found in a cave, which earned them each six thousand dollars in gold pieces. Since then, he has been adopted by the genteel and good-hearted Widow Douglas. She calls Huck a "poor lost lamb" and kindly but persistently encourages him to wear respectable clothes, mind his manners, and stop smoking. The widow's skinny sister, Miss Watson, has recently moved in, and she, too, tries to "sivilize" Huck. She relentlessly grills him on spelling and lectures him about heaven – where there is nothing to do but play the harp and sing – and "the bad place" – which sounds appealing to Huck because Tom Sawyer is bound to be there. She nags him saying, "Don't put your feet up there, Huckleberry," and "Don't scrunch up like that, Huckleberry." Miss Watson owns a big slave named Jim.

For several months, Huck attends school where he quickly learns to read and write. One day, he sees an unusual boot-print and realizes that his cruel father, presumed dead by many, is back in town. Huck quickly attends to business, negotiating with Judge Thatcher, keeper of Huck's treasure: the money is safe, but Huck is not. Pap shows up, "fish-belly white" and as evil as ever. He tricks a naive new judge in town, wins custody of Huck, and hides him in a log shack in the woods. A routine is quickly established: Pap drinks whiskey all day and beats Huck all night. A plucky if lonely survivor, Huck fears for his life and decides to run away.

One day, when Pap leaves the shack, Huck elaborately fakes his own murder. He smashes the front door with an axe; slaughters a pig and splashes the blood around; pulls out some of his own hair and sticks it on the bloody axe; and drags a bag full of rocks down to the river. After attending to every detail, Huck climbs into a canoe and sails away from Pap and from the "sivilizing" efforts of the well-meaning town folk. He has had enough of both.

For several lonely but peaceful days, Huck camps out on nearby Jackson's Island. He watches from behind a log as a cast of familiar characters, including Pap, float by on a ferry-boat looking for Huck's dead body. The boy soon discovers that he is not alone on the island: Jim, Miss Watson's slave, has run away and is hiding there, too. When they meet, it takes some time to convince Jim that Huck is not a ghost, not that Jim is afraid: "I awluz liked dead people, en done all I could for 'em," he says. Huck and Jim confide in each other, explaining how they escaped and why. Though slavery is condoned and endorsed by both church and state, Huck promises not to tell on Jim, even if it means being labeled a "low down Ablitionist."

They set up camp in a high cave just before a fierce storm shakes the island and causes the river to flood. In the next few days, many things float by, including a section of a lumber raft, which they salvage. When an entire house floats by, they go aboard and make "a good haul," finding a tin lantern, candles, knives, clothing, blankets, and other useful items. They also find a dead man. Jim protects Huck from seeing too much or identifying the corpse: it is Pap.

Eager to hear the local gossip, Huck disguises himself in a calico dress and bonnet and takes the canoe to the Illinois shore. Arriving at the house of a talkative woman, he learns that people along the coast are looking for whoever murdered poor Huck Finn. Some say it was the boy's own father; others suspect a runaway slave. The woman tells Huck that smoke has been seen rising from Jackson's Island and bounty hunters are on their way. As soon as Huck gets back to the island, he warns Jim, "There ain't a minute to lose. They're after us!" In fact, no one is after Huck, but with this famous warning, Huck ties his fate to Jim's. They are in this together.

The abused child and the escaped slave make their getaway on the raft and, for a time, the river is their universe. Jim builds a wigwam on the raft to provide cover from sun and rain, and to protect their things. Hiding during the day and floating downstream at night, they find life on the river peaceful for a time.

*We catched fish, and talked, and we took a swim now and then to keep off sleepiness. It was kind of solemn, drifting down the big still river, lying on our backs looking up at the stars, and we didn't ever feel like talking loud, and it warn't often that we laughed, only a little kind of a low chuckle.*

The river, peaceful as it is, is also a place of peril. When they come upon a wrecked steamboat, Huck and Jim climb onboard and find themselves in the company of two thieves who are plotting to kill a third. When their raft breaks loose and floats away, Huck and Jim are stranded with the felons on a sinking ship, but a stroke of luck puts them in a getaway skiff with the thieves' loot. They eventually recover their raft and watch helplessly as the thieves drown.

They formulate a plan: when they reach Cairo, they will sell the raft and buy tickets for a steamboat ride up the Ohio River to freedom. They pass Cairo in a dense fog, however, and then, for a time, lose each other when Huck takes off in the canoe. Returning to the raft, he convinces Jim that it was all just a bad dream. Confused, Jim proceeds to interpret the dream, until he realizes that Huck has tricked him. After a dignified rebuke, Huck hangs his head in shame. It takes fifteen minutes for the white child to apologize to the black man, but he does.

Huck and Jim do not realize that they have missed Cairo and are drifting farther

into the deep South. Jim talks about freedom and his plan of earning enough money to buy his wife and children. Hearing this, Huck again wrestles with his conscience. According to both church and state, it is wrong to steal or, in this case, to assist Miss Watson's valuable property in getting away. Huck gets into the canoe, determined to see that Jim is returned to Miss Watson, but Jim begins an exuberant tribute to Huck, calling him, not only his *best* friend, but his *only* friend. Soon, Huck's conscience pulls him in the other direction. At this critical juncture, two slave hunters with guns approach in a skiff. Huck makes up a quick story about his parents and sister, sick with the dreaded smallpox. As he knew they would, the slave hunters make a quick exit. Huck's lie has protected Jim.

The muddy Mississippi is suddenly full of danger and bad luck. Huck and Jim learn that they have missed Cairo; the canoe becomes unleashed and floats away; and the raft is destroyed when it collides with a steamboat. After the accident, Jim disappears, but Huck washes ashore and finds shelter with an aristocratic southern family, the Grangerfords. He introduces himself as George Jackson and enjoys the good life in a mansion filled with books and paintings, while Jim is rescued by slaves and hidden in a nearby swamp. Huck is shocked to learn that the Grangerfords are deeply entrenched in a decades-old feud with another genteel family, the Shepherdsons. No one in either family can remember why they hate each other, but they do. When the feud erupts into bloodshed, Huck witnesses the slaughter and, in the chaos, flees with Jim, back to the comfort and relative safety of the repaired raft.

After a few days of peace, Huck takes onboard two con men on the run. After concocting a variety of unlikely identities, they proclaim that they are each of royal birth: one is a duke and the other, not to be outdone, says that he is the "pore disappeared Dauphin, Looy the Seventeen." Gullible, good-hearted Jim is impressed by all this displaced royalty, but Huck knows that they are just "hum-bugs and frauds."

What follows are eleven chapters of adventures in towns along the Mississippi River, with Huck as a reluctant participant in a variety of cons, some silly, some serious. The king and duke fool a variety of audiences; they parade naked in a scam called the Royal Nonesuch and, in another scheme, present themselves as "world renowned tragedians," mangling Hamlet's soliloquy, passionately reciting, "To be, or not to be: that is the bare bodkin that makes calamity of so long life." In another con, the king attends a revival meeting and poses as a repentant pirate, ready to help "save" other wayward pirates. At the preacher's urging, the faux pirate passes the hat and returns to the raft triumphant, with eighty-seven dollars and a jug of whisky. By now, Huck and Jim, evicted from their own wigwam, are miserable.

Huck has convinced the swindlers that Jim is not a runaway slave, saying, "Goodness sakes, would a runaway nigger run south?" For Jim's safety, it is agreed that he must remain on the raft. For good luck, the duke paints Jim's skin blue, dresses him in a King Lear costume, and hangs a shingle on the raft bearing the legend, SICK ARAB – BUT HARMLESS WHEN NOT OUT OF HIS HEAD.

In their most complex scheme, the king and duke pose as the British uncles of three recently orphaned girls of the Wilks family and the rightful inheritors of the family's wealth. Huck, moved to sympathy by the vulnerable children, does what he can to foil the villainous plot. After many twists and turns, the con men's scheme is discovered. Huck escapes back to Jim and the raft, almost managing to leave behind the king and duke, but not quite.

The crowded raft floats past trees overgrown with Spanish moss, and the mock royal racketeers keep up their pathetic schemes, but have little luck. At last, broke and desperate, the two resort to their lowest stunt and sell Jim for "forty dirty dollars," claiming that he is a runaway slave from New Orleans. Jim is taken into custody at Silas Phelps' farm, two miles south of town, to be handed over to his rightful owners as soon as they can be located.

Distraught, Huck returns to the raft to wrestle with his conscience. By the dictates of both church and state, he should have contacted Miss Watson long ago with information about her runaway slave; not to have done so is both a sin and a crime. Huck gets out paper and pencil and jots a note to Miss Watson and momentarily feels washed clean of sin. Then, his heart pulls him in the other direction, and he reminisces about his time with Jim:

*I'd see him standing my watch on top of his'n, stead of calling me, so I could go on sleeping; and see him how glad he was when I come back out of the fog . . . and do everything he could think of for me and how good he always was.*

This is the moment of truth. "All right, then, I'll go to hell," he declares in the novel's most famous sentence. He tears up the note and makes a plan to steal Jim out of slavery.

Huck makes his way to the home of Silas and Sally Phelps, a "little one-horse cotton plantation," where Jim is locked in a hut. In a wild turn of events, the Phelpses are Tom Sawyer's aunt and uncle. They mistake Huck for Tom, the nephew they have never met but whose visit they have been anticipating. When Tom himself shows up, he quickly devises a scheme, assuming the identity of his brother Sid. Huck's plan to rescue Jim is quick and efficient, but is immediately dismissed by Tom who says, "What's the good of a plan that ain't no more trouble than that?" Tom labels the escape an "evasion" and outlines a farfetched scheme that ranks high in "style" because it is dramatic and risky for all involved, most of all for the prisoner himself. Once set in motion, Tom's plan

wreaks havoc in the Phelps' household, causes fear and panic throughout the slave community, and results in misery and torment for Jim. The slave's fate is in the hands of young, white boys who are playing games with his life, but he endures with dignity.

During the attempted escape, Tom is shot in the leg by local farmers. Huck runs for help while Jim, refusing to leave Tom, is recaptured and almost lynched. Recovering from his gunshot wound, Tom confesses all, explaining the mysterious thefts and pranks that he and Huck have committed while trying to mastermind Jim's "evasion." When Tom learns that Jim has been caught and is being held captive in heavy chains, he shocks everyone with news that he has been keeping to himself: Miss Watson, who died two months earlier, had set Jim free in her will.

To everyone's surprise, Tom's Aunt Polly shows up, reveals the true identity of each boy, and confirms the news that Jim is a free man. In what is almost a party atmosphere, Jim is brought into the house and given all the food he wants. With truths being divulged, Jim tells Huck that the corpse they saw on the floating house was Pap. Huck accepts this as good news.

The book's conclusion is sweet and happy, but open-ended. Huck's closing words suggest that there are more adventures to come:

*So there ain't nothing more to write about, and I am rotten glad of it, because if I'd a knowed what a trouble it was to make a book I wouldn't a tackled it and ain't agoing to no more. But I reckon I got to light out for the Territory ahead of the rest, because Aunt Sally she's going to adopt me and sivilize me and I can't stand it. I been there before.*

## The Story behind the Story

Twain kept Hannibal in his back pocket like a well-worn compass; whenever he lost his way, he would take it out and let it lead him home. During the summer of 1876, while America celebrated its Centennial, Twain was in a mood to reject the restrictions of polite society as he restlessly awaited publication of *Tom Sawyer*. Ensconced in his writing gazebo at Quarry Farm, he was once again flooded with boyhood memories.

Copyright © Dave Thomson

In "Huckleberry Finn" I have drawn Tom Blankenship exactly as he was. He was ignorant, unwashed, insufficiently fed; but he had as good a heart as ever any boy had. His liberties were totally unrestricted. He was the only really independent person – boy or man – in the community.

Twain remembered the slow, steamy summer days on his uncle's farm, the prototype for the Phelps farm, and Uncle Dan'l, a slave who lived there. In the autobiography, Twain would call him a "good friend, ally, and advisor" and describe him as a man "whose sympathies were wide and warm and whose heart was honest and simple and knew no guile." He lived again as Jim.

With Huck and Jim and the farm in place, he began writing. "I am tearing along on a new book," he wrote to Mother Fairbanks at the beginning of August. A week later, with hopeful excitement and confusing dread, he wrote to William Dean Howells:

> Began another boy's book – more to be at work than anything else. I have written 400 pages on it – therefore it is very nearly half done. It is Huck Finn's Autobiography. I like it only tolerably well, as far as I have got, and may possibly pigeonhole or burn the MS when it is done.

Fortunately, he did not burn his manuscript, but he did put it aside and fiddled with it in "fits and starts" over the course of the next seven years. During this long stretch, Twain traveled to Europe and back and wrote and published other major works including *A Tramp Abroad* and *The Prince and the Pauper*. In the spring of 1882, he returned to the mighty Mississippi and boarded the *Gold Dust*. He sailed to New Orleans, then went back up the river to pay a visit to Hannibal. Everything had changed except the mud: "It, at least, was the same," he wrote in his notebook. When he returned home to Hartford, the river was in his blood, and Huck was calling his name.

Twain finished writing *Life on the Mississippi*, then returned to Huck's story in May, 1883. He wrote to his mother, "I am piling up manuscript in a really astonishing way. . . . This summer it is no more trouble to me to write than it is to lie." It took until the next April to revise and tighten the manuscript for publication, eight long years after its inception.

*Huckleberry Finn* almost capsized again when an advertising sample had to be recalled because someone had altered an illustration to make Uncle Silas look like he had an erection. The "obscenity" was reported on the front page of the *New York World* with the headline: MARK TWAIN IN A DILEMMA – A VICTIM OF A JOKE HE THINKS THE MOST UNKINDEST CUT OF ALL. The presses were shut down until the defiled pages could be recalled and the engraved plate mended; then the book was on its way to publication. There is one other publication oddity: this great American novel, like its predecessor *Tom Sawyer,* was first published in England and in Canada.

### The Mystery of the Missing Manuscript

The *Huckleberry Finn* manuscript is famous for appearing and disappearing, as if in the mists of the river that runs through it. It was proclaimed "lost" the first time by the author himself. In 1885, James Fraser Gluck asked Mark Twain to donate his handwritten manuscript to the Buffalo Young Men's Library Association (later, the Buffalo and Erie County Public Library). Twain was honored and sent the second half of the manuscript with a note explaining that the first half had been lost by the printer. When the first half turned up two years later, Twain promptly sent it to the library. Gluck (which rhymes with Huck and bad luck), presumably intended to get the new pages bound, but died suddenly in 1897. The first half of the manuscript got mixed in with other papers, neatly tucked away in a big trunk. There they remained until 1990 when they were discovered in an attic in Los Angeles by Gluck's granddaughter. Opening the old trunk she had inherited from her family, she recognized a treasure when she saw one. First, she called her sister; then she called Sotheby's auction house. News of the remarkable find broke in 1991, to an astonished world. The *New York Times* put it on the front page. In July, 1992, the pages were ceremoniously reunited with the second half of the manuscript at the library in Buffalo.

### Of Critics and Controversies

The river of response to *Adventures of Huckleberry Finn* began pleasantly enough as a trickle of positive notices. Then, suddenly, the book drifted into the shallow waters of intolerance as some readers denounced Twain's unprecedented use of the vernacular, claiming that it was an affront to the public's good taste and moral standards. In March 1885, the Concord Public Library in Massachusetts excluded the book from its new acquisitions because, "all through its pages there is a systematic use of bad grammar and employment of rough, coarse, inelegant expressions." Other libraries banned the book, and Louisa May Alcott added her voice to the critics who denounced it as "trash of the veriest sort." Twain was both amused and bothered by the well-publicized objections, predicting that news of the censorship would sell at least twenty-five-thousand copies. He was right.

One reader's "trash" is another reader's treasure. The language, dialects, folklore traditions, warnings, and remedies used by Huck and other characters have been considered a treasure trove of Americana. Mark Twain listened to the voices of the voiceless and recorded them for posterity. Whereas some wanted to "clean up" *Huckleberry Finn*, new voices called out in the fog to defend the book and guide it back into the rushing waters of independent thought. By the time the second edition was published, it was being called a masterpiece. Over time, some of the world's most respected writers would sing the book's praises and write of its significance.

Credit: www.twainquotes.com, courtesy Barbara Schmidt

*All modern American literature comes from one book by Mark Twain called* Huckleberry Finn. ~ Ernest Hemingway

*Huckleberry Finn . . . was the first to look "back" at the republic from the perspective of the West.* ~ F. Scott Fitzgerald

*So we come to see Huck himself in the end as one of the permanent symbolic figures of fiction; not unworthy to take a place with Ulysses, Faust, Don Quixote, Don Juan, Hamlet and other great discoveries that man has made about himself.* ~ T. S. Eliot

As American readers, in both academia and in the wider population, continued to grapple with this strange and wondrous book, the culture changed and, with it, our reading and our questions. In 1945, the National Association for the Advancement of Colored People (NAACP) charged that Twain's book was a work with "belittling racial designations." By the mid-1950s, as the Civil Rights Movement rocked the nation, *Huckleberry Finn* was dropped from recommended-reading lists for middle and high-school students. Today, though it remains on library shelves, many schools across the nation discourage teaching it in the classroom.

"Nigger," an old word which has been offensive since its inception, is used over one-hundred-and-fifty times in this novel. What was Twain thinking when he repeatedly subjected his readers to this taboo word? Some say that he was holding up a mirror to America and saying, "take a good look." Slavery was a fact of life in Huck's America: the church preached it, the government endorsed it, the law enforced it. Nothing would have led Huck to question slavery, and yet, he does question it. We grow, with Huck, and slowly shift our point of view. We, the readers, are meant to contemplate our racially divided history, and to see ourselves on that small raft, black and white together, struggling toward freedom.

Huck's odyssey toward increased awareness of the evil of slavery is not unlike Twain's. The author confessed: "In my schoolboy days, I had no aversion to slavery. I was not aware that there was anything wrong about it. No one arraigned it in my hearing. . . ." Only in adulthood would

Twain question slavery, after marrying into an abolitionist family and developing close bonds with people who not only loathed slavery, but worked against it, conscious of the impact white racism had on American society. Twain's mind and heart were opened, old assumptions were reviewed and revised, and Huck Finn burst forth, a child on a journey.

It is precisely the word "nigger," an offensive, dehumanizing word that still touches a raw nerve today, that identifies the oppression of slavery and the slave-holding mentality. It is the word of America's national shame. Some readers have asserted that, by removing the book from our schools or the N-word from the text, censors are covering up the harsh, racist reality of American history. When Twain scholar Shelley Fisher Fishkin visited Hannibal in the summer of 1995, she attended a two-hour pageant about Mark Twain and his major characters. During intermission, she chatted with a local teenager who knew the pageant well and was told that Jim's character had been omitted, his lines given to white characters. Fishkin wrote, "In this 'delightful' pageant, the black presence in Hannibal and in Mark Twain's work was simply erased." Fishkin wrote, "A whitewashed fence is one thing, I thought. A whitewashed history is another."

There are others, however, who find that this grappling with American racism is a lesson that comes at too high a price, especially for black students. In a 1982 editorial in the *Washington Post*, educator John H. Wallace, conceding that the book has a place on library shelves and in college classrooms, argued passionately against the use of the book in middle and high school classrooms. He recalled his own sense of humiliation and embarrassment as a black student, forced to study the book.

*I maintain that it constitutes mental cruelty, harassment and outright racial intimidation to force black students to sit in a classroom to read this kind of literature about themselves. . . .*

*For years, black families have trekked to school in just about every district in America to say that "This book is bad for our children," only to be turned away by insensitive and often unwittingly racist teachers and administrators responding that "this is a classic." Classic or not, it should not be allowed to continue to make our children feel bad about themselves.*

## The Problem with the Ending

The controversy that leads some to label *Huckleberry Finn* a racist book, is compounded by the book's strange ending. The last ten chapters of the book, devoted to the freeing of Jim and commonly referred to as the "evasion chapters," have perplexed readers and scholars since publication.

In 1895, Twain wrote in his notebook that *Huckleberry Finn* is "a book of mine where a sound heart and a deformed conscience come into collision and conscience suffers defeat." Readers cheer Huck's "sound heart" and yet, the moment he appears, Tom Sawyer seizes the action, the voice, the style; we, the readers, are appalled to see Huck forget everything he has learned on this journey to nowhere. After standing up to the whole slaveholding society, Huck suddenly seems cowed by his reckless, self-indulgent friend. The same boy who saw through the crass hypocrisy of the king and the duke, himself plays duke to Tom's king and joins in causing all kinds of misery to Aunt Sally and Uncle Silas, certainly, but more significantly to long-suffering Jim. For his survival, Jim must endure days of psychological and physical torture, mindful that he is in the hands of two egocentric young teens, white and male. It is painful to see Jim victimized for the sake of a game; when we learn that he is already free, our outrage is complete. We close the book, feeling foolish and cheated. If Twain meant us to laugh, very few of us do.

How do we make sense of this? Some say that the author was too worn out to care how his book ended. Others, like scholar Charles H. Nilon, maintain that Twain intended the ending to describe, metaphorically, what was happening in the South while he was writing the book. The Civil War was over and slavery had ended, but Reconstruction was a disaster, with one concession after another robbing the black population of power, not unlike Tom and Huck's game of "freeing" the already freed Jim. According to Shelley Fisher Fishkin, "Faulting Twain for how his story ends is blaming the messenger for the message."

*What is the history of post-Emancipation race relations in the United States if not a series of maneuvers as cruelly gratuitous as the indignities inflicted on Jim in the final section of* Huckleberry Finn? *. . . Why were black Americans forced to go through so much pain and trouble just to secure rights that were supposedly theirs already? You think importing rats and snakes to Jim's shack is crazy? How about this: give blacks the vote, but make sure they can't use it.*

## Major Images and Themes

### The River

It is no accident that the story of "Moses and the bullrushers" is introduced in the opening pages. Huck is not interested in Moses, but we are. According to the Bible story, Moses was a child in danger, who floated down a big river, lived in disguise, took courageous action, and helped lead slaves to freedom; all of which parallel Huck's adventures. Our American Moses, however, is unaware, uninformed, and heading the wrong way.

The shore, in Huck's experience, is a place of extremes, where life swings wildly between gentility and barbarism, morality and sin. The river, on the other hand, is a place of freedom and movement, though not necessarily of peace. It is a place of floods, death, danger, thick fog, sand bars, and steamboats that crash down on smaller crafts. One can be lost, then found. The river is a refuge from trouble, but trouble can find you, even there. On the shore, even in the best of times, you watch your back. You do that on the river, too, but the view is wider. T. S. Eliot wrote:

*It is Huck who gives the book style.*
*The River gives the book its form. . . .*
*At sea, the wanderer may sail or be*

*carried by winds and currents in one direction or another; a change of wind or tide may determine fortune. . . . But the river with its strong, swift current is the dictator to the raft or to the steamboat.*

Lionel Trilling wrote that *Huckleberry Finn* is a book about a boy who loves the Mississippi River as one would adore a god, aware of its divine nature.

*After every sally into the social life of the shore, he returns to the river with relief and thanksgiving; and at each return, regular and explicit as a chorus in a Greek tragedy, there is a hymn of praise to the god's beauty, mystery, and strength, and to his noble grandeur in contrast with the pettiness of men.*

### Freedom

To the other boys of St. Petersburg, Huck represents the childhood ideal of freedom from adult supervision. He is free to skip school, come and go as he pleases, wear rags, sleep wherever he can. A free spirit, Huck is, nevertheless, not free to be a part of the community; he is always on the outside, looking in. As the story progresses, he seeks freedom from his increasingly violent father, as well as from the well-meaning town folk who have failed to protect him.

Jim urgently seeks freedom from bondage and from the imminent decision by Miss Watson to sell him away from his family. His dream is to get to a "free state." Jim and Huck are not free, even on the raft, but must travel by night, hiding from "civilization" by day. The raft provides an illusion of freedom, as it sails through America's heartland; but that heart beats a hard rhythm. David L. Smith,

an African-American educator and scholar, concludes:

*Ultimately,* Huckleberry Finn *renders a harsh judgment on American society. . . . Indeed, the novel suggests that real individual freedom, in this land of the free, cannot be found. "American civilization" enslaves and exploits rather than liberates. It is hardly an appealing message.*

### Family

Huck bounces from one family to another, experiencing a number of configurations, most of them unsatisfactory. He and Pap make a nightmare family, with Pap, a mean drunk, alternating physical abuse with neglect. Huck is invited to be part of the family of the Widow and her sister, Miss Watson, but this is a family with an agenda, the civilizing of a homeless child; it cramps and stifles. Tom Sawyer, though an orphan, is housed in a respectable family consisting of his aunt, a cousin, and a half-brother. It is a place where love is expressed through an abundance of rules and punishments. Huck is constantly calling Tom away with a "meow" at the window, and, time and again, Tom will answer this call to escape the confines of "family."

Jim, as a slave, is almost a peer to Huck, but, as they journey, he increasingly plays the role of parent and protector, sheltering the homeless child, greeting him with kind words. We learn that Jim is a loving father, lamenting an unintended act of violence against his deaf daughter, yearning for reunion with his family, willing to risk everything in the hope of that reunion. In a discussion with Huck, Jim is outraged by the biblical story of Solomon who orders a child cut in half to determine custody. Jim says, "De 'spute warn't 'bout a half a chile, de 'spute was 'bout a whole chile." The biblical story parallels Huck's situation, with the Widow on one side and Pap on the other. Jim is the true father, the one who sees and loves the whole child.

Huck washes ashore and is taken in by the Grangerfords who seem, at first, to represent the ideal of Southern gentility, with the patriarch at the head of a tight and loving family, one with proper manners and nice things. Ultimately, Huck flees in terror from this family, which is caught in a bloody feud. Later, Huck, passing as Tom at the home of Aunt Sally and Uncle Silas, finds a family that is homey and kind, albeit one that owns slaves. The slaves on this plantation have a network of extended families that suffer and sing, worry and laugh together.

Huck rarely finds a place to rest his head. He will hold them all at arm's length and, in the end, anticipate lighting out for the Territory alone, having long since given up on the notion of "family."

# Map of Huck and Jim's River Journey

· · · · · · · · · · ·

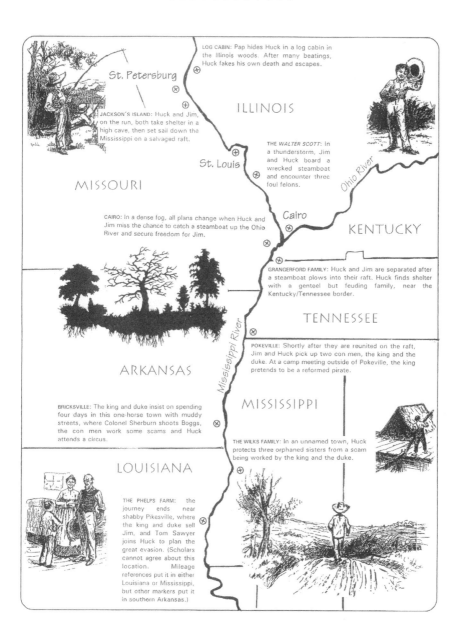

LOG CABIN: Pap hides Huck in a log cabin in the Illinois woods. After many beatings, Huck fakes his own death and escapes.

St. Petersburg

ILLINOIS

JACKSON'S ISLAND: Huck and Jim, on the run, both take shelter in a high cave, then set sail down the Mississippi on a salvaged raft.

THE *WALTER SCOTT*: In a thunderstorm, Jim and Huck board a wrecked steamboat and encounter three foul felons.

St. Louis

MISSOURI

Ohio River

CAIRO: In a dense fog, all plans change when Huck and Jim miss the chance to catch a steamboat up the Ohio River and secure freedom for Jim.

Cairo

KENTUCKY

GRANGERFORD FAMILY: Huck and Jim are separated after a steamboat plows into their raft. Huck finds shelter with a genteel but feuding family, near the Kentucky/Tennessee border.

TENNESSEE

Mississippi River

POKEVILLE: Shortly after they are reunited on the raft, Jim and Huck pick up two con men, the king and the duke. At a camp meeting outside of Pokeville, the king pretends to be a reformed pirate.

ARKANSAS

BRICKSVILLE: The king and duke insist on spending four days in this one-horse town with muddy streets, where Colonel Sherburn shoots Boggs, the con men work some scams and Huck attends a circus.

MISSISSIPPI

THE WILKS FAMILY: In an unnamed town, Huck protects three orphaned sisters from a scam being worked by the king and the duke.

LOUISIANA

THE PHELPS FARM: the journey ends near shabby Pikesville, where the king and duke sell Jim, and Tom Sawyer joins Huck to plan the great evasion. (Scholars cannot agree about this location. Mileage references put it in either Louisiana or Mississippi, but other markers put it in southern Arkansas.)

# A Whortleberry by Any Other Name ... or, What the Heck's a Huckleberry?

· · · · · · · · · · · ·

As early as 1670, American colonists began using the word *huckleberry* as a variation of *hurtleberry*, the common name for the whortleberry, a fruit similar to one they had known in Europe, native to North America, east of the Mississippi River. A huckleberry is little and blue, so blue, in fact, that it is often mistaken for a blueberry. When Mark Twain first arrived in Hartford, he saw children collecting huckleberries in buckets on the hillsides outside of town. He wrote, "I never saw any place where morality and huckleberries flourished as they do here."

The word "huckleberry" is a long word for something so little. By the 1830s, it was used to mean a tad or a small unit, a small person or someone of little importance. There is a home-grown American feel to the word huckleberry; it sounds friendly and sun-kissed, a little bit dreamy and drifty. By the mid-1800s, "huckleberry" was American slang meaning the right person for a job. "I'm your huckleberry!" meant, "I'm just the one you are looking for." "A huckleberry over your persimmon," meant that something was just beyond reach.

Our Huckleberry is a true blue American original, like the berry, unpretentious, earthy, and innocent. There is an "aw shucks" quality to the name Huck. No wonder it pops up now and then, as it did in the 1950s with the cartoon character Huckleberry Hound, an unhurried blue dog with a southern drawl, a homespun wanderer, perpetually looking for his place in the world, but never quite finding it; he usually came out on top through sheer luck or persistence.

In 1961, Americans were humming about a "huckleberry friend" after Holly Golightly, a lost waif in the big city, curled up on her fire escape and sang "Moon River" in *Breakfast at Tiffany's*. It was a melancholy song about a river and two drifters, and Johnny Mercer's award-winning lyrics left us dreamy and nostalgic for that friend, "waiting 'round the bend."

Which brings us back to our Huck, whose name rhymes with luck (sometimes he has it and sometimes he doesn't). Inevitably, the name "Huckleberry" calls to mind our nature-child, who survives on the margins of society, unspoiled, open, vulnerable, and wise. To some eyes, he seems small and insignificant, but we know that he is the right one for the job, a cut above the others, last seen floating through the bluish mist of the Mississippi.

# Huck Honey and Mars Tom

. . . . . . . . . . .

## Two Boys Together, Worlds Apart

Huck and Tom, two boys joined together in our collective imaginations, are as different from each other as "right brain/left brain." Jim, the escaped slave, knows this in his bones: his very survival depends on such discernment. He instinctively holds Huckleberry Finn close to his heart, calling him just plain Huck or sometimes "Huck, honey." Scholar Leslie Fiedler put a homoerotic spin on this in his notorious 1948 essay "Come Back to the Raft Ag'in, Huck Honey," but to most readers the familiar designation is understood to convey only a level of comfort, trust, and affection. Huck is "honey," but Tom Sawyer is "Mars Tom" which means "master," a title of presumed respect and a little fear. Tom is held at a distrustful distance by the slave.

Whereas Jim proceeds with caution, other characters see Tom as a smart-alecky scamp who frequently needs to be reined in. An orphan, Tom is part of a solid middle class, albeit fatherless, family. Aunt Polly's is a house full of rules; Tom will break them and take the consequences, safe in the knowledge that the boundaries and his battle with them define his place in the world. Huck is not an orphan, and that is his great misfortune. He has no mother, but he has a father, the town drunk, a brute. Huck is better off on his own, away from his abusive father.

Tom, a prankster, is not so much malicious as oblivious. He lives in his head, which is full of adventures borrowed from books. Huck's adventures, on the other hand, are real. He has little time for the romance of fiction. Fending for himself, he has to keep his eyes open, stay alert. Tom is the ultimate show-off. He takes comfort in bravado-laced death fantasies because he knows that he would be missed and mourned. Huck, on the other hand, never imagines himself as the center of anyone's attention, though the Widow Douglas and Jim are protective of him. He is a child so marginalized that he is easily mistaken for dead. Pap, hallucinating, thinks his son is the "Angel of Death," and, when Huck stages his own murder, it is not hard for the townspeople to believe that this abused child is dead. He is greeted as a ghost by Jim and later by Tom. Though he is a tough kid, his life is fragile. Huck knows solitude and loneliness, and finds death around every corner. He hears it when the breeze quivers the leaves, "as if long-dead spirits are whispering."

Tom turns life into a game, which is his privilege as a middle-class child. He is a born leader and a master manipulator, a profit-motivated capitalist, cleverly turning every situation to his advantage. Like a skillful chess competitor, he thinks several moves ahead, anticipating a variety of outcomes, all in his favor. This is the genius of the fence-whitewashing scheme and also why Mark Twain referred to Teddy Roosevelt, the imperialistic hero of San Juan Hill, as "the Tom Sawyer of the political world," and meant it as an insult.

Both boys are well schooled in frontier superstitions, but for Tom, they are part of the game; for Huck, they are rules to live by. When Huck is prevented from throwing spilled salt over his left shoulder, he knows that bad luck is around the corner. There are other causes of misfortune: Huck says, "I've always reckoned that looking at the new moon over your left shoulder is one of the carelessest and foolishest things a body can do." Huck and Jim explain most of the disasters that befall them as the result of Huck touching a snakeskin, "the worst bad luck in the world." There are a few signs of good luck; when a little green worm lands on Tom's leg, he anticipates getting new clothes, hoped to be a pirate's outfit.

Huck has empathy for everyone, even the many "rapscallions," crooks, and kings he encounters. He grows and deepens throughout the course of his adventures, but Tom does not: his conscience is engaged now and then, as when he risks his own life to tell the truth about Muff Potter's innocence and when he gallantly takes a punishment for Becky; but he is less consistent than Huck. His empathy is all but absent at the conclusion of Huck's book. A mischief-maker with a mean streak, he knows that Jim is already free, but withholds that crucial information in order to make a game of "freeing" him. Tom is the hero, director, and stage manager of this drama, more concerned with the props than with Jim, who suffers in this white boy's game.

In *Tom Sawyer*, Huck is a slow thinker. When he gets to tell the story in his own voice, however, we realize that he has an agile mind. A child alone in a harsh universe, Huck is shrewd, but he is not one for jokes: he never gets the punch line. When Buck Grangerford asks him where Moses was when the candle went out, Huck is clueless. Even when Buck gives the answer to the old riddle, that Moses was in the dark, Huck is simply confused, not recognizing a joke. He says, "Well, if you knowed where he was, what did you ask me for?"

For survival, Huck uses false names and story lines to get what he needs; information, shelter, protection. Tom, by contrast, is always "Tom" or "Tom Sawyer, the Black Avenger of the Spanish Main." A child in an adult's world, his name is sometimes, ominously "pronounced in full," as when the schoolmaster is about to dole out a punishment or when he is called upon in Sunday School or when he testifies at Muff Potter's trial. When Becky calls him "Thomas Sawyer," he replies, "That's the name they lick me by. I'm Tom when I'm good." At the end of his *Adventures* tale, Huck does not take the name of Tom Sawyer, but accepts it when the name is thrust upon him. Mark Twain scholar James M. Cox noted in an essay:

*There is bitter irony in Huck's assumption of Tom's name because the values of Tom Sawyer are so antithetical to the values of Huck Finn; in the final analysis, the two boys cannot exist in the same world. When Huck regains his own identity at the very end of the novel he immediately feels the compulsion to "light out for the territory" because he knows that to be Huck Finn is to be the outcast beyond the paling fences.*

Tom and Huck are depicted in a statue in Hannibal, sculpted by Frederick C. Hibbard and dedicated in 1926; one of the earliest statues depicting fictional characters. It shows Tom with a knapsack swinging from a stick over his shoulder, his body leaning forward into the future. Huck, however, is depicted with his hand on Tom's arm, as if he wants to stay in the present. Tom is eager to grow up and leave behind his pal who, like Peter Pan, will stay forever young. As critic Harold Bloom has written, "Huck is already his final self, even as a boy."

# Encounters with the A-List

· · · · · · · · · · · ·

There must have been times when Sam Clemens wanted to pinch himself to make sure he was not dreaming. Born in a shack in a two-bit prairie town, he grew up to hobnob with the world's rich and famous. This child of poverty, in turn, threw lavish dinner parties in his elegant home, where he regaled his guests with stories or songs. In 1892, amazed at the crowds that gathered around her father in Berlin, eleven-year-old Jean told Twain, "If it keeps on like this, there won't be anybody for you to get acquainted with but God." Below is a partial listing of names of noteworthy persons who encountered the remarkable Mark Twain.

- Alexander II (Emperor of Russia). In 1867, he received Mark Twain and other *Quaker City* passengers at his summer palace near Yalta.
- Matthew Arnold (English poet and literary critic). In 1883, Twain entertained the Arnold family in Hartford, but later publicly criticized Arnold's cultural snobbery.
- P. T. Barnum (showman whose traveling circus was billed as the "Greatest Show on Earth"). Barnum

lived fifty miles from Hartford; he and Twain visited and wrote to each other, and Barnum was referenced in a number of Twain's short stories.
- Henry Ward Beecher (orator, author, pastor of the Plymouth Congregational Church in Brooklyn). Twain visited the church in 1867 and later contracted to publish Beecher's book, a project that never reached fruition because of the pastor's untimely death.
- Sarah Bernhardt (legendary French actress). In 1905, Twain appeared with her in New York at a benefit for Russian Jews.
- Josh Billings a.k.a. Henry Wheeler Shaw (popular humorist). After they met on the lecture circuit in 1869, Billings and Twain developed a friendship. Twain included a number of his original writings in *Mark Twain's Library of Humor*.
- Robert Browning (English poet). Twain met Browning in 1873 and later led study groups on the poet's work.
- Andrew Carnegie (industrialist and philanthropist). Five *days* Sam

Clemens' senior, Twain tried to interest the steel magnate in investing in the doomed Paige compositor in the 1890s, but all he got was some advice: "Put all your eggs in one basket, and watch that basket."

- Lewis Carroll a.k.a. Charles Dodgson (British author of *Alice in Wonderland* and *Through the Looking Glass*). Painfully shy, he sat in silence when he and Twain met in London in 1873.
- Grover Cleveland (U.S. President). Shortly after he was elected to office, he told Twain a joke that later appeared in *Connecticut Yankee* as Sir Dinadan's "old joke."

Charles Darwin

- Charles Darwin (British naturalist who developed the theory of evolution by natural selection). Twain traveled to meet Darwin in 1879 and referenced his work in several short pieces.
- Charles Dickens (British novelist). Twain sat beside Olivia, his wife-to-be, to hear the author read from *David Copperfield*. Twain claimed that he reread *A Tale of Two Cities* every two years.

- Mary Mapes Dodge (author of *Hans Brinker, or the Silver Skates* and editor of *St. Nicholas Magazine*). Though their families summered together in the Catskills in 1890, the two had a falling-out after Dodge, who serialized *Tom Sawyer Abroad* in her magazine, corrected Huck Finn's grammar and removed all swearing and references to drinking.
- Frederick Douglass (escaped slave, abolitionist, journalist, and lecturer). Twain met Douglass in 1869 while courting Olivia. He later helped Douglass obtain a post in the administration of President Garfield.
- Thomas Alva Edison (über inventor). In 1888, Twain traveled to New Jersey to meet Edison and referenced him in a number of his writings. Edison, in turn, produced a short film with the only known footage of Twain.
- Edward VII (King of England from 1901 to 1910). The two met when Edward was Prince of Wales in 1892 and again at Windsor Castle when Edward was king.
- Ralph Waldo Emerson (transcendentalist, philosopher, poet). Hard-of-hearing, the poet took no offense at Twain's spoof at the 1877 Whittier birthday celebration.
- Maxim Gorky (Russian writer/activist, father of Socialist Realism). In 1906, Twain introduced Gorky at an anti-czarist fundraising dinner in New York, but distanced himself later because Gorky was traveling with his mistress.

Ulysses S. Grant

- Ulysses S. Grant (commander of the Union Army and U.S. President). Twain and Grant became close friends during the last year of Grant's life, when the ailing war hero signed a contract to have Twain's publishing company bring out two volumes of his memoirs.
- Horace Greeley (founder of the New York *Tribune*, abolitionist, and reformer). Twain attended Greeley's sixty-first birthday celebration in New York with other celebrity-intellectuals.
- Joel Chandler Harris (creator of "Uncle Remus"). Twain respected Harris's attempts at recreating black dialect in his retelling of American folk tales. After meeting in New Orleans, Twain described Harris as "the bashfulest grown person I have ever met."
- Bret Harte (author of frontier stories including "The Luck of Roaring Camp" and "Outcasts of Poker Flat"). Half-a-year Twain's senior, the two met in San Francisco, and Harte assisted in editing *Innocents Abroad*. In 1876, Harte stayed with Twain in Hartford and collaborated on a play, but the visit turned sour and the two

parted ways. Twain later wrote, "In the early days I liked Bret Harte and so did the others, but by and by I got over it; so also did the others."
- John Hay (statesman and author, President Lincoln's secretary and Secretary of State under McKinley and Teddy Roosevelt). Twain and Hay met in 1871, and they remained good friends.
- Oliver Wendell Holmes, Sr. (essayist, poet, physician). Twain gave Holmes a copy of *Innocents Abroad*, but later confessed that he may have unconsciously plagiarized the dedication. Twain spoke at a birthday dinner honoring Holmes, who later published a poem honoring Twain.
- William Dean Howells (critic, author, editor of the *Atlantic Monthly* [1871-81], and first president of the American Academy of Arts and Letters). Twain and Howells enjoyed four decades of friendship. Howells penned rave reviews of Twain's works, and, in 1910, published a memoir titled *My Mark Twain*, naming Twain "the Lincoln of our literature."
- Helen Keller (blind and deaf American author and lecturer). Keller was fifteen and a fan of Twain's work when they met. Twain was instrumental in raising funds for her education and later hosted a party to promote her book, *The World I Live In*.
- Rudyard Kipling (Indian-born English author). In 1889, Kipling, not yet famous, traveled to Elmira to meet Twain. The two remained friends. Twain enjoyed reading aloud from Kipling's works. In 1907, both Kipling and Twain received honorary degrees from Oxford.

- Henry Wadsworth Longfellow (American poet, author of narrative poems). Twain admired Longfellow's poems and apologized to him for any offense at Whittier's birthday banquet.
- Thomas Nast (German-born U.S. political cartoonist, creator of the symbols for the Democrats [donkey] and Republicans [elephant]). Twain and Nast, friends from the mid-1860s, dreamed of touring together, with Twain as speaker and Nast as sketch artist.
- Henry Huttleston Rogers (Standard Oil Company executive). A fan of Twain's work, the wealthy industrialist served as Twain's business manager and tried to help the author out of his financial troubles. The two enjoyed playing billiards, yachting, and traveling to Bermuda.
- Franklin Delano Roosevelt (U.S. President). Roosevelt claimed to have met Twain as a child. He borrowed the term "New Deal" from *A Connecticut Yankee*.
- Theodore Roosevelt (U.S. President). In 1905, Twain dined at the White House and enjoyed Roosevelt's company, but dismissed him as the "Tom Sawyer of the political world."
- Bram Stoker (Irish writer, author of *Dracula*). Stoker visited Twain often when both were in London and invested in the Paige compositor: Twain eventually returned his money.
- Harriet Beecher Stowe (author of *Uncle Tom's Cabin*). Twain's neighbor in Hartford, Stowe regarded *The Prince and the Pauper* as the "best book for young folk that was ever written."
- Alfred, Lord Tennyson (appointed by Queen Victoria as England's Poet Laureate, 1850–92). The two met in London in 1873.
- Ivan Turgenev (pro-Western Russian writer). Twain met him in London in 1873.
- Artemus Ward, a. k. a. Charles Farrar Browne (traveling showman and humorist). Twain and Ward became friends in Virginia City, and Twain was influenced by the popular humorist's deadpan delivery and use of the dramatic pause.
- Booker T. Washington (African-American educator and author). The two admired each other's work and first met in London in 1899. At Twain's death, Washington wrote a tribute.
- James Whistler (American artist). Twain and Whistler met in London in 1879.
- John Greenleaf Whittier (abolitionist, Quaker, New England poet). Invited to speak at a banquet in honor of the poet's seventieth birthday, Twain regretted his over-the-top speech.
- Oscar Wilde (Irish playwright and wit, persecuted for his homosexuality). Twain and Wilde met in passing, greeting each other at the German spa city of Bad Nauheim in 1892.
- Wilhelm II (Emperor of Germany and king of Prussia, 1888–1918). In 1892, the Kaiser out-talked Twain over dinner. He claimed that *Life on the Mississippi* was his favorite American book.
- Woodrow Wilson (U.S. President, awarded the 1920 Nobel Peace Prize). A month before he died, Twain played miniature golf with the future president in Bermuda.

# The Investor

. . . . . . . . . . . .

## (1880–91)

After a year and a half in Europe, Mark Twain had seen enough of the Old World, with its castles and smutty postcards. Changes loomed on the horizon: Livy was pregnant, and Twain's hair, now gray, would turn even grayer. America was eager to get to the new century, a better world was at hand, and a faster one. Though Twain kept his long drawl and funny, duck-footed walk, the rest of the nation was striding ahead, rushing their words into telephones and phonographs and lighting up their big city streets with electricity.

Illustration by Kate Carew

## New Inventions

With the rest of the country, Twain was ready to turn a new page, literally. One night in Hartford, over the hard smack of billiard balls, a friend told Twain about a young machinist-turned-inventor named James Paige who was tackling a problem dear to Twain's heart; how to improve the tortuously repetitive process of setting type. It had changed little since Gutenberg had invented movable type in the 15th-century. Paige's invention would be operated by one person seated at keyboard, like the maestro of a great orchestra, and would perform six times faster than a person doing the same work by hand. Twain began to invest a fortune, heavily and consistently, ignoring the competition. Linotype, slower but less complicated and more reliable, would win the day, but in 1880, no one knew that.

In America, the air was thick with all things new, and Twain was in the mood to invest. He reached into his deep pockets, bought the patent for a process for making engraved printing plates, and set up the Kaolatype Engraving Company in New York City, naming himself president and principal stockholder. Who knew that new photographic etching techniques would prove more cost efficient and turn out a better product than Kaolatype ever could, or that the man Twain hired to oversee the business would turn out to be a crook?

Sure that he would soon turn a profit from his new investments, Twain poured money into renovating the Hartford house. In 1880, the last daughter was born to Sam and Livy. They named her Jane after Sam's mother, but from the start, they called her Jean. They hired someone to help with the baby; Katy Leary, the child of Irish immigrants. Nanny, seamstress, nursemaid, and housekeeper, Leary would stay with the Clemens family to the bitter end, literally. Hers was the face last seen by Susy, Livy, and Mark Twain himself as she nursed each on their deathbeds, and she would find Jean dead in her bath on Christmas Eve, 1909. Blessedly, she would also be present to assist in the birth of Twain's only grandchild, the doomed Nina Clemens Gabrilowitsch.

In 1880, the Wheel of Fate seemed to be on the ascendant. Too bad Twain didn't look closer and observe that the fickle goddess Fortuna had her fingers crossed.

Newly infatuated with all things American, Twain felt the need to vent some of his frustrations about the Old World. He had finished writing *A Tramp Abroad* in January. Now, he eagerly returned to a project he had been toying with for almost a decade, his first historical novel, about two boys in 16th-century London. Twain's pen raced and the pages stacked up quickly. By September, the first draft of *The Prince and the Pauper* was completed.

## Time Out on the Mississippi

Twain turned his attention back to his investments and began to have worries about the Kaolatype business. He hired his niece's husband, Charles Webster, to be his general business manager. By the beginning of 1882, the Kaolatype business had collapsed, and Twain was out fifty-thousand dollars. Unsettled, he returned to the river of his youth, needing the Mississippi to take away the sting of failed business; but new towns and cities had grown up along the river's banks, and small islands had disappeared forever. Twain wrote, "The river is so thoroughly changed that I can't bring it back to mind. . . . It is like a man pointing out to me a place in the sky where a cloud has been." America was in love with railroads now, not dreamy steamboats. The South, post–Civil War, was lost and suffering. Cynicism and greed were the hallmarks of the new world.

After his visit to the heartland, Twain had enough material to fill two books. The first, *Life on the Mississippi*, came hard, though half of it was previously published articles. When it was published in

May 1883, he called it a "wretched God-damned book." In July, however, the words were flowing and easy as he returned to the manuscript abandoned seven years earlier, about a boy named Huck. The manuscript pages piled up. It was a very good summer, one commonly thought to be the high point of Twain's creative life.

In 1884, America experienced a small but devastating financial panic. Twain needed to make money fast. Partnering with George Washington Cable, the two went on the lecture circuit, billed as the "Twins of Genius." By the end of the tour, Twain was depressed; the two men had made money, but they didn't like each other. The panic of 1884 also devastated former President Ulysses S. Grant, whose only valuable asset was his memory. Twain signed a mutually beneficial contract to publish the *Personal Memoirs of U.S. Grant*. Grant died in July, shortly after he finished writing his manuscript. His *Memoirs* sold so many copies that Twain was able to give Grant's widow the largest royalty payment ever made. In March 1886, the second volume was published, again to great acclaim and financial reward for Grant's family and for Twain's.

Twain launched a new novel, aptly, one full of modern gadgets and machines. In *A Connecticut Yankee in King Arthur's Court*, Twain's hero, Hank Morgan, finding himself in the age of Camelot, introduces industrial-age inventions: telephones, telegraphs, phonographs, typewriters, sewing machines, bicycles. As his dream of an informed and educated population crumbles, Hank introduces guns, electric fences, warships, and dynamite torpedoes.

While he was blowing up inventions on the page, Twain was still investing in the Paige typesetter, paying the inventor to keep tinkering with it, and promising to raise the money to manufacture it once it was ready. "Paige," Twain would write, "is the Shakespeare of mechanical invention." There were other inventions that needed his backing as well, including a steam pulley, a marine telegraph, and a steam generator; all were destined to fail, as was the *Memory-Builder* board game Twain patented in 1885. The one invention he chose not to sink money into was a hot new gadget called the telephone. Twain was sure the public would never want such an intrusive device, though he claimed he was the first in all of New England to have one installed in his home for private use. In one Christmas letter he wrote:

> It is my heart-warm and world-embracing Christmas hope and aspiration that all of us, the high, the low, the rich, the poor, the admired, the despised . . . may eventually be gathered together in a heaven of everlasting rest and peace and bliss, except the inventor of the telephone.

Another new invention that caught Twain's eye was the typewriter. He had bought one in 1874 and pecked out notes to friends. Later, he would boast that *Tom Sawyer* was the first manuscript in the world to be typed, but it was *Life on the Mississippi*, typed by assistants.

In June 1888, Twain visited Thomas Alva Edison in his Orange, New Jersey lab. There, Edison recorded Twain's voice, though the records would be lost in a fire. The two men admired each other's works. Twain put Edison's inventions in his *Connecticut Yankee*. Edison made a short film of *The Prince and the Pauper*, with the only known footage of Twain himself.

Twain spent thirty-thousand dollars on household expenses, tutors, and elaborate dinner parties at a time when the average annual wage in the U.S. was five-hundred dollars. He played the stock market with abandon. "I must speculate in something, such being my nature," he quipped, unaware that he was standing on financial quicksand. Later, he would say that there are two times a man should not speculate, "when he can afford it, and when he can't." With dollar signs in his eyes, Twain again put aside his own writing to publish the works of others, but bad luck and an embezzling bookkeeper brought Webster & Company to its knees. Blaming his nephew for all the disasters, Twain was happy to grant him a leave for health reasons; Webster never returned.

Paige kept tinkering, and Twain kept sinking thousands of dollars into the invention every month. "Don't imagine that I am on my way to the poorhouse," he wrote defensively to Orion, still half believing that Paige would eventually get it right. "All good things arrive unto them that wait – and don't die in the meantime." Twain cajoled investors in the name of progress, but the only thing that actually progressed was Twain's steady march toward bankruptcy.

Now, Fortuna didn't even bother with the spinning; she sadistically locked the Wheel of Fate in its downward position and watched Twain squirm. He developed severe rheumatism in his writing arm, and his publishing company was in debt. *Connecticut Yankee* came out to damning reviews and reader bewilderment. The month Susy went off to college at Bryn Mawr, Twain's mother died after complications from a stroke. The funeral over, Twain rushed to Elmira to comfort Livy whose mother lay dying as well. These sorrows were interrupted by another: daughter Jean had the onset of epilepsy and needed attention immediately. Twain jotted notes for a new book in which Tom and Huck, aging and desolate, die together.

Each time Paige tried to demonstrate the wonders of his machine, something failed to function. "I have been an author for twenty years and an ass for fifty-five," Twain said, as the family closed up the home they could no longer afford. They would live in exile for nine years, and return, heartbroken, to America; but never again to their beautiful home in Hartford.

# A Connecticut Yankee in King Arthur's Court

· · · · · · · · · · ·

Setting: England
Periods: 6th and 19th centuries

Mark Twain steps into the opening pages of this novel as witness and participant. He claims that he was taking a guided tour of Warwick Castle during a visit to England, when another tourist, a curious stranger, whispered something about the "transposition of epochs," time travel. The tour guide droned on about the age of King Arthur, a time before the invention of firearms, then pointed to a display of armor and said, "Observe the round hole through the chainmail in the left breast: can't be accounted for." Twain distinctly heard the stranger mutter, "I did it myself."

That evening, the stranger showed up at Twain's hotel room for a few drinks of Scotch whiskey. He introduced himself as Hank Morgan, an American from Hartford. He had been the superintendent in an arms factory, until one bad day when a worker hit him over the head with a crowbar. When he regained consciousness, he was sitting under an oak tree in the middle of King Arthur's Camelot. Luckily for Twain, and for us, Hank kept a journal.

Awakening in the 6th century, Hank knows the reputations of the people he meets from the popular tales of the knights of the Round Table: Sir Launcelot, Sir Galahad, Morgan Le Fay, Queen Guenever, Merlin. Meeting them face-to-face, Hank soon learns the truth: the people of Camelot are superstitious, ignorant, and utterly at the mercy of the king's foolish knights and of the Roman Catholic Church. Fortunately, Hank meets an enterprising page named Clarence, who will become his right hand.

Early in the story, Hank, about to be burned at the stake on trumped up charges, cleverly uses his knowledge of history to anticipate a total eclipse of the sun. Before the eclipse is over, Hank is not only untethered, but promoted to second-in-command. He has King Arthur and most of the population convinced that he is a greater magician than Merlin, and that they had better cooperate or he will blot out the sun forever.

There are other tests of Hank's powers, but he manages to manipulate the gullible population. Once free, 6th-century England becomes his blank slate on which to try out the advances of the 19th century. Hank hopes to zap Camelot into a virtual utopia with his democratic ideal of universal suffrage and his knowledge of technology. He proclaims himself "The Boss" and takes stock of the kingdom. There are no matches or mirrors, no maps, books, pens, paper, or ink, nor is there coffee, tea, tobacco, or sugar: worst of all, there is no soap. Hank opens a patent office and promptly "invents" the telephone and telegraph, electric lights, the printing press, and bicycles. He institutes schools (Man Factories) and a secret military academy, and founds Camelot's first newspaper. To introduce the novel notion of cleanliness throughout the kingdom, he insists that his knights wear sandwich boards over their armor, advertising soap, toothbrushes, and toothwash.

Hank is ordered to assist a young woman who pleads for help on behalf of forty damsels-in-distress who must be rescued from an ogre. Her name is Demoiselle Alisande de la Carteloise, but Hank just calls her Sandy. He dons a suit of armor, but he is tormented to tears: he cannot get at his handkerchief or swat a fly or scratch an itch. Hank and Sandy scour the mapless land for the ogre's castle, which, to Hank's amazement, turns out to be a pigsty and the maidens, pigs. He frees them from bondage.

Hank continues to build his new world. He lectures "freemen" (who work the land but do not own it) about their need for a "new deal." Visiting the dungeon of Morgan Le Fay's castle, he insists that captives be set free. One, a wretch whose only crime was uttering his belief in the equality of all people, is not only freed by Hank but sent to the Man Factory to be educated. Hank prepares for his new world, in between outrageous adventures. He and King Arthur travel incognito. Passing themselves off as peasants, they encounter everything from smallpox to slavery. Increasingly, Hank turns to his knowledge of arms and explosives to get his way. He dynamites two knights and their horses, delighting in the "steady drizzle of microscopic fragments of knights and hardware and horseflesh." In a duel with Sir Sagramore, Hank first wows the crowd with lasso tricks (a first in this cowboyless land); when this fails to end the duel, he pulls out a revolver and shoots his opponent. (This accounts for the hole in the chain-mail observed by the museum guide at the beginning of the story.) Hank then pulls out another revolver to shoot the remaining challengers.

Following an abrupt interval of three years, the world of Camelot has changed. The Boss rules; the land is prosperous and happy, with schools, colleges, newspapers, railroads, and a stock market. There are steamboats on the Thames and a fleet of ships that Hank intends to send on a mission to discover America. The people have telephones, phonographs, typewriters, sewing machines, and a new sport – baseball – though the players insist on wearing full armor. Hank is blissfully married to Sandy, and they have a baby girl named Hello Central. The world's first mass-produced book is a volume of jokes by Sir Dinadan the humorist; Hank, recognizing a joke that will survive the centuries, has the book suppressed and its author hanged.

Hello Central becomes ill with croup and, when she recovers, the doctor recommends a vacation. Hank and his family, accompanied by two hundred and sixty others, set sail for France. After one month, Hank sends the ship back to England for supplies, expecting it to return in three or four days. Again, Hello Central slips near death and is nursed back to health. Worried because the supply ship has been gone more than two weeks, Hank returns to England and is shocked at what he finds. His "civilization" has ended. King Arthur has been killed in battle. The Church has banned the electric light. Most of Hank's converts have reverted and are willing to do the Church's bidding once again. "Did you think you had educated the superstition out of those people?" Clarence asks a disillusioned Hank: he has assembled a fighting force, fifty-two boys.

Once the Father of Civilization, Hank now becomes the Father of Destruction in all-out war. With his band of boys, he retreats to one of Merlin's caves in the sand belt along the coast. The remainder of the story is gruesome, a testimony to the power of modern warfare: electrocution ("silent lightning"), bombs, and torpedoes. Hank, almost giddy with the power at his fingertips, presses a button to set off a series of explosions that shake "the bones of England loose from her spine." Moments later, Hank is stabbed: his old rival, Merlin, disguised as a woman, puts a spell on him so that he will sleep for thirteen centuries. When the nasty magician loses his balance and reels against an electrified wire, he literally dies laughing, his mouth frozen into a grimace. Clarence dutifully tucks the manuscript beside the body of his "dear good chief," where Hank finds it when he awakens in the 19th century.

Mark Twain returns as a character at the end of his own novel. He has read the remarkable memoir throughout the night and, upon returning it, finds Hank on his death bed, in the throes of an hallucination. Thinking Twain is his 6th-century love, he cries out, "O, Sandy, you have come at last," and dies.

## The Story behind the Story

One day in 1884, while on tour in Rochester to publicize *Huckleberry Finn*, Twain was caught in a rainstorm and ducked into a bookstore where he found a copy of Malory's *Le Morte d'Arthur*. After that, Twain and his tour companions played with the "quaint language" of Malory's book in hotels and on the train. Later, Twain jotted a note in his journal:

*Dream of being a knight errant in armor in the middle ages. Have the notions & habits of thought of the present day mixed with the necessities of that. No pockets in the armor. . . . Always getting struck by lightning. Fall down, can't get up.*

Twain began to plan a holiday book to be entitled *The Lost Land*. In it, a character traveling back to Camelot is devastated by all that has been lost and, in the end, commits suicide. This strange mix of holiday reading and death remains a quality in this story that is part utopian vision, part apocalyptic nightmare. In November 1886, Twain wrote to Mother Fairbanks, "The story isn't a satire peculiarly, it is more especially a 'contrast.'"

After publication, a journalist accused Twain of plagiarizing his story "The Fortunate Island," about a professor who, finding a community of people still living in the 6th century, introduces modern inventions.

Twain denied this charge in 1890 in the *New York World*. While he claimed the story as his own, he, like many authors, did not feel that the story was ever finished. In a letter to William Dean Howells after its publication, Twain wrote:

*Well, my book is written – let it go, but if it were only to write over again there wouldn't be so many things left out. They burn in me; they keep multiplying and multiplying, but now they can't ever be said; and besides, they would require a library – and a pen warmed-up in hell.*

*The Brave Sir Mark*

*A Yankee Writer at King Arthur's Court*

Copyright © Dave Thomson

# "The Sweet Bye and Bye"

. . . . . . . . . . .

As Mark Twain would remember it, "The Sweet Bye and Bye" (variously spelled) was *their* song, his and Livy's, because they heard it playing when they met in December, 1867. No doubt Twain remembered it that way, but memory can be a funny thing: the hymn was composed by a depressed violinist in a Wisconsin drugstore one winter day in 1867, and was not yet available to the world when Twain and Livy met.

According to the legend of the song's composition, Joseph Webster, nearly despondent, stopped by a drugstore run by fellow bohemian-wannabe, Dr. Bennett, one cold afternoon. Webster's song "Lorena" had been a hit during the Civil War, but sheet music sales were down. Where once he had accompanied the Swedish Nightingale, Jenny Lind, he now ran a saloon. To cheer his melancholy friend, the inspired pharmacist picked up a pen and jotted down a few verses that came to him "like a revelation."

*There's a land that is fairer than day,*
*And by faith we can see it afar;*
*For the Father waits over the way*
*To prepare us a dwelling place there.*

[Refrain] *In the sweet bye and bye,*
*We shall meet on that beautiful*
*shore.*
*In the sweet bye and bye.*
*We shall meet on that beautiful*
*shore.*

Webster glanced at the words as Dr. Bennett scribbled them, picked up his ever-present Stradivarius (destined to be lost in the 1871 Chicago fire), and composed the music on the spot. Two customers entered the store and witnessed the creation of the hymn.

"The Sweet Bye and Bye" first appeared in print in 1868. By the time Sam married Livy in 1870, the hymn was a national bestseller. It is quite believable that they enjoyed singing it together at home. Twain claimed that he always thought of Livy when he heard it. Livy must have been amused, therefore, when her husband used "their song" as a gag in several stories.

In *A Connecticut Yankee in King Arthur's Court,* when Hank first arrives at the castle of the wicked Morgan Le Fay, a band serenades those feasting on wild boar in the banquet hall with a crude version of the "The Sweet Bye and Bye." Hank concedes that it should have been better rehearsed, but he is startled when the queen orders the song's composer to be hanged after dinner. Then, the queen is informed that the Yankee is a powerful wizard. As Hank tells it:

*The poor queen was so scared and humbled that she was even afraid to hang the composer without first consulting me. I was very sorry for her. . . . I therefore considered the matter thoughtfully, and ended by having the musicians ordered into our presence to play that Sweet Bye and Bye again, which they did. Then I saw that she was right, and gave her permission to hang the whole band.*

"ORIGINAL AGONY."

Twain used the song again in "The Invalid's Story," a macabre little tale about two men riding through a snowstorm on a railway car with what they believe is a corpse in a coffin. They do not know that the coffin has been switched with a box of rifles or that someone has left a package of ripe Limburger cheese on top of it. When the doors of the car are closed, the air fills with a foul odor. The old expressman hums "The Sweet Bye and Bye," just before he exclaims, "He's pretty ripe, ain't he!" By the end of the journey, imagination has felled both men.

In Twain's story "The Loves of Alonzo Fitz Clarence and Rosannah Ethelton," Alonzo, talking with his aunt via long distance telephone, hears someone singing "The Sweet Bye and Bye" in the background. The angelic voice is that of Rosannah, and the two fall in love. Later, when a jealous rival, impersonating Alonzo, rudely tells Rosannah to stop singing *that* song, the bride-to-be is hurt, calls off the wedding, and disappears. After much heartache, the two will be reunited to sing "The Sweet Bye and Bye" to their hearts' content.

In "What Is Man?" Young Man complains to Old Man about how maddening it is when a song or jingle gets into one's head and goes on and on, over and over for a week. He uses as an example, "In the Swee-eet By and By."

*Yes, the new popular song with the taking melody sings through one's head day and night, asleep and awake, till one is a wreck. There is no getting the mind to let it alone.*

# The American Claimant

· · · · · · · · · · · ·

**Setting:** A castle in England; Washington, D.C., and environs

**Period:** Two months during the Reconstruction Era in the 1880s

This novel, commonly described as a social satire, borrows several characters from Twain's first novel, *The Gilded Age*, most notably Colonel Sellers (the claimant), an eccentric inventor, always scheming a way to get a taste of the good life.

Young Lord Berkeley, pining away in an English castle, wishes he could renounce all aristocratic privilege; he intends to change places with an American relative. A letter arrives from Colonel Sellers claiming that, because the chosen relative has died, *he* is next in line for the earldom. Sellers lives in a shabby house in Washington, D.C., with his wife Polly and his servants. He has invented a game called "Pigs in the Clover" and is refining a process to materialize the spirits of the dead.

Washington Hawkins, also from the previous novel, visits Sellers with news about a bank robber, One-Armed Pete, whose capture will bring a reward. The men plot a way to catch the thief and, simultaneously, work at marketing the game. Meanwhile, Lord Berkeley boards a ship for America, eager to experience life as an ordinary bloke, without access to unearned power and privilege. Class confusion affects unpretentious, levelheaded Sally Sellers, too; her father has ordered her home from college and taken to calling her Lady Gwendolen.

Sellers and Hawkins, dreaming of the reward money, successfully trick One-Armed Pete into coming to D.C., where they observe the cowboy-suited bandit, checking into the same hotel as the suave Lord Berkeley. The reward-seekers plan to capture Pete the next day, but that night there is a fire in the hotel. Lord Berkeley rushes out of his room with only his diary in hand. Needing clothes, he stumbles into another guest's smoke-filled room, grabs some clothes, gets dressed, and rushes off to find other accommodations. What he has hurriedly put on is a cowboy suit, with five-hundred dollars cash in the pocket.

The next day, the paper reports that Lord Berkeley has died heroically in the hotel fire and that One-Armed Pete has most likely died in the fire as well. Berkeley is overjoyed at this chance to discard his aristocratic identity. He discovers the money and puts most of it in a hard-to-access bank account. Then, he changes his name to Howard Tracy, and cables his father the news that he is not really dead. Free to manage on his own, Berkeley checks into a cheap boardinghouse and starts looking for work, but weeks go by. Just when he is truly desperate, he secures a job as an artist's assistant, filling in paintings with cats, pianos, and rocks.

Sellers, meanwhile, distressed at the thought of losing the chance of a reward, works on "materializing" Pete's spirit. When he and Hawkins see Berkeley dressed in the cowboy suit, they assume he is One-Armed Pete, freshly materialized from the dead. A chance encounter brings Berkeley to Sellers' shabby home, where he is believed to be the materialized bank robber, though Sellers and Hawkins are mystified as to why the ghost of a one-armed American bank robber has come back with two arms and a British accent.

Berkeley, meanwhile, realizes that he is in the home of the American claimant. When Sellers hires him to restore several paintings, he and Sally take one look at each other and fall in love. Later, Hawkins is shocked to see Sally kissing a dead man, albeit one that has been "materialized." Hawkins and Sellers have a puzzle on their hands and a problem. The *puzzle* is why the dead man has two arms, an accent, and can kiss and eat. The *problem* is that they like him and no longer want to turn him in for the reward money. Sally has a problem too: she is worried that her sweetheart loves her only for her assumed upper-class status. When she confesses that she is not really an aristocrat, Berkeley, amused, reassures her of his love.

The charm of being powerless and penniless having worn off, Berkeley writes to his father asking to be reinstated as the rightful heir to the earldom. When he reveals his true identity to Sally, however, she does not believe him and sends him

away. Now, Berkeley is desperate for proof of his social status. While he is struggling, Sellers and Hawkins are reaping hefty profits from the "Pigs in the Clover" game, enough for Sellers to buy a ticket to England where he intends to claim his earldom. Hawkins, disgusted that Sally is dating a materialized spirit, makes up a story to end the relationship; he says that Berkeley is a depraved ruffian in disguise whose name is "Spinal Meningitis Snodgrass." Far from turning her against Berkeley, however, this story makes Sally pity her forlorn and friendless sweetheart.

The novel ends like a Shakespearean comedy, with all the players tying up the loose ends, resolving misunderstandings, revealing true identities, reconciling hurt parties. Plans are made for all to gather for a tasteful wedding ceremony, which takes a back seat to Sellers' new money-making project; a scheme to rearrange the tropics and open a resort at the Arctic Circle.

**The Story behind the Story**

After *The Gilded Age* was published in 1873, an unauthorized version of the story was dramatized, exaggerating the eccentric qualities of Colonel Sellers. Twain bought the rights to the play, then persuaded William Dean Howells to collaborate on writing a new play. The result was *Colonel Sellers as a Scientist*, a decided flop. In 1891, Twain continued tinkering with the play, refashioning it as a novel, keeping the Colonel's offbeat inventions but adding his pursuit of the earldom. In just two months, Twain finished *The American Claimant*, sure that it would be a success. His confidence was misguided.

This story was initially serialized in the *New York Sun*, appearing in the Sunday editions for three months of 1892. It was published later that year as a book.

# Tom Sawyer Abroad

· · · · · · · · · · ·

## by Huck Finn, edited by Mark Twain

Setting: A hot-air balloon floating over Missouri, the Atlantic Ocean, Africa

Period: Pre–Civil War

"Do you reckon Tom Sawyer was satisfied after all them adventures?" Huck asks in the opening sentence of this sequel to *Adventures of Huckleberry Finn*. He answers his own question, telling us that Tom was hailed as "the Traveler" back home in St. Petersburg, until the postmaster, Nat Parsons, one-upped him by traveling all the way to Washington to seek a pardon from the President for failure to deliver a misaddressed letter.

Tom knows he has to find a new adventure and reads in the St. Louis papers about a hot-air balloon that will soon set sail for Europe. Tom, Huck, and Jim head for the balloon and find it surrounded by people mocking the pale genius who plans to fly it across the ocean. The Professor, as he is called, exchanges insults with the crowd as Tom and his two friends climb aboard the basket hanging under the balloon for a tour with other curiosity seekers. Last to

debark, they suddenly see the city dropping from under them and become unintended travelers.

The shocked Professor teaches Tom how to work the controls, but then turns, with a wild look in his eyes, spouting a tirade of paranoia and holds the three hostage, waving a revolver over his head. Tom begins to plot ways to get free from their kidnapper while he sleeps, saying, "It's no good politics sailing around like this with a person that's out of his head." When they begin to sail over a vast ocean, Tom begs the nutty Professor to let them return home, but the kidnapping genius just waves his revolver. The balloon flies into a storm, and the Professor lunges at Tom, screaming, "Overboard you go!" but it is the Professor who falls into the ocean as thunder roars around them. Tom, Huck, and Jim are on their own.

Tom teaches Jim and Huck to steer the well-stocked balloon and jots a note to Aunt Polly, planning to mail it when they reach London. The next morning, however, they discover that they are flying over Africa not England. In the distance, they see a procession of camels and men in long white robes. When robbers ambush the distracted caravan, Tom, Huck, and Jim watch in horror as six-hundred men battle each other, and the sand is littered with the dead. The water stored in the basket of the balloon soon becomes stale, so the travelers are overjoyed when they spot a lake in the distance and "pam trees" with coconuts; only a mirage, it quickly disappears. When this happens again, Jim is convinced that the lake is a ghost and that the desert itself is haunted. Tom knows about the desert from reading the *Arabian Nights*. Keeping a lookout for a magic hill full of incredible treasures, he finds the hill but not the door to its secret chamber. The balloon flies over another caravan, but, when the sun suddenly turns "blood red," the people scatter, flinging themselves down on the hot sand. From across the desert comes a wide wall of sand. It takes several minutes for the sandstorm to pass, burying everyone in the caravan; camels and all.

They reach the pyramids. Jim has heard a lot about Egypt and the Exodus story in the Bible, of Moses leading the enslaved people out of bondage. After they almost collide with the Sphinx, Tom hitches a hook onto the massive figure's lower lip and leaves Jim on top of the Sphinx's head with an American flag for protection. From a distance, Huck and Tom reflect on the Sphinx. Huck writes:

*It made us feel quiet and kind of solemn to remember it had been looking out over that valley just that same way, and thinking its awful thoughts all to itself for thousands of years, and nobody can't find out what they are to this day.*

Lost in their revery, Tom and Huck think they see bugs crawling up the

Sphinx's back. Looking through the telescope, they see that the bugs are men with guns and hurry to rescue Jim.

The balloon floats over the narrow streets of Cairo, crowded with copper-colored people in turbans and Whirling Dervishes who spin around like tops. Huck writes, "They was all Moslems, Tom said, and when I asked him what a Moslem was, he said it was a person that wasn't a Presbyterian." They find a man in baggy trousers and a blue silk jacket to be their guide in Mecca, Medina, and Central Africa. By dinnertime, they are floating over the place where the Israelites crossed the Red Sea.

Just after they take in the grandeur of Mount Sinai, something happens that brings the meandering adventure to a halt: Tom's old corncob pipe, held together with string and bandages, crumbles from age and over-use. This is nothing short of a disaster, because there are no corncob pipes in that part of the world. Tom remembers the pipe hidden over the kitchen stove back home and, in a matter of sentences, Jim and the Arabian guide are on their way to Missouri, while Tom and Huck wait on top of Mount Sinai. In a flash, the balloon returns, but Jim reports that Aunt Polly is not at all happy; Tom is to return immediately. Huck writes only this: "So then we shoved for home, and not feeling very gay, neither."

## The Story behind the Story

In 1892, Twain had moved his family to Europe, no longer able to afford life in Hartford, thanks in part to the Paige compositer, which was bleeding Twain dry. Is it any wonder that he conjured up an inventor, part dreamer, part madman, who holds Tom, Huck, and Jim captive in a balloon, adrift at the mercy of the wind? Not long into the story, Tom throws the mad inventor over the side of the balloon, to his death.

This novella was written quickly, forty thousand words in four weeks, for money, not art. Twain finished editing the book in a villa near Florence. He hoped that the book would be the beginning of a new series featuring Tom and Huck, the way the popular Horatio Alger books recycled its hero and stock characters. While he made out-lines of several stories, Twain would complete only one other book featuring his young heroes, *Tom Sawyer, Detective*. He sold his ersatz Jules Verne story to *St. Nicholas*, a magazine for children, where it appeared in six issues in 1893. Twain was furious when Mary Mapes Dodge, editor and moral guardian of the magazine, took the liberty of revising the story, removing references to Tom and Huck's drinking, smoking, and swearing.

# The Wanderer

· · · · · · · · · · ·

## (1891–1904)

As if he were Tom Sawyer crawling out of the window and sneaking off in the night, Mark Twain crawled out of Hartford, pulled Susy out of college, and set sail for Europe with his family in June 1891. The Clemens family would drift from one hotel to another, and one country to another for the next nine years; and so the restless roaming began. After four days in Paris, Sam and Livy moved the girls to Geneva, then spent five weeks in a health spa in the south of France, hoping the sulfur baths would relieve Twain's rheumatism. Next, it was off to a Wagner Festival in Germany. Livy bought tickets for nineteen performances, much to Twain's deep regret. He wrote, "I wish I could see a Wagner opera done in pantomime once."

In September, Twain left his family in Lausanne and spent ten days sailing down the Rhone through France, stopping to visit villages along the way. He briefly thought of writing a new book, *The Innocents Adrift*, but abandoned the idea. Meanwhile, daughter Susy was sending lovesick letters home to her college friend, Louise Brownell, writing "If you were here

I would kiss you hard on that little place that tastes so good just on the right side of your nose." Clara, on the other hand, was waltzing with men in bright uniforms: Twain, panicked at the thought of his daughters dancing their way out of his control, locked her in a room for several days.

The winter was spent in Berlin. Then, the family was on the move again: France, Italy, another spa city in Germany. Everywhere, Twain was cheered as a celebrity. He was writing again: travel sketches for papers back home, short stories and essays, and a novel, *The American Claimant*. In a cavernous villa overlooking Florence, he immersed himself in reading about Joan of Arc, churned out *Tom Sawyer Abroad*, and then wrote a book about racism, *Pudd'nhead Wilson*. Though he found solace in work, he could not shake off his financial woes and wrote to a friend, "I have never felt so desperate in my life." Leaving his family behind, he crisscrossed the Atlantic to tend to business, hat in hand. Twain looked for investors to rescue Webster & Company, which was frantically publishing everything from Tolstoy to *One Hundred Ways of Cooking Eggs*, but

even Andrew Carnegie looked the other way. Livy wrote to her husband, "If failure comes we shall not be cast down and you must not allow yourself to be."

The stock market crashed in 1893, wiping out businesses and employment for two-and-a-half-million people. Then, when all seemed most hopeless, Twain found a friend in Henry Huttleston Rogers, a founder of Standard Oil, who unabashedly described his occupation as "capitalist" and whom others described as "ruthless." Twain wrote of him, "He's a pirate all right, but he owns up to it and enjoys being a pirate." A fan of Twain's work, Rogers tossed a few thousand dollars at the mountain of debt, then recommended voluntary bankruptcy. He pulled as many strings as he could, even persuading the *Chicago Herald* to test Paige's machine: it was deemed a dud, hopelessly unreliable. (James Paige continued to invent, but never found success. He died, destitute, in 1917. One of his compositors is on display in the Mark Twain Museum in Hartford; the other was dismantled and used for scrap-metal during World War II.)

Other writers might have been paralyzed by such public humiliation and loss of place in the world, but not Twain. He picked up the pen and wrote an homage to Joan of Arc, the vulnerable teen who, against all the odds, marched into battle with a pure heart and was martyred while the masses wept. Each evening, he read aloud to his wife and children from the pages he had written that morning. Susy, still chronicling their lives, wrote, "Many of Joan's words and sayings are historically correct and Papa cries when he reads them."

Twain was determined to earn enough money to pay back his creditors. There was only one way to do this; return to lecturing. Almost sixty and rheumatic, Twain was desperate: he signed a contract for an around-the-world tour. Susy opted to stay home, and Jean had too many health complications for a five-continent tour, but Sam, Livy, and Clara set out to span the globe. Twain, suffering with gout and other ailments, climbed on one stage after another, drawled his slow drawl, and kept a straight face while the crowds roared.

Mark Twain and Empire—a Laughing World

He held the audiences in the palm of his hand all across the northern United States and then across the Pacific to Australia in time for Twain's sixtieth birthday, then on to Ceylon, India, and South Africa. Everywhere, the crowds came out to greet the American author with the wild white hair and the funny way of talking.

One year after the start of the tour, Twain sailed for England. He had earned back a quarter of the amount he had hoped to raise to pay off his debt. The family had planned to be reunited, but news came that Susy was ill and her trip would have to be postponed. Livy and Clara left immediately for the States, while Twain stayed behind to find lodging for the family. He was alone on August 18, 1896, when he received word that Susy, at twenty-four, had died of spinal meningitis. Years later, Twain would say, "It is one of the mysteries of our nature that a man, all unprepared, can receive a thunderstroke like that and live." He stayed in England, holding onto a cue stick for dear life. "I play billiards, and billiards, & billiards, till I am ready to drop – to keep from going mad with grief & with resentful thinking," he wrote. "It would bankrupt all vocabularies of all the languages to put it into words," he eked out in faint script.

The family rejoined Twain in London in a house without laughter. At the end of October, he immersed himself in the task of writing up his recent tour, to be published the next fall as *Following the Equator* (British edition, *More Tramps Abroad*). He wrote for six months straight, all through the long, damp London winter and into the spring, holed up in his study. Rumors circulated that Twain was not only destitute but dying, and then that he was dead. A young reporter knocked on the Clemens's door holding instructions from

James Ross Clemens, a
cousin of mine was seriously
ill two or three weeks ago, in London,
but ~~he~~ is well now. The report of
my illness grew out of his illness, the
report of my death was an
exaggeration.
Mark Twain

Credit: www.twainquotes.com, courtesy Barbara Schmidt

his editor: IF MARK TWAIN HAS DIED IN POVERTY SEND 1000 WORDS. The occasion prompted Twain to give his most famous wisecrack, "The report of my death was an exaggeration." It became the quip heard 'round the world; everywhere, people rejoiced.

Twain claimed indifference to his life now, marveling only that a part of him continued to function in the world, to write and be clever. According to Twain biographer Justin Kaplan:

*For about two years after Susy died Clemens lived in a sort of deliberate, self-induced dream state in which the reality was what he dreamed and the fantasy was what he lived by day.*

Twain and the family set off for a summer in Switzerland and then moved to Vienna so that beautiful Clara could study with a world-famous pianist. Now, it seemed that Twain's pen was truly "warmed

up in Hell." He began to write about Satan visiting the earth in one guise or another and about happy families suddenly caught in nightmares. He stopped and started manuscripts that would be published posthumously, if at all, writing at a furious pace for eight or nine hours at a stretch. Ink became air, the very stuff of life.

Elegant, café-crowded, intellectual Vienna was bursting at the seams with creativity and life and more than a touch of the anti-Semitism that would later turn the world upside down. Counted among Vienna's citizens were Dvořák, Freud, and Clara's future husband, a dashing Russian-Jewish pianist and conductor named Ossip Gabrilowitsch. Twain was inspired by the city, though alarmed at the prejudice against the Jews, something he noted in his writings. In December, word came that Orion had died. Within months, Twain would experience other significant losses: a friend from the Wild West whose pen name was Dan De Quille and his *Quaker City* friend, Mother Fairbanks.

At the beginning of 1889, Lady Luck roused herself out of her long stupor to give the Wheel-of-Fortune an upward spin for a change. Henry Huttleston Rogers wrote that, through a series of clever manipulations and with the monies garnered from Twain's tour and writings, the one-hundred-thousand-dollar debt had been paid off at last.

## Return of the Prodigal Son

After a short stint in Sweden searching for a cure for Jean's seizures, the family headed home to America. They docked on October 15, 1900, to the roar of a welcoming crowd. The "people's author" had returned to the people; newspaper headlines across the country proclaimed: MARK TWAIN COMES HOME, followed by MARK TWAIN WANTS TO BE PRESIDENT.

There was no going back to Hartford, the place of heartbreak for the Clemens family. They found a home in New York City's Greenwich Village, where Twain was in a mood to be more than amusing. He began holding forth on a variety of political themes, supporting women's right to vote, Russian efforts to over-throw the czar, and workers' efforts to unionize. He denounced United States and Christian imperialism, saying, "I am opposed to having the eagle put its talons on any other land." His publishers and friends worried that he would offend readers; but, more than ever, Twain was the toast of the town, followed by crowds of adoring strangers.

Having come out of seclusion, Twain seemed to thrive, but Livy began a downward spiral into virtual invalidism. Twain moved her out of the hectic rush of the Village and into quiet Riverdale

in the Bronx, overlooking the Hudson River in what is now known as Wave Hill, but the flow of visitors remained constant. Daughter Jean continued to suffer seizures. Clara, against her parents' wishes, briefly returned to Europe to continue her music studies. Twain could not hold still; he needed to move. He took a cruise through the Caribbean aboard the luxury yacht of his friend Henry Rogers, then headed west, returning to Hannibal, where the whole town turned out to greet their native son. Twain posed for photographs and marveled at all the Toms, Hucks, and Beckys. On his last night, addressing five hundred guests at the Labinnah Club ("Hannibal" spelled backward), he broke down and wept in the middle of a comic routine. The next day, the whole town waved good-bye at the train station. One old friend in the crowd shouted out, "Same damned fools, Sam!" as the train pulled away.

Back home, vacationing in Maine, Livy suddenly couldn't breathe. Doctors diagnosed it as "nervous prostration" and consigned her to bed for eight months. Clara was called back from Paris to tend to her mother, and Twain was ordered to stay away from his wife. Forbidden to see each other except for several minutes each evening, Sam and Livy sent each other little notes, each miserable in their separation. When Livy murmured "Florence," Twain immediately began making plans for their return. Whatever Livy wanted, Twain would strive to deliver. He hurried to tie up loose ends, arranging, finally, for the sale of the Hartford house where they had all once been so happy. He instructed his agent, "For the Lord Jesus H. Christ's sake *sell or rent that God damned house. I would rather go to hell than own it 50 days longer.*" In October, 1903, Twain set sail for Italy with Livy, Clara, Jean, Katy

Leary, Livy's secretary Isabel Lyon, and a nurse.

Livy's dream of warm and sunny Florence turned quickly to nightmare, with the primary villain being their American landlady, who sadistically toyed with her renters; turning off the water, imposing nonsensical rules, refusing entry to Livy's doctors. The weather was as miserable as the landlady, providing only a bone-deep cold and overcast skies. Sam and Livy were allowed to see each other only for a few minutes each evening, per doctor's orders, though Livy continued to read and comment on Twain's daily writings. As Livy suffered, so suffered her family. Clara cursed her life and everyone in it, though she managed to give a concert; Jean endured more seizures. Twain developed a persistent cough and a twitch in his right cheek.

In June 1904, after months of misery, Livy seemed like her old self, alert and eager to talk. She was allowed to spend half-an-hour with her husband that night, after which Twain sat down at the piano and sang some African-American spirituals he loved, including "Swing Low, Sweet Chariot," a song about the angels coming to carry the dying home to heaven. Livy turned to Katy Leary and smiled, saying, "He is singing a good-night carol to me." Moments later, she was dead. After sobbing with his daughters, Twain picked up his pen and wrote to a friend:

*An hour ago, the best heart that ever beat for me and mine was carried silent out of this house and I am as one who wanders and has lost his way.*

# Of Stolen Watermelons and Golden Arms

· · · · · · · · · · · ·

## Mark Twain on Stage

Mark Twain's hunger for applause may have gotten its start back in Hannibal, the time the "mesmerizer" came to town. For three nights, Sam Clemens went up on stage. Determined and sincere, he nevertheless failed to lose himself to the hypnotist's control, while a boy named Hicks stole the show. On the fourth night, it dawned on Sam that the whole thing was a game. He out-Hicked Hicks and faked his way through a variety of staged acts, squirming at imaginary snakes and smooching with invisible girls. He hammed it up for the audience, and they loved it.

The next time he knew the kiss of an audience's affection was in 1856. Sam was working for his big brother, Orion, at the Ben Franklin Book and Job Office in Keokuk, setting type. Orion revered Ben Franklin and had arranged a banquet commemorating the forefather's one-hundred-and-fiftieth birthday. After a parade of ho-hum speakers, Sam was urged to say a few words. He took the stage and improvised; the people applauded until their hands were sore.

A decade later, in 1866, after Twain returned to California from his tour of the Sandwich Islands, he was shocked to learn that his published reports had made him a celebrity, and he decided to test his name-recognition on the lecture circuit. Twain worked up a lecture and rented a hall. His handbills were one part vital information, one part joke:

A SPLENDID ORCHESTRA
*Is in town, but has not been engaged.*
*Also*
A DEN OF FEROCIOUS WILD BEASTS
*Will be on Exhibition in the next Block.*
MAGNIFICENT FIREWORKS
*Were in contemplation for this occasion,*
*but the idea has been abandoned.*

At the bottom of the flier were these words:

Doors open at 7 o'clock.
The Trouble to begin at 8 o'clock.

Twain gave out some free tickets, convinced that no one would show up, and was amazed to find a packed house; even the aisles were full. Twain's first and last experience of stage fright lasted only a few minutes. The audience was at least as entertained by Twain's eccentric mannerisms and long Missouri drawl as they were by what he had to say about his adventures. The next day, the newspapers called his lecture "side-splitting" and proclaimed it a hit. In just one night, he made four-hundred dollars after expenses, a lot of money given his circumstances. Suddenly,

people were paying to hear *what* he had to say and *how* he had to say it, in towns and cities throughout northern California and western Nevada.

After establishing a reputation for himself in the West, Twain hoped to claim the same respect in New York City. With the help of a flamboyant acquaintance, he booked the Great Hall at Cooper Union, where Lincoln and other famous orators had spoken. May 6, 1867, was a busy evening in the city, and it didn't look good for the ingénue, Mark Twain, when his fifty-cent tickets failed to sell. His friend came to the rescue, distributing free tickets to teachers, "the most intelligent audience." That evening, the Hall was packed, and, though Twain had to introduce himself, he feasted on favorable newspaper reviews the next morning.

## 1868–69 Tour

In January 1868, fresh from his cruise aboard the *Quaker City*, Twain began receiving invitations to speak. One night, he was the twelfth of fifteen speakers at the Washington Correspondents' Club banquet and, afterward, some said that it was the best dinner table speech they had ever heard. When portions of the speech were reprinted in the next day's papers, Twain wrote to Mother Fairbanks, "They had no business to report it so *verbatimly*." He promised to reform.

By April, Twain was back in San Francisco, where he wasted no time in setting up a lecture tour. People who had heard him before, lined up to hear him talk about his *Quaker City* tour. In town after town the laughter fell flat, however, when he poked a little too much fun at "sacred things." Clergymen called him a "son of the devil," and newspaper reviewers decried him as a "miserable scribbler." Twain took it all in stride, holding that a little notoriety was not a bad thing. By November 1868, Twain was back East, wooing the great love of his life, Livy Langdon. Needing to make money, he embarked on the "American Vandal Abroad" tour, which took him from Cleveland, through parts of Pennsylvania, New York, Michigan, Indiana, Illinois, and Iowa. Audiences roared as he described the various antics of his fellow tourists, a few of them incorrigible relic-gatherers.

In Iowa City, after receiving a bad notice that labeled him a vulgar comic humbug, Twain fell on the ice and landed hard on his left hip. He endured lost luggage and missed connections, cold lecture halls, and uncharitable audiences. Lonely and exhausted, Twain despaired to think that his gift for the stage would trap him in the vagabond's life, a hell with no escape. After forty-two lectures, he protested that he was "wearied to death with travel." After lecturing in Lockport, New York, he wrote to Livy, "The long siege is over, and I may rest at last."

### 1869–70 Tour

But it wasn't over. Twain signed up with James Redpath, a liberal reformer and the manager of the Boston Lyceum Bureau, which represented Henry Ward Beecher, Ralph Waldo Emerson, Horace Greeley, Julia Ward Howe, and Henry David Thoreau. In November, Twain was on the road again, talking about the Sandwich Islands. Again, he got high marks for spontaneity on stage, although he rarely improvised. In fact, he wrote out his lectures and, using an original system of mnemonics, memorized his talks, including the stammers, pauses, gestures, and inflection.

He sometimes gave reviewers written copies of his speeches in advance so that, when they quoted from them, they would be accurate. A reporter would later describe Twain's style:

*Hardly changing his position, never moving the muscles of his face, speaking in a tone which is almost melancholy, with what the French call "tears in his voice," when he is saying the funniest things, the lecturer is the only person in the room who preserves a semblance of gravity or maintains any personal dignity. The closest attention is demanded from the audience, for often the finest bits of humour . . . are quietly dropped out parenthetically, as if the speaker either wasn't aware there was any fun in them or didn't notice it himself.*

### 1871–72 Tour

In October 1871, Twain, now a married man with a child and needing a quick source of money, returned to the lecture circuit, with Redpath as his manager. The speech he settled on was filled with anecdotes from *Roughing It.* He wrote to Mother Fairbanks, "Shall be studying it in the cars till midnight, and then sleep half the day in Toledo and study the rest. If I am in good condition there, I shall deliver it."

Livy was miserable with their separation and wrote in a letter, "I *can not* and I WILL NOT think about your being away from me this way every year, it is not half living." The reviews on this tour were mixed, but Twain attracted large crowds and, in the end, paid off his bills. Having patched together three different lectures for this one tour, Twain would call it, "the most detestable lecture campaign that ever was."

## 1873–74 Tour

For awhile, Twain managed to avoid another lecture tour, although he was frequently called upon to give informal after-dinner speeches. It was not until late 1873 that he returned to the lecture circuit; this time, in England. Livy and little Susy were with him, touring between engagements. When Twain began his London lectures on the Sandwich Islands in October, Livy was homesick and pregnant again. Twain escorted his family back to Hartford, then returned to England and continued his speaking tour. Before Christmas, he wrote to Livy, "I am so tired of lecturing." Though he was hailed as a great success, he cancelled a number of speaking engagements to return to the States in mid-January.

## 1877 Birthday Speech Catastrophe

Mark Twain's biggest public speaking disaster was in Boston one December evening, at the seventieth birthday celebration of revered New England journalist and poet, John Greenleaf Whittier. Hosted by the *Atlantic Monthly*, the literary magazine of note, the evening was one of refinement and gentility. Those honoring Whittier included big names: Ralph Waldo Emerson, Oliver Wendell Holmes Sr., Henry Wadsworth Longfellow. Then, Mark Twain stood up. He did not talk like the New England giants, nor look like them. He delivered an impolite burlesque, meant to be amusing, to counterbalance the bloated and haughty accolades. In his story, Holmes, Longfellow, and Emerson, are drunken ruffians who show up at a lonely miner's log cabin, spouting bits and pieces of their famous (albeit misattributed) verses. As Twain remembered it, his story

fell flat and hard, and was met with a stone-cold, deadly silence.

It may not have been as bad as Twain seemed to think. The *Boston Advertiser* reported: "The humorist of the evening was next introduced and the amusement was intense . . ." Twain, nevertheless, wrote letters of apology to each of the spoofed luminaries. Although they reassured him that they had taken no offense, it is widely believed that Twain's embarrassment prompted him to leave the country with his family for two years.

## 1884–85 Tour

In November 1884, after a long hiatus, Twain took to the stage again, but, by this time, the lecture circuit was a thing of the past. Charles Dickens had launched a new form of literary performance: author's readings. For this trip, Twain would share the stage with a Southern writer, George Washington Cable, whom he considered "the South's finest literary genius." James Pond, hired to promote the tour, billed Twain and Cable "Twins of Genius" and sent them on one-hundred-and-four speaking engagements. The two men read at cities and towns in Connecticut, New York, Pennsylvania, parts of Canada, Michigan, Ohio, Kentucky, Indiana, Missouri, Iowa, Illinois, Minnesota, Wisconsin, New Jersey, and Washington, D.C.

Twain primarily read from *Adventures of Huckleberry Finn*, hot off the press, while Cable both read and sang. By the end of the tour, Twain was sick of his sidekick, a stingy man and "pious ass" Presbyterian who, Twain concluded, was "the pitifulest human louse I have ever known." He wrote to a friend that Cable had taught him to "abhor & detest the

Sabbath-day & hunt up new & troublesome ways to dishonor it."

## 1891 at Bryn Mawr

When nineteen-year-old Susy Clemens enrolled in Bryn Mawr, Twain readily accepted an invitation from the college to give an address. Susy was cautious; what would her sophisticated friends think of her offbeat, albeit celebrity, father? She asked of him only one thing: do not tell "The Golden Arm." Twain had heard this classic European ghost story masterfully told on his uncle's farm, sitting at Uncle Dan'l's feet beside the slave children. As the repeated question grew louder and louder, "Whoooo got my golllllden arrrrm?" little Sammy had anticipated the moment the ghost would point an accusing finger and shout, "*You've* got it!" In adulthood, Twain made the story his own and told it often. He worked the timing, the rhythm, the pause perfectly and told it the way he had first heard it, in black dialect. In 1895, he wrote specific instructions on delivering the story in his essay, "How to Tell a Story." Susy had enjoyed the story as a child, but, as a Bryn Mawr scholar, she worried that it was low-bred and uncouth. She begged her father not to tell it, and he promised not to. As he addressed her classmates in the college chapel, however, he could not help himself: he launched into "The Golden Arm," and Susy ran from the chapel in tears.

## 1895–96 Tour

At the close of 1894, Twain's publishing company declared bankruptcy. The weary and rheumatic celebrity made plans for an around-the-world-tour, hoping it would get him out of his debt of one-hundred-thousand dollars. The plan was to lecture in cities and towns across North America; tackle Australia, New Zealand, Ceylon, India, and South Africa; then meet up with his family in England, where he would write a book about his adventures. He rented the Hartford house, crawled out of a sickbed, and, with Livy and Clara, waved good-bye to Susy Clemens, by then a twenty-three-year-old "brimming with life and the joy of it." It was July 14, 1895: they would never see her again.

Twain got off to a rough start in hot and steamy Cleveland, where he shared the stage with two-hundred newsboys. Despite this, Twain's opening-night story, about the time he stole a green watermelon, was a success. In his long, slow drawl, Twain told how he had returned the melon to the farmer and lectured him about selling green fruit. By the time he reached Vancouver, the sold-out crowds and standing ovations had done Twain a world of good.

With Livy, and Clara, he set sail for Australia on the *RMS Warramoo*, a weather-beaten vessel full of rats and cockroaches. The ship stopped at Honolulu, but was quarantined due to a cholera scare. In Australia and then New Zealand, crowds followed him everywhere. One man walked seventy-five miles to hear him speak. Then, it was on to Ceylon (Sri Lanka), and then India, where he stayed for almost three months, gathering curious and appreciative crowds in Bombay, Darjeeling, and Calcutta. In South Africa for two months, Twain spoke to crowds in Pretoria, Johannesburg, and Cape Town. He was disgusted by the blatant European colonialism and wrote, "There are many humorous things in the world; among them the white man's notion that he is less savage than the other savages."

A year and a day after they began their journey, Twain, Livy, and Clara headed for England. He had made thirty-five-thousand dollars toward paying off his debt; his notebooks were filled with ideas for a final travel book, *Following the Equator*. Exhausted and eager to reunite his family in England, Twain could not wait to see Susy again, but it never happened: she died, suddenly, of spinal meningitis. Twain would give another two-hundred speeches here and there, but his heart was rarely in it; as if there was nothing left worth saying.

Illustration by Joseph Keppler, *Puck*, December 1885

"MARK TWAIN,"
AMERICA'S BEST HUMORIST.

# The World Was His Oyster

## Twain's Travel Books

Believing himself to be an American Everyman, Mark Twain packed his bags and traveled the world with a smirk, shaking his head at tourist trade hype. Notebook in hand, he recorded what he saw, from the trashy to the transcendent, and let himself experience everything from the fake awe to the genuine lump-in-the-throat-goose-bump-experience.

### Tart-tongued Tourist in the Old World

#### *The Innocents Abroad* (1869)
Twain's first full-length book has a full-length title, the longest in the Twain canon: *The Innocents Abroad, or The New Pilgrims' Progress; Being Some Account of the Steamship Quaker City's Pleasure Excursion to Europe and the Holy Land*. It was the book that put Mark Twain on the map and led to his worldwide fame.

On June 8, 1867, the *Quaker City* set off on the first American pleasure cruise to the Old World. Twain's way was paid by San Francisco's *Alta California*, a daily paper that gladly gobbled up the fifty letters he sent them during the five-month tour. These formed the basis for his book, a wickedly witty memoir of American tourists fumbling their way through Europe, around the Mediterranean, and back. Twain kept careful notes of overheard conversations, comical and tragic sights, reactions to ancient marvels and modern day realities, as he and his fellow travelers gaped and grunted through the Azores, Gibraltar, Tangier, France, Italy, Greece, Russia, Turkey, Syria, Palestine, Egypt, Spain, and Bermuda. To our delight, we, the readers, will see it all through the eyes of a "night-hawk," who dares to sneak out past curfew and who scoffs at the strange ways of the world, with its misery and its mirth.

Twain turned the tourist experience on its head and inserted ridicule where reverence is generally expected, putting into words what it feels like to find a souvenir kiosk in the middle of a panorama the glossy brochures had promised would be awe-inspiring. Inevitably for Twain, the destinations look better when observed at night or from a distance, away from the sound and the fury, the smells and the flies. "In the glare of the day," he wrote, "there is little poetry about Venice, but under the charitable moon her stained palaces are white again."

All along the way, the "pilgrims," as he called his fellow travelers, helped themselves to relics. In Jerusalem, at the Church of the Holy Sepulcher, the stone on which the body of the crucified Jesus had been laid is hidden under a marble slab to protect it from ardent tourists. As Twain explained, "Pilgrims were too much given to chipping off pieces of it to carry home." Everywhere, he saw how tourist "vandals" desecrated ancient sites and trampled over the local citizenry, turning them into beggars or servants if they weren't already.

Once home and ready to write the book, Twain relied on the writings of his fellow passengers as well as the scrapbook of his published writings, letters, and news clips which his sister Pamela had meticulously assembled. He had to fight the *Alta* for the rights to quote from his own writing. Bret Harte, whom Twain would famously come to loathe, helped edit the manuscript, and Livy Langdon, soon to be his wife, helped with proofreading. Twain earned advance publicity for the book with his lecture tour, "The American Vandal Abroad." The book became wildly popular, although Twain himself would eventually consider the writing crude.

### A Tramp Abroad (1880)

The running gag in this book is that an American narrator (the unnamed Mark Twain) and his sidekick, Mr. Harris, boast of their ambitious intention to *tramp* across parts of Europe on foot, when, in fact, they manage to hitch rides on everything from donkey carts to trains and boats.

These burlesqued travels are based on the time Twain's best friend and pastor, Joe Twichell, joined him for a tour of the Swiss Alps and on his excursions in Germany, Switzerland, France, and Italy in 1878–79. In the book, Twichell became the colorless, much put-upon Mr. Harris, who reluctantly agrees to go to the opera but refuses to jump off Riffelberg Mountain with an umbrella for a parachute. Rabidly anti-Catholic, Harris finds that everything is better in the Protestant districts of Switzerland; from the flower boxes to the dogs. Twain comically exaggerates the experiences he and his travel companion have, as when the two set out for a mountain climbing excursion in full evening dress, with an entourage which includes seventeen guides, fifteen barkeepers, and

INNOCENT DREAMS.

three chaplains. They cannot figure out how to navigate a large rock, let alone climb a mountain. And so it goes, as Twain laughs at himself and other overly ambitious travelers, bogged down by bravado, baggage, and big dreams.

Twain struggled to write this book; he quickly lost interest, but persevered, churning out page after page. Distracted, he wrote too much, and had to cut the excess verbiage. Some of the cut stories or chapters became parts of other books.

## Nostalgic Note-taker of the New World

### Roughing It (1872)

Between publishing two books about European travel, Twain wrote *Roughing It*, playing fast and loose with the truth of events as they happened during his years out West (1861–66). He did not start writing the book until 1870, by then dependent on his memory, Orion's notes, news clippings, and his imagination, useful for embellishment.

The first twenty-one chapters describe the cross-country stagecoach trip, during which Sam Clemens bumped along beside Orion and a six-pound dictionary. As the stagecoach passed through prairie towns, he saw his first buffalo, antelope, jackrabbit, and coyote. The brothers gave "a whoop and hurrah" to the Pony Express rider who went by so fast that he seemed to be "a flash of unreal fancy;" nervously wended their way through hostile Indian territory; heard shots and shouts one night and mysteriously woke up to a new stagecoach driver; and, in Wyoming, enjoyed breakfast one morning with a man named Slade, a notorious but soft-spoken desperado, who murdered twenty-six people. Twain wrote, "I was afraid he had not killed anybody that morning, and might be needing diversion." After stopping in Salt Lake City, where Sam pondered polygamy, the stagecoach crossed unmeasured stretches of desert.

*Imagine a vast, waveless ocean stricken dead and turned to ashes. . . . there is not a sound – not a sigh – not a whisper – not a buzz, or a whir of wings, or distant pipe of bird – not even a sob from the lost souls that doubtless people that dead air.*

127

Three weeks after beginning their trip, the Clemens brothers reached Carson City. The Wild West was crowded with outlaws, gold and silver miners, speculators, and "nabobs," swaggering men who had gotten rich overnight. Never a nabob, Sam remained at the other end of the spectrum. Eventually, he traded in mining in the camps for writing in Virginia City, a rough and nearly lawless town. After a stint as journalist in San Francisco, he headed for a mining camp where Dick Baker told tall tales about his cat, the remarkable Tom Quartz. Sailing to the Sandwich Islands, Sam soaked up the lush world as if he had been parched from his days in the desert and offered descriptions of the food, the people, their myths, and their music. One night, a volcano erupted, spewing a pillar of fire; the next day, with the volcano still grumbling, he and a fellow tourist walked down into the crater, though the guides refused to accompany them. Back on the mainland, Sam trembled through a bout of stage fright on the lecture circuit. The long book comes to a quick close with the return home by boat, and hints of excursions to come.

By the time Twain assembled his notes and wove them into this book, he had known great success with *Jumping Frog* and *The Innocents Abroad*. Readers could not get enough of this new voice, which was and would always be more storyteller than accurate chronicler. Since its first publication, *Roughing It* has remained in print as one of Twain's most popular books.

### Life on the Mississippi (1883)

This book is a love song to the Mississippi River. Twain, the unnamed narrator, takes us back to the days when he was a boy in Hannibal, describing the thrill that pumped through the town whenever a steamboat docked, and the town turned from torpid to turbulent.

*Once a day a cheap, gaudy packet arrived upward from St. Louis, and another downward from Keokuk. Before these events, the day was glorious with expectancy; after them, the day was a dead and empty thing. Not only the boys, but the whole village felt this.*

With the cry, "Steamboat a-comin'!" the town drunkards stir and people pour out of their houses to see the chimneys spewing the black smoke, the pilot house "all glass and 'gingerbread,'" the texas deck ornamented with white railings, and flags "gallantly flying from the jackstaff." The upper decks would be lined with passengers, and all would look for the captain who stood by the big bell, "calm, imposing, the envy of all." We follow the young narrator to New Orleans, where he gives up his dream of going to the Amazon; instead, he becomes a cub pilot under the watchful eye of Horace Bixby. The words splash along, drenching each scene with excitement. We are given a picture of life in the heyday of river travel.

By chapter twenty-two, we are with the author on his return visit to the river in 1882. Traveling in disguise, he feigns ignorance of the river and is given a "tranquil pool of lies"; when he reveals his

"I WAS GRATIFIED TO BE ABLE TO ANSWER PROMPTLY, AND I DID. I SAID I DIDN'T KNOW."
—Life on the Mississippi, Ch. 6

© Tom Tenney

identity, everyone has a good laugh. The laughter evaporates as the narrator observes how the river has changed, a victim of modernization, and how the post-Civil War South has suffered, subjected to brutal modifications. This is a lamentation of the fast-paced age of the railroad and the loss of romance. New Orleans is described as a vulnerable city, in words that make readers in post-Katrina America tremble. He writes, "There is nothing but that frail breastwork of earth [the levee] between the people and destruction." All is not bleak, however. We will hear wildly exaggerated tall tales, reminiscences, legends, jokes, superstitions. The pages are full of colorful characters, remembered or newly met.

Twain was inspired to pen his memories of days as a steamboat pilot after reminiscing aloud with his Hartford friend, Joe Twichell, in 1875. The result was a series of articles for the *Atlantic Monthly* titled "Old Times on the Mississippi." Seven years later, Twain returned to the river with his publisher, James R. Osgood, and a stenographer. They sailed down-river on the *Gold Dust*, spent a week in New Orleans, boarded Bixby's steamboat to St. Louis, then toured the northern river towns. Back home in the East, Twain combined his earlier writings with new ones. The publisher omitted one chapter, fearing that it would offend Southern readers.

## Galavanting Globe Trotter

### Following the Equator (1897)

From July 1895 to July 1896, Twain circled the globe with his wife Livy and daughter Clara, addressing packed houses on stages across northern United States, Australia, New Zealand, Ceylon, India, and South Africa. He also visited the Fiji Islands and Mauritius. Everywhere he went, he peered out from under his wild eyebrows and scribbled in his notebooks, filling them with anecdotes. In Australia he scans the night sky for a constellation called the Southern Cross: "It is ingeniously named, for it looks just as a cross would look if it looked like something else."

Benares

In Benares, a city in India, which Twain describes as "a religious hive, whose every cell is a temple, a shrine, or a mosque," he visits Sri 108 Swami Bhaskarananda Saraswati, a "most pleasant and friendly deity." The 108, Twain notes, "stands for the rest of his names." They spend the afternoon conversing, then exchange autographs. Twain wrote:

*I gave him a copy of* Huckleberry Finn. *I thought it might rest him up a little to mix it in along with his meditations on Brahma, for he looked tired, and I knew that if it didn't do him any good it wouldn't do him any harm.*

In South Africa, Twain finds beauty in the "liquid voices" of the African women and in their language which is rounding and flowing. He finds little to admire in the Boers of the veldt (South Africans of Dutch or Huguenot descent), whose clothing sets a record for "miracles of ugly colors inharmoniously associated."

Twain offers these bits and pieces of history and life, tossing them on this path around the world, like Hansel and Gretel tossing breadcrumbs in the dark woods. We will follow him, eager to see the places he visited and the people he met. There is humor here and scattered tall tales, but there is also attention to human suffering at the hands of oppressors and invading tourists. By now, Twain has seen how the tourist trade impacts the native cultures and understands it as the by-product of privilege and imperialism.

Written in the months of anguish after the death of his daughter Susy, Twain felt himself to be "in hell" as he looked back on this marathon journey. He consciously worked to lighten his tone. The American edition was published after major cuts and revisions; the British edition, titled *More Tramps Abroad*, had only minor edits and is closer to Twain's original manuscript.

# Out of this World

· · · · · · · · · · ·

## Twain's Science Fiction and Fantasy

Mark Twain may have gotten his start with a story about a frog weighed down with lead pellets, but his mind was destined to explore the vast reaches of space and time. Could any less be expected from an über-genius who was born and would die under the spell of a comet?

Never bound by the laws of gravity or nature, Twain unleashed his imagination early and often. In 1874, he penned "A Curious Pleasure Excursion" in which he proposed that certain corrupt politicians be given complimentary tickets for a luxury cruise into outer space.

In "Captain Stormfield's Visit to Heaven," after the title character dies, he zooms through space on a speeding comet and engages in a drag race with another comet carrying brimstone, "cargo for Satan." When Stormfield arrives at a place that is hellishly bright, he is relieved to learn that it is heaven. He has arrived at the wrong gate, however, and must stand aside as myriads of sky-blue aliens, each with seven heads and one leg, file past. Eventually, he is sent to the American sector of heaven. Later, he notes:

*The learned men from other planets and other systems come here and hang around a while . . . and then go back to their own section of heaven and write a book of travels, and they give America about five lines in it.*

In *No. 44, The Mysterious Stranger*, Twain's title character enjoys visiting planet Earth because it always holds the element of surprise. "Number 44, New Series 864,962" is a precursor to *Star Trek's* omnipotent albeit mischievous "Q." He freely travels through time and space on a whim, gawking at Pharaoh's army as it flounders in the sea, racing ahead to yet undiscovered America to pick up some hot corn-pone from Arkansas.

Time travel is a primary feature in *A Connecticut Yankee in King Arthur's Court*. Hank Morgan is sent back in time to Camelot, where he attempts to introduce the technological and sociological advances of the late 1800s: soap and suffrage, phonographs and telephones, colleges and newspapers. Twain could not sustain the vision; the utopian fantasy unravels into a dystopian nightmare. By story's end, floodlights illuminate fields of corpses.

In "The Curious Republic of Gondour," Twain envisioned a society that, disappointed by its tradition of universal suffrage where anyone can vote, develops a system weighted in favor of property owners and those who are educated. Since then, women have been elected to top offices and the government has been free of corruption.

Twain tackled a utopia gone bad in "The Great Revolution in Pitcairn." In this story, an American stumbles upon a stress-free island in the South Pacific and takes up residence. After four months, he has introduced money, established a military force, and proclaimed himself emperor, but the people revolt, take back their island, and return to their peaceful ways.

Twain looked into the future when he wrote "The Loves of Alonzo Fitz Clarence and Rosannah Ethelton," in which the title characters meet, fall in love, and court each other in a series of long-distance phone calls. Written in 1877, he anticipated long-distance phoning, which was not possible until 1915. Twain looked into the future again in "From the *London Times* of 1904." In this story, a new invention called the telelectroscope is used to relay visual communication around the world. Written in 1898, before the development of television, people viewing a telelectroscope screen observe that a Polish inventor, presumed dead, is alive and well and living in China.

In addition to speculative fiction, space and time travel, and fantasies of long-distance telephones and television, Twain played with the plasticity of gender. "A Medieval Romance" is a gender-bender set in 1222, in which a girl is brought up as a boy so that she can inherit the throne. In "1002d Arabian Night," Scherezade tries to evade the executioner's blade one more night by telling the Sultan a bizarre tale about two children whose gender identities are switched at birth by a witch. Twain's short story "Wapping Alice" also ends with a gender-bender surprise.

It did not take much for Twain to enter the realm of the fantastical, something he did increasingly with age. As early as 1876, he wrote a bizarre fantasy entitled "The Facts Concerning the Recent Carnival of Crime in Connecticut" in which his conscience materializes in the form of a shriveled imp covered in fuzzy, green mold. The encounter is not pretty; the Twain-like narrator does battle with his diminutive conscience and eventually exterminates it.

Several pieces left unfinished by Twain easily fit the category of either science fiction or fantasy. In "The Enchanted Sea Wilderness," Captain Elliot Cable (a Mark Twain stand-in) sails a ship straight into an imaginary region of the Indian Ocean, the "Devil's Race-Track," where compasses spin out of control. Trapped in the dead-calm center, called "Everlasting Sunday," the ship drifts through the utter stillness, passing other ships, whose crews, long dead, are nothing but bones. In "The Great Dark," a happy father and two daughters of a prosperous family, look through a microscope at a drop of water and its minuscule animal life. Suddenly, the whole family is aboard a ship, sailing across that same drop of water. "Three Thousand Years Among the Microbes" is the story of a man who has been turned into a cholera germ by a magician. He lives in the bloodstream of a scurvy, unwashed tramp. From the germ's point of view, the beggar's ravaged body is a "grand and awe-compelling" planet. In "Which Was the Dream?" a U.S. senator and his happy family endure a series of disasters. Stripped of wealth and power, the narrator wakes up and wonders if he has been asleep for eighteen months or one hour.

David Ketterer, who has edited a collection of Twain's fantastical stories, asserts that Twain might have replaced H. G. Wells as the significant author of modern science fiction, had he managed to polish and publish some of his unfinished pieces.

Dave Thomson Collection.

# Pudd'nhead Wilson, A Tale

· · · · · · · · · · ·

**Setting**: Dawson's Landing, Missouri
**Period**: 1830–53

Despite the whimsical title, this slim volume is densely packed with grim twists and turns, dealing deftly with issues of prejudice and slavery in pre–Civil War U.S.A. Its three distinct story lines are cleverly woven together to make one tangled tragedy.

As in *The Prince and the Pauper*, this novel, too, begins with the birth of two boys at opposite ends of the class spectrum. This time, however, the setting is not 16th-century London, but 19th-century Dawson's Landing, located a little south of St. Louis. One baby, Valet de Chambre (Chambers), is born to Roxana (Roxy), a domestic slave belonging to Percy Driscoll. She was impregnated by Colonel Cecil Burleigh Essex, one of the town's leading white citizens; something she will keep secret until after his death. Both Roxy and her child are fair: Roxy is 1/16th Negro and her blond, blue-eyed son is 1/32nd Negro, which means that they are both Negro, not Caucasian, in the eyes of the law. The other baby, born the same day and in the same household, is Thomas à Becket Driscoll (Tom). His parents are a prominent white couple in town; his uncle is a prosperous judge.

When Mrs. Driscoll dies of childbirth complications within the week, Roxy must tend both babies. As she fusses over the boys, it occurs to her that they look very much alike. How unfair it is that her little baby will be doomed for the hard, cruel life of a slave, while the other, through no merit of his own, will be blessed with a life of opportunity and luxury.

That same month, David Wilson, a young lawyer from the East, moves into town to set up his practice. When he makes a clever remark that goes over the heads of his listeners, he is dubbed "Pudd'nhead Wilson," a nickname that ruins his law career for two decades. With no clients seeking his legal assistance, Wilson turns to accounting. His hobby is fingerprinting, a very new tool of criminal investigation; in his spare time, he collects the fingerprints of his neighbors. His other hobby is the development of a calendar with clever maxims sprinkled throughout. Wilson has occasion to see Roxy with the two babies and playfully involves her in his hobby, taking fingerprints from both infants and filing them away in his collection.

One day, Roxy and the rest of the slaves in the Driscoll household are accused of theft. The others confess their guilt and are sold down the river to the Deep South. Roxy, though spared, is scared by the close call. She contemplates the two babies in her care, one lucky, the other doomed. In an act born of desperation, she switches the babies. With nothing but a change of clothes and cradles, their lives have now reversed course. When Wilson wants to fingerprint the babies again, Roxy lets him and is relieved when he does not suspect their switched identities.

The boys grow up together, never guessing their true circumstances. Tom, the name of the one born a slave but reared a child of privilege, is sickly, pampered, and demanding. He showers Roxy with insults and abuse, never guessing that he is her son. Chambers, born privileged and now a slave, develops into a physically robust youth but learns to keep his mouth shut and his head down.

When the boys are fifteen, their fathers both die. Percy Driscoll, who believes himself to be Tom's father, frees Roxy on his deathbed; she leaves town to become a chambermaid on a steamboat. Judge York Driscoll, who has bought Chambers, also takes on the care of his nephew, Tom. The judge will soon promise to leave him his estate, since Tom inherited nothing from Percy. Tom is sent to Yale for his education where his manners improve but his character flaws deepen, specifically his addiction to drinking and gambling.

Angelo and Luigi Capello, Italian twins of Florentine nobility, arrive in town. They charm the townspeople and receive many social invitations, the first of which is for a drink with David Wilson. As Wilson waits for the twins to arrive, he contemplates something he saw that morning when he

glanced into the window of Judge Driscoll's house; a strange woman was moving around Tom's bedroom. Tom is due home for a visit.

Roxy has worked on a riverboat for eight years, carefully depositing her meager earnings in a bank in New Orleans. Forced to retire because of rheumatism, she attempts to collect her savings, but learns that the bank has gone out of business. Penniless, she returns to Dawson's Landing, where she is warmly welcomed by Judge Driscoll's slaves. Chambers greets the woman he believes is his mother and tells her the latest gossip about Tom, who is drinking and gambling. When Tom comes home for a visit, Roxy is waiting for him. Predictably, he treats her with disrespect. She tells him her sad story and begs him for money, but he responds with a sneer. Appalled by Tom's ingratitude and his rudeness, Roxy turns the tables, telling him all she knows about his recent bad behavior and threatening to tell the judge. This scares Tom, but Roxy is not finished; she instructs him to meet her later at the haunted house.

That night, Roxy tells Tom her big secret: she is not his old slave, but his mother. Stunned to learn that he was born black and enslaved, Tom agrees to split his fifty-dollars-a-month allowance with her. The problem is that he is three-hundred dollars in debt, and his only plan for recouping the money is theft. Roxy approves.

Over the next few months, Tom raids various homes and, by selling the hot loot, gets out of debt, but immediately gambles his way back in.

On the day the Italian brothers arrive in town, Tom sneaks back into town disguised as a woman. Later, after learning about that evening's reception for the twins, Tom loots the homes of the party guests. After the party, Angelo and Luigi stop by David Wilson's place. To their surprise, Tom shows up and teases Wilson about his fingerprinting hobby. Intrigued, the twins ask for a demonstration, and Wilson collects fresh fingerprints from all three of his guests. Wilson also tells his guests about another interest, palmistry, which leads to the awkward discovery that Luigi once killed a man while saving Angelo's life and retrieving a special knife, a gift to the twins from an Indian prince. The men end the evening drinking at an anti-temperance meeting, where Tom gets into a dispute with Luigi.

Tom refuses to challenge Luigi to a duel, which is interpreted as cowardice. To save the family honor, Judge Driscoll challenges Luigi to a duel the next night. Happily, both live to enjoy the respect of the whole town. Meanwhile, everyone is talking about the rash of thefts in the neighborhood. Someone has stolen the twins' special knife, and they want it back. Tom gets nervous when he hears that Wilson and the Italian twins have set a trap for the thief. He turns to Roxy, who tells him to negotiate with the St. Louis creditors, offer to pay interest on his debt until his inheritance comes through, and sell all the stolen loot to pay that interest. If he fails in any way, Roxy says, she will tell everyone the truth about his identity.

A town election is approaching. Wilson is, at last, being recognized for his leadership abilities and has accepted the invitation to run for mayor. The Italian brothers have been accepted into Dawson's Landing, especially since Luigi had the courage to participate in a duel. Their popularity assured, they apply for citizenship and run for city council. All of this is irksome to Tom. He tells his uncle that Luigi once committed murder. Hearing this, the judge denounces the Italian twins and vows to make sure that Luigi and Angelo will lose in the upcoming election.

Tom, meanwhile, is the victim of a theft: someone steals his stolen goods. He is almost glad when Roxy arrives in St. Louis and showers him with a mother's pity. She makes an astonishing offer; that Tom forge ownership papers and sell her upstate, as his slave, to cover his debt. She is worth at least six hundred dollars. Tom agrees to the plan, but, instead of selling her to a kindly farmer upstate, he sells her down the river to an Arkansas cotton farmer.

Back at Dawson's Landing, Judge Driscoll rewards his nephew's improved behavior with access to the family safe. At the same time, the judge has spread nasty rumors about the Italian twins and their supposedly "stolen" knife, publicly called them frauds, and implied that they are killers. On the day of the town election, Wilson wins for mayor, but the twins lose. There is talk that Luigi may challenge the judge to another duel.

The next time Tom returns to St. Louis, he is followed by a shabbily dressed man; it is Roxy in disguise. Having escaped, she tells Tom how she was forced to work in the Arkansas fields under harsh conditions. This time, Roxy has had enough. She orders Tom to go to his uncle and ask for the money both to pay off his gambling debts and to purchase her freedom. When Tom objects that his uncle will disinherit him, Roxy shrugs, saying that if he does not do this, she will tell his uncle who Tom really is. "He'll sell you down de river," she says, holding her son at knife point, "en you kin see how you like it."

At Dawson's Landing that night, the Italian twins are out for an evening stroll when Tom sneaks into his uncle's house intending to steal the money. He disguises himself as an elderly black woman and grabs the twins' special knife he has in his possession. Creeping down the stairs, he finds his uncle napping on the sofa, beside a stack of banknotes. When Tom reaches for the money, his uncle wakes up, and Tom stabs him to death. In a panic, he flees, leaving the knife behind. After cleaning up, he takes a canoe upstream to catch a steamboat to St. Louis. There, he will use the stolen money to buy Roxy's freedom and pay off his debts.

The Italian brothers, returning from their evening stroll, hear the judge's cries and rush to help. They are the ones standing by the dead body when others arrive; their special knife is the murder weapon. Luigi, the one with the public grudge against the judge, is charged with homicide, and Angelo is charged as an accessory. Wilson vows to defend them in court, although the case appears to be open-and-shut. Almost everyone has turned against the twins. The only hope Wilson has is to call on witnesses who might testify about the veiled woman seen running from the Driscoll house at the time of the murder, but she remains a mystery. Tom, meanwhile, returns to Dawson's Landing, acting shocked and sad at the news of his uncle's brutal murder.

One evening, Wilson examines his fingerprint collection, hoping that one of the female sets will match some prints taken off the murder weapon. Tom stops by to harass the lawyer and casually picks up the glass with Roxy's prints. Later, Wilson looks at the glass again and, seeing Tom's prints, suddenly begins to put two and two together. The only thing is, Tom's adult prints do not match the prints taken when he was an infant.

The next day in court, Wilson surprises everyone. First, he points out that the twins stayed at the murder scene, something they would not have done if they had committed the crime. He talks about the murder weapon, the motive, and the mystery woman. Finally, he pulls out his fingerprint plates. The townspeople begin to laugh derisively, until Wilson patiently explains the scientific evidence and gives a compelling demonstration of this form of identification. The people filling the courtroom are impressed. In a dramatic conclusion, Wilson, no longer considered a "pudd'nhead," not only reveals the killer to be Tom Driscoll, but also reveals that Tom and Chambers were switched at birth. The man known as Chambers is actually Driscoll's nephew and rightful heir. The man known as Tom was actually born a black slave. With this, Roxy falls to her knees, begging God for mercy, while Tom is led away in handcuffs.

In the final chapter, we learn that the twins, though exonerated, have had enough of America and cannot wait to leave. Roxy has been given a pension to live on, but her spirit is broken. Tom has confessed; instead of being sent to prison, however, he is sold down the river. As for the true Tom Driscoll, he is now understood to be both white and rich, but he is also illiterate and uneducated, with the mannerisms of a slave and the dialect to match. He ends this story as a lost soul.

## The Story behind the Story

With this novel, Mark Twain became the first author to make use of fingerprinting as a devise in a story line. Fingerprint identification was developed by Sir Francis Galton, who published his theory in 1892, only two years before Twain wrote this novel.

Written almost entirely while Twain was living in Europe, the story was originally titled "Those Extraordinary Twins." He conceived it as a farce about "Siamese twins" who, though conjoined, disagree with each other about everything. A year later, Twain was calling the story "Pudd'nhead Wilson" but the twins were still conjoined; the story was oversized and rambling. Twain rewrote the story, strengthening the Roxy-Tom-Chambers story line, separating the twins, and removing the comedy. What is left is tragedy. The book continued to go through painfully elaborate rewrites. In the end, no one was quite sure what the title was, a confusion that lasts to this day.

# Twain's Twins and Doubles

· · · · · · · · · · · ·

twain (twān), *adj., n.* two.

An obsession with the twos of nature is inherent in the pen name chosen by Sam Clemens: a nautical term, *mark twain* also served to accent the author's fascination with twins and doubles, switched-identities and disguises.

In his early thirties, Twain wrote an essay, "The Personal Habits of the Siamese Twins," exaggerating the strange reality of Chang and Eng Bunker (1811–74). The famous conjoined twins became American citizens, got married and fathered twenty-two children. In Twain's fiction, the strange possibilities of such a life are magnified: one is Baptist, the other Catholic; one is a teetotaler, the other a heavy drinker; one fights for the Confederacy, the other for the Union, and they take each other prisoner.

In 1891, Twain saw the Tocci brothers, Giovanni and Giacomo, who shared one torso and a pair of legs. Inspired, Twain changed their names to Angelo and Luigi Capello and wrote the beginnings of a novel, in which the conjoined twins, almost incompatible, take turns controlling their shared body. One smokes, the other doesn't. When one sings a hymn, the other drowns him out with a vulgar song. They run for office, opposite each other. In the end, one of the conjoined twins is lynched, while the other is left hanging, as it were.

The Tocci twins

Eventually, Twain separated the Capello brothers and expanded the story for

*Puddn'head Wilson*, incorporating the tale of two boys, one black, one white, who look almost identical. When the mother of the black child switches them in their cradles, their lives are forever changed. A similar experiment with switched identities occurs in the more streamlined story, *The Prince and the Pauper*. Here, two boys are born on the same day, but one is born in the London slums whereas the other is born in a palace. As adolescents, the two meet and, playing, exchange clothes and are each mistaken for the other.

Tom Sawyer and Huck Finn could pass for twins. The same age and size, they are bosom buddies; but Tom leads with his head, thinking up mischievous adventures, whereas Huck leads with his heart, feeling his way toward the complicated truth. Midway through his adventures, Huck gets a glimpse of what his life might have been had

The Capello brothers

he been born into a genteel Southern family, but his near-twin, a boy named Buck, meets an untimely death in a fatal family feud; Huck is glad to be himself, homeless but free.

In *Tom Sawyer, Detective*, the boys must untangle a murder mystery involving actual twins. Tom's Uncle Silas is on trial for killing Jubiter Dunlap. Tom stuns the courtroom when he reveals that Jubiter is not dead at all, but is sitting in the audience wearing a fake beard. The victim was his twin brother, Jake.

Twins, doubles, and mistaken identities appear in Twain's short works as well. In "An Encounter with an Interviewer," the narrator confounds a reporter with peculiar life details. He claims, for example, that he was a twin, but that something went very wrong:

> We got mixed in the bath-tub when we were only two weeks old, and one of us was drowned. But we didn't know which. Some think it was Bill. Some think it was me.

In "Lucretia Smith's Soldier," a young woman lavishes all her attention on a severely wounded soldier for several weeks, nursing him back to health, only to learn, when the bandages are removed from his head, that the soldier is not her fiancé.

Sunday-school lessons are debunked in twin stories, "The Story of the Bad Little Boy" and "The Story of the Good Little Boy." In the former, a prankster matures into a murderous villain, but is nevertheless revered and elected to office, while in the latter, Jacob Blivens strives for perfection and encounters nothing but disaster. This theme was repeated in "Edward Mills and George Benton: A Tale," which describes orphaned cousins who, adopted, grow up as brothers. Edward strives to live a good life, being industrious and kind, but meets with defeat and disgrace. George, on the other hand, is selfish and destructive, but is treated sympathetically.

Justin Kaplan, author of the much-acclaimed biography *Mr. Clemens and Mark Twain*, wrote about "the troubled twainness of Mark (or dark) Twain and his creator and Siamese twin, Samuel L. Clemens." Tormented by nightmares from childhood, Twain's bad dreams continued and multiplied with age. Sometimes, he would stand alone on a dream stage and announce, "I am Mark Twain," but no one would believe him. In story after story, he began to explore two realities, one experienced while awake, the other while asleep. Inevitably, he would ask the question; which was the "real" existence? He wrote of his "dream self" as "my double, my partner in duality, the other and wholly independent personage who resides in me." In Twain's novel, *No. 44, The Mysterious Stranger*, set in an Austrian village in 1490, the printers go on strike and "Duplicates" appear, like some demented vision of union-busting scabs. No. 44, the title character, explains to his teenaged friend August Feldner, that the Duplicates are solidified Dream-Selves.

*You know, of course, that you are not one person, but two. One is your Workaday-Self, and 'tends to business, the other is your Dream-Self, and has no responsibilities, and cares only for romance and excursions and adventure. It sleeps when your other self is awake.*

Later, August realizes that there is more to the story: "Each human being contains not merely two independent entities, but three – the Waking-Self, the Dream-Self, and the Soul." The first two selves die when the body dies, but the Soul is immortal. Just when he thinks he has figured out the nature of reality, August learns that the Waking-Self and the Soul are fictions. No. 44 tells him, "Nothing exists; all is a dream."

In 1868, in order to draw attention to a lecture he was about to give in Cleveland, Twain penned a comical sketch titled "A Mystery," in which he claimed that an imposter using his name was traveling the country running up bar bills. He listed some ways in which he differed from this Double: "It gets intoxicated – I do not. It steals horses – I do not. It imposes on theatre managers – I never do. It lies – I never do. It swindles landlords – I never get a chance."

At least twice, Twain took on the role of a twin. He was paired with a Southern writer, George Washington Cable, for a four-month lecture tour called the Twins of Genius (1884–85). Like most of Twain's twins, he and Cable did not get along.

On January 1, 1907, the *New York Times* ran an article with the headline, MARK TWAIN AND TWIN CHEER NEW YEAR'S PARTY. It was an account of a party at Twain's home the previous evening, during which the humorist had appeared tied by a ribbon to a man introduced only as his Siamese twin, their arms draped around each other's shoulders. The more the "twin" drank, the louder Twain lectured on temperance, and a jolly time was had by all.

# Short Works of the 1890s

. . . . . . . . . . .

1891 "Down the Rhone" (Essay)
Twain describes what he sees on the river and along the shore during a ten-day trip down the Rhone River, through France, aboard a flatboat.

1891 "Marienbad – A Health Factory" (Essay)
Twain spent some time at a health resort where the visitors were rude and self-absorbed, with no other topic of conversation than their aches and pains.

1892 "Some National Stupidities" (Essay)
Twain laments that patriotic pride prevents people from sharing inventions and new ideas across national borders.

1892 "The £1,000,000 Bank-Note" (Short story)
Poor Henry Adams, swept out to sea, is rescued by a British brig. Arriving in London, dirty and penniless, he meets two elderly men who hand him an envelope and send him on his way. What Adams does not know is that the two men are rich and eccentric brothers who have made a bet with each other about what would happen to a poor but honest man, given a million-pound bank note.

1892 "The Californian's Tale" (Short story)
An unnamed narrator visits the tidy home of a prospector named Henry in a California mining town. Henry is eagerly awaiting the arrival of his beloved wife. After several days, Henry collapses, and his friends tuck him into bed, telling the narrator the sad truth: Henry's wife died nineteen years earlier, and he has been insane ever since.

1893 "The Esquimau Maiden's Romance" (Short story)
This is the sad story of a charming Inuit woman, Lasca, who is dressed in furs that would be the envy of Manhattan's upper crust. Everyone wears furs in her village, but it is her father, the man with the most fish hooks, who is considered wealthy. One day, a handsome stranger named Kalula comes to town. He and Lasca fall in love and are engaged to be married. When Lasca's father discovers that a hook is missing, Kalula is accused of theft, given a trial by

water, and thrown into the sea. Months later, on the day of the Great Annual Sacrifice, when the women wash and comb their hair, Lasca finds the fish hook in her own tangled locks. She and her remorseful father moan, "We murdered him."

1893  "Is He Living or Is He Dead?" (Short story)
Lamenting that artists often struggle and starve, only to attain fame with death, four friends draw lots. The one who "wins" serves as a pallbearer at his own faux funeral and lives a secret life, reaping the benefits of being a dead artist. The story later became the basis for Twain's play *Is He Dead? A Comedy in Three Acts*, which, remarkably, opened on Broadway in the fall of 2007.

1893  "Traveling with a Reformer" (Sketch)
A clever narrator manipulates public servants by using tricks of diplomacy to reform bothersome or unfair regulations, such as the prohibition against Sunday card-playing.

1894  "In Defense of Harriet Shelley" (Essay)
Condemning it as a literary cake-walk, Twain rips apart Edward Dowden's biography of Percy Bysshe Shelley, especially his cavalier treatment of the suicide of Shelley's first wife.

1895  "How to Tell a Story" (Essay)
After outlining the elements of the humorous story, Twain analyzes "The Wounded Soldier" and "The Golden Arm," of the latter warning, "You must get the pause right."

1897  "Wapping Alice" (Short story)
In London's Wapping district, a maid marries her lover, then confesses that she is male.

1898 "About Play Acting" (Essay)
Twain laments that the New York theater scene offers too much "mental sugar," a steady fare of comedy and farce.

1898 "A Memorable Assassination" (Essay)
Twain was living in Austria when that nation's Empress Elizabeth was stabbed by an Italian anarchist. He marveled at the power of modern media to rapidly convey news.

1898 "The Austrian Edison Keeping School Again" (Essay)
Jan Szczepanik, a brilliant young inventor, developed an early form of television (telelectroscope) as well as a copy machine. Twain was outraged that the government ordered him to teach school every two months for half a day in a far away village.

1898 "From the *London Times* of 1904" (Sketch)
Jan Szczepanik, the inventor, appears again in this science fiction sketch set in the near future when a new invention brings visual communication around the world, but fails to stop the execution of a wrongly accused man.

1899 "My Boyhood Dreams" (Essay)
Twain's accomplished friends longingly reconsider their childhood aspirations of being cowboys, circus ring-masters, buccaneers, auctioneers.

1899 "My Début as a Literary Person" (Essay)
Twain recalls interviewing the survivors of a shipwreck in Hawai'i and his excitement at getting his report published in *Harper's*.

1899 "My First Lie and How I Got Out of It" (Essay)
"All people are liars from the cradle onward, without exception," Twain writes. He has forgotten his first lie, but his second was when he pretended to be stuck by a diaper pin in order to get attention. Lies of silent assertion are insidious, he claims, because they provide the rationale for slavery and other forms of injustice.

1899 "How to Make History Dates Stick" (Essay)

This essay for children was written and illustrated by Twain. It outlines several of his tried and true memory-enhancing techniques.

1899 "Concerning the Jews" (Essay)
In this essay, inspired by the case of Alfred Dreyfus, a Jewish officer in the French army who was falsely accused of treason, Twain examines why Jews are persecuted and concludes that it is because of resentment for their accomplishments.

1899 "The Death Disk" (Short story)
Set in 17th-century England and based on a true story, three military men are charged with disobeying orders. Oliver Cromwell has decided to let an innocent child select one man to be executed. When little Abby is brought in, Cromwell hands her three wax disks and tells her to give them to the prisoners. Thinking it is a game, the child approaches the shackled men and presents her father with the prettiest disk, the red one signifying execution.

1899 "Diplomatic Pay and Clothes" (Essay)
Twain ponders why America outfits its military generals in impressively decorated uniforms while sending its diplomats to formal events in plain clothes.

# The "Dontcareadamn Suit"

. . . . . . . . . . . .

## Clothing in Twain's Life and Fictions

When Mark Twain was seventy-one, he began wearing his trademark white "dontcareadamn suit." He introduced the outfit in December 1906, when he addressed a Congressional committee on copyright laws. According to biographer Justin Kaplan, "When his turn came, he stripped off his long overcoat; he was dressed from shoulder to foot in white serge, and, with his great mane of white hair, he stood out in the dimly lighted committee room at the Library of Congress like a blaze of sunlight." He joked to a *Chicago Daily Tribune* reporter: "This suit, I may say, is the uniform of the Ancient and Honorable Order of Purity and Perfection, of which organization I am president, secretary, treasurer, and sole member."

Wearing white in all seasons lifted his spirits and satisfied his obsession with cleanliness. "I prefer to be clean in the matter of raiment – clean in a dirty world," Twain said, "absolutely the only cleanly-clothed human being in all Christendom north of the Tropics. And that is what I am."

Claiming his role as "the most conspicuous person on the planet," Twain shunned black, but was not averse to other colors. He wrote,

> I would like to dress in a loose and flowing costume made all of silks and velvets, resplendent with all the stunning dyes of the rainbow, and so would every sane man I have ever known; but none of us dares to venture it.

Visiting Ceylon in 1896, Twain was impressed with the brightly clothed people, "each individual was a flame, each group a house afire for color." Into this vision of paradise marched grim children wearing the missionary school uniform, "repulsive as a shroud." He felt ashamed of the Western influence on this vibrant society. Twain

got his chance to wear a swirl of colors when he was awarded an honorary degree at Oxford and was presented with a scarlet-and-gray gown. It became his favorite costume; later, he wore it at Clara's wedding, upstaging the bride.

## "Au Natural" vs. Civilization's Stifling Attire

Twain explored the power of clothes to affect mood, perception of power, and expression of freedom or bondage, throughout his writings. For Tom and Huck, the fewer the clothes the better. When his cousin Mary helps him get dressed for church, Tom feels "exceedingly improved and uncomfortable." Huck, too, is at war with clothing from the first page of his adventures. Taken in by the Widow Douglas, he complains about his new clothes: "I couldn't do nothing but sweat and sweat, and feel all cramped up." To Huck's abusive father, nice clothes represent exclusion from the good life he will never have; confronting Huck at the mansion, he sneers, "Starchy clothes – very. You think you're a good deal of a big-bug, *don't* you?" In most illustrations, Huck sports a floppy straw hat and, like Jim the slave, wears clothes that are patched and several sizes too big. In fact, for much of *Adventures of Huckleberry Finn*, the adolescent and his adult companion wear nothing at all. "We was always naked, day and night," Huck tells us, "whenever the mosquitoes would let us."

Twain extolled the innocence of those who live in societies where clothing is optional. In his writings about Adam and Eve, the transition from naked to clothed is experienced as loss. In his travel books, Twain wrote that notions of what constitutes the outfit of a well-dressed person vary considerably. "About the most becoming get up I ever saw in my life," Twain wrote, "was out in the Sandwich Islands thirty years ago, where a native who wanted to appear at his best usually appeared in a pair of eyeglasses."

## Clothing as Mask

For Twain, all clothing was, in some sense, camouflage, a costume designed to influence perception. In "The Czar's Soliloquy," written a decade before the Russian Revolution, Twain imagines the skinny Czar, after his morning bath, standing naked in front of a mirror, musing, "There is no power without clothes. . . . Naked officials could exercise no authority; they would look (and be) like everybody else – commonplace, inconsequential. A policeman in plain clothes is one man; in his uniform he is ten."

In *Huckleberry Finn*, two con men, the king and the duke, use clothing as disguise. When the king puts on black, store-bought clothes, Huck marvels at the transformation, writing, "he did look real swell and starchy. I never knowed how clothes could change a body before. Why, before, he looked like the orneriest old rip that ever was."

The plots of two novels rest almost entirely on an exchange of clothing. In *Pudd'nhead Wilson*, Roxy, a light-skinned black slave, notices that her baby looks almost identical to a white baby, except that the white child wears ruffled soft muslin and a necklace. Roxy changes their destinies merely by dressing them in each other's outfits. Similarly, in *The Prince and the Pauper*, when circumstances conspire to let Tom Canty and Edward Tudor exchange clothes, the little prince says, "Fared we forth naked, there is none could say which was you, and which the

Prince of Wales." Suddenly separated, their experiences are dictated by the clothes they wear.

In his essay, "Diplomatic Pay and Clothes," Twain laments that American ambassadors are sent to formal events plainly dressed while foreign representatives wear clothes that distinguish them from "the unofficial throng." To remedy the sorry situation, Twain suggests that we confer on our ambassadors the rank of admiral or general, because these persons, even after retiring from military service, are allowed to wear uniforms blazing with color and gold.

Only Twain's idealized Maid of Orléans, in *Personal Recollections of Joan of Arc*, is able to dismiss and reverse the assumptions made by costume. Joan's simple peasant garb, in all its purity, proves more impressive than the dazzling ornamentation of the Dauphin's court, in all its splendor. When she is escorted into the court, a crowned imposter sits on the throne in a deception designed to dupe the peasant girl; but Joan is destined to become a saint, in part, because she is not fooled by surface appearance. She easily identifies the Dauphin, dressed in plain clothes, hiding in the crowd.

© Mark Dawidziak

# Personal Recollections
# of Joan of Arc

· · · · · · · · · · · ·

**Setting: France**
**Period: 15th century**

Twain takes two steps back, doubly dis-guising his authorship of this novel by presenting it as a memoir by the eighty-two-year-old Sieur Louis de Conte, as translated by Jean Francois Alden. As the book opens, de Conte, now elderly, remem-bers the France of his childhood, defeated and demoralized by the English, when the dead lay in heaps on the streets of Paris. Orphaned and traumatized, he was sent to live with a priest in the village of Domremy. The church property was adjacent to the garden of Jacques d'Arc, who had a daugh-ter named Joan; they became lifelong friends. De Conte recounts many stories of the remarkable Joan, whom the children of the village gave a range of nicknames: the Bashful, the Patriot, the Beautiful, the Brave. De Conte was the Scholar, because he could read and write.

Central to the childhood experience in Domremy is the magical tree at the edge of the oak forest, beneath which the fairies have danced for hundreds of years.

According to the village legend, all people reared in Domremy become Children of the Tree and see it in a vision before their deaths. When conditions in France grow worse and Domremy is ransacked, Joan boldly proclaims, "France will rise again. You shall see." One day in 1428, de Conte finds Joan beneath the enchanted tree, pleading aloud, "But I am so young! oh, so young to leave my mother and my home and go out into the strange world to undertake a thing so great!" De Conte confronts Joan who tells him about the "Voices" which have been talking to her, informing her that God wants her to win back France. The day before Joan's seventeenth birthday, she tells de Conte that the Voices have in-structed her to meet with the Dauphin within two months.

Joan begs the governor of Vaucouleurs for an armed escort, but he delays, wonder-ing whether she is a witch or a saint. Frus-trated, Joan foretells an imminent military defeat and begins to assemble her own tiny army; five men and a horse. The governor, impressed, belts his own sword around her waist and provides her with a mounted escort of men-at-arms. With twenty-five men now under her command, Joan sets off across France to meet with the Dauphin.

After many setbacks, the day comes when the peasant girl, dressed in simple clothes, is escorted into the court's gaudy presence. The authorities try to trick Joan by putting an imposter on the throne. Joan is not fooled. She looks carefully at the lines of standing courtiers and, though she has never seen him before, recognizes Charles VII. Throwing herself at his feet, she calls him the "dear and gentle Dauphin!" Other words to describe the Dauphin might be vapid, ungrateful, self-serving, and weak. He looks slightly astonished when Joan commands, "Thou art lawful heir to the King thy father, and true heir of France. God has spoken it. Now lift up thy head, and doubt no more, but give me men-at-arms and let me get about my work." Convinced, the Dauphin sends Joan and her army to Courdray Castle, accompanied by his guard of honor. Along the way, crowds cheer for the Joan, the Maid, the one sent from heaven.

The weak-willed Dauphin, influenced by advisers, turns Joan over to bishops and theology professors for three weeks of questioning. The robed inquisitors eventually determine that Joan has been sent by God, not Satan. The Dauphin names her "General-in-chief of the Armies of France" and, with this announcement, a thousand caps fly into the air. De Conte marvels at his childhood friend, who, just months earlier, had brought home a starving kitten to cuddle and feed. "And now – the kitten had hardly had time to become a cat, and yet already the girl is General of the Armies of France."

Joan dictates a letter to the English commanders at Orléans and orders them to leave France. As a suit of armor is made for her, she names de Conte her page and secretary and sends for a crusty veteran, La Hire, to train the recruits. A "Vesuvius of profanity, forever in eruption," La Hire is baffled to learn that Joan not only wants every recruit to attend mass twice a day, but that he, too, is expected to attend. The old soldier argues, but Joan wears him down. Soon, Joan and La Hire are inseparable, reviewing the troops in a camp that is clean and orderly.

When the battles begin in earnest, Joan must deal with delays caused by her jealous and doubting male generals. Despite this, she leads her men to their first victory. A few days later, on May 8, Joan is wounded in battle but continues to fight, inspiring another victory by her courage and determination. The grateful Dauphin asks the Maid to name her reward, but she only begs the king to hurry to his coronation. Ignoring her pleas, he ennobles her and all her kin, saying, "Rise, Joan of Arc, now and henceforth surnamed Du Lis, in grateful acknowledgment of the good blow which you have struck for the lilies of France." Joan assembles eight-thousand men and forces the English to surrender in village after village. Now proclaimed the "Savior of France," she celebrates the victory and predicts that it means English power in France is broken for a thousand years.

After the king is finally crowned, Joan passionately argues against the cautious advice of his counselors, begging permission to march to Paris. In the end, her impassioned plea moves the entire assembly, and the King hands his own sword to Joan, proclaiming, "There, the King surrenders. Carry it to Paris." Where the story should lead to victory, however, the weak King and his sniveling advisors turn all progress toward defeat. De Conte writes bluntly, "Joan of Arc, who had never been defeated by the enemy, was defeated by her own King." Camped outside of Paris, Joan is denied the troops she needs; then, the King orders that her army be disbanded. For eight months, Joan travels with the King, leading small skirmishes. Captured on May 24, her military career ends.

Twice, Joan tries to escape from her imprisonment and fails. The king offers no assistance, but political deals are in the wind. The Duke of Burgundy ransoms Joan to Bishop Cauchon who has been promised a promotion to archbishopric of Rouen. Now, Joan will be brought to trial for religious crimes. De Conte, heartbroken when he learns of Joan's plight, hurries to Rouen and gets a job as clerk with a priest named Manchon, fated to be the chief recorder at Joan's trial. All the while, Joan is chained to her bed by the neck and hands, and deprived of female attendants. Though a minor, she is forbidden counsel; tricks are played on her and traps set for her. Brought into court, she takes a moment to lift her colorless face to a shaft of sunlight, then refuses to reveal what the Voices have told her. Joan maintains her dignity and presence of mind while the officers of the court dicker and argue. This is only the bitter beginning.

Time and again, the judges are confounded by her clear, forthright answers to their devious questions. They increase the number of judges to sixty-two and put Joan before a cunning theologian, "an old hand at tricks and traps." He questions her about the Voices and about her male attire, but Joan is more than a match for all the judges and the trickster theologian. When Bishop Cauchon realizes that the court is losing ground, he closes the proceedings to the public. Joan, ignorant of her rights, is led away in chains.

At her third trial, Joan is charged with sixty-six offenses, including that she is a sorceress, false prophet, and dealer in magic. This trial, too, ends without result. The fourth trial lists only twelve charges. Parisian theologians are sent the documents and, while they confer, Joan grows ill. As secretary to Manchon, de Conte is alarmed when he sees Joan in chains in her dungeon cell, where the interrogation continues. He barely recognizes the frail creature with the sad face. Even after the Parisian theologians find her guilty on all twelve counts and fifty judges call her to renounce her "errors," Joan calmly refuses to cooperate with her accusers.

For the first time, Joan is led to the stake; when she sees the hot coals before her, however, she succumbs and agrees to sign a confession. This earns her a reprieve from the stake, but she is condemned to perpetual imprisonment, not in a church prison, as she had been promised, but in the English dungeon devoid of female matrons, the same iron cage where she has spent the last months. The realization that she has been lied to again slowly dawns on the exhausted girl, and she is led away, sobbing.

Two days later, street criers call out, "Joan of Arc has relapsed! The witch's time has come!" Her prison guards had hidden her gown and put male clothing in its place, giving her no choice but to wear the forbidden clothes. Bishop Cauchon and other clerics descend to the dungeon one more time, gloating. One judge momentarily ponders how it was possible that Joan had access to men's clothes in her cell, but he is quickly silenced. No longer agitated, Joan is serene as she recants her earlier confession and gives the *responsio mortifera*, the fatal answer. She will no longer deny that the Voices of St. Marguerite and St. Catherine speak to her. Manchon conveys a message to de Conte; it is a request from Joan, that he write to her mother and say that she has seen the vision of the tree of Domremy. De Conte recognizes this as a message of comfort for Joan's family and friends, signifying her acceptance of imminent death.

Crowds flock to see the tragedy at the Old Market, their faces lined with dumb sorrow. A priest hears Joan's confession and gives her communion, then a dunce cap is put on her head bearing the inscription HERETIC, RELAPSED, APOSTATE, IDOLATER. Placed in a cart, sunlight illumines the white-robed Maid while thousands of peasants whisper "a vision! a vision!" At the Old Market, Joan weeps and kneels to pray, not for herself, but for the King of France. Now, every heart is touched, even Cauchon's. As the world gazes up at her, Joan waits alone at the top of the stacked wood. De Conte is forced to look away, unable to witness the torture.

**The Story behind the Story**

According to Twain legend, one day in Hannibal, a page torn from a history book blew into young Sam's hands. It was a dramatic passage about Joan of Arc. This was the beginning of his lifelong interest, not only in the Maid of Orléans, but in medieval history. Later, it took twelve years of research, reading five texts in French and five in English, before he was ready to pick up the pen. He drew on the actual heresy trial transcripts, published in the 1840s. Twain began writing the book in 1892, while living in Florence. He wrote quickly, weaving into the straight historical narrative some fictional characters and modeled much of Joan's youthful beauty and spirit

on his daughter Suzy. In a letter to Clara, Suzy wrote:

*Papa is progressing finely with his "Joan of Arc" which promises to be his loveliest book. The character of Joan is pure and perfect to a miraculous degree. Hearing the M.S. read aloud is an up-lifting and revealing hour to us all. Many of Joan's words and sayings are historically correct and Papa cries when he reads them.*

Twain finished writing the book in February 1895. In an essay, he wrote of the feeling of desolation that swept over him when he entered his study the next day.

This book, he claimed, was written "for love not for lucre," and, at first, Twain hid his authorship, not wanting it dismissed as the work of a humorist. Readers were to think that it was the newly translated work of one of the Maid's contemporaries, Sieur Louis de Conte, known in actual history as the page and secretary to Joan of Arc. Significantly, if one counts the title Sieur, the secretary's initials match those of the true author's, SLC, Samuel Langhorne Clemens. Twain loved this book and considered it his best and most important work.

*I like Joan of Arc best of all my books; and it is the best; I know it perfectly well. And besides, it furnished me seven times the pleasure afforded me by any of the others; twelve years of preparation, and two years of writing. The others needed no preparation and got none.*

# Best Loved Witty
# Sayings of Mark Twain

· · · · · · · · · · ·

~ A Crossword Puzzle ~

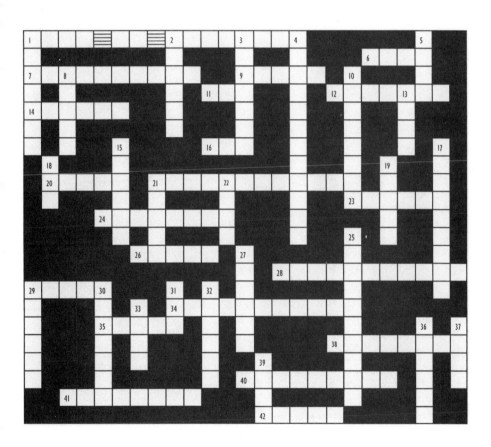

## ACROSS:

1. It is better to be a young June-bug than an old (three words) .
6. Consider the ____! – incomparably the bravest of all creatures of God, if ignorance of fear were courage.
7. Let us endeavor so to live that when we come to die even the _____ will be sorry.
9. When angry, count four; when very angry, _____.
11. Next to a wife whom I idolize, give me a ____ .
12. _____. This is one of the peculiarly dangerous months to speculate in stocks in. The others are July, January, September, April, November, May, March, June, December, August, and February.
14. [Referring to Bermuda] You go to _____ if you want to – I'd druther stay here.
16. As to the Adjective: when in doubt, strike it ____ .
20. It is by the goodness of God that in our country we have those three unspeakably precious things; freedom of speech, freedom of conscience, and the prudence _____ to practice either of them.
21. _____ is a limitless multiplication of unnecessary necessaries.
23. _____ has no longer any charm for me. I have seen all the foreign countries I want to see except heaven and hell, and I have only a vague curiosity as concerns one of those.
24. It could probably be shown by facts and figures that there is no distinctly native American criminal class except _____.
26. The man with a new idea is a _____ until the idea succeeds.
28. _____ is nothing but cabbage with a college education.
29. The first time that I ever _____ a watermelon . . . I carried that watermelon to a secluded bower in the lumber yard, and broke it open and it was green.
34. You can't depend on your judgment when your _____ is out of focus.
35. It were not best that we should all think _____; it is difference of opinion that makes horse-races.
38. Always do right. That will gratify some of the people, and _____ the rest.
40. By trying we can easily learn to endure_____. Another man's, I mean.
41. Good _____ consists in concealing how much we think of ourselves and how little we think of the other person.
42. Hardly any cats are affected by _____, but these [mine] are; when I sing they go reverently away, showing how deeply they feel it.

## DOWN:

1. Man is the only animal that _____. Or needs to.
2. When I write _____ I do not get any wages; often I lose money by it.
3. Get your facts first and then _____ them as much as you please.
4. The report of my death was an _____.

5. In my age as in my youth, night brings me many a deep remorse. I realize that from the cradle up I have been like the rest of the race – never quite _____ in the night.

8. Every time I see or hear a new wonder . . . I have to postpone my _____ right off.

10. Name the greatest of all inventors. _____.

13. If you pick up a starving dog and make him prosperous, he will not _____ you. This is the principal difference between a dog and a man.

15. The secret source of humor itself is not joy but _____. There is no humor in heaven.

17. I was young and foolish then; now I am old and _____ .

18. I have not yet come across a living ___ that seemed to have any more sense than a dead one.

19. It is my rule never to smoke when asleep, and never to refrain when _____.

21. I have made it a rule never to smoke more than one _____ at a time.

22. There are many humorous things in the world; among them the white man's notion that he is _____ savage than other savages.

25. The holy passion of _____ is of so sweet and steady and loyal and enduring a nature that it will last through a whole lifetime, if not asked to lend money.

27. "Classic." A book which people _____ and don't read.

29. [Declining an invitation] Won't go to any banquet, not even the Last _____.

30. Few things are harder to put up with than the annoyance of a good _____.

31. One of the most striking differences between a cat and a ____ is that a cat has only nine lives.

32. Nothing so needs reforming as other people's _____.

33. Even popularity can be overdone. In Rome, along at first, you are full of regrets that Michelangelo _____; but by and by you only regret that you didn't see him do it.

36. I believe in early _____ – for everyone but myself.

37. Summer seas and a good ____ – life has nothing better.

39. What a good thing ____ had – when he said a good thing, he knew nobody had said it before.

*Answers can be found at the end of the book.*

# He Said a Lot, But He Didn't Say This

. . . . . . . . . . . .

## Quotes Mistakenly Attributed to Mark Twain *

Giving up smoking is easy. I've done it hundreds of times.

Wagner's music is better than it sounds.

When I feel the urge to exercise, I go lie down until it passes.

Better to keep your mouth shut and appear stupid than to open it and remove all doubt.

Everybody talks about the weather, but nobody does anything about it.

There are three kinds of lies: lies, damned lies, and statistics.

The man who does not read good books has no advantage over the man who *can't* read them.

When the end of the world comes, I want to be in Cincinnati because it's always twenty years behind the times.

The devil is alive and doing well because he has so many damned helpers.

There is nothing so annoying as to have two people go right on talking when you're interrupting.

When I was a boy of fourteen, my father was so ignorant I could hardly stand to have the old man around. But when I got to be twenty-one, I was astonished at how much the old man had learned in seven years.

So I because a newspaperman. I hated to do it, but I couldn't find honest employment.

I don't exaggerate; I just remember big.

* List compiled by Twain authority Jim Zwick (*www.boondocksnet.com/twaintexts/quotes_not_twain.html*), who drew on the research by Kim A. McDonald, Shelley Fisher Fishkin, and others.

# Tom Sawyer, Detective

· · · · · · · · · · · ·

Setting: St. Petersburg, the Mississippi
River, and Arkansas
Period: Pre–Civil War

Tom's Aunt Sally and Uncle Silas need a
diversion from their worries: Brace
Dunlap, a rich, widowed farmer, who lives
up the road, wants to marry their innocent
daughter, Benny. They have been staving
off the pushy farmer and trying to appease
him by hiring his no-good brother, Jubiter
(so nick-named for the mole on his leg that
looks like the planet "Jubiter" and its
moons). Jubiter had a twin named Jake, also
no good, who disappeared seven years ago.
All of this has gotten on Uncle Silas's
nerves: he does not seem to be himself.

Tom and Huck, accepting an invitation
to visit, catch a ride on a sternwheeler.
Right away, Tom learns that there is a genuine mystery on the boat: Phillips, the man
in the next cabin, has locked himself in,
and keeps his boots on day and night. The
boys disguise themselves as waiters and
deliver the mystery man's breakfast one
morning. "Jubiter!" Tom exclaims. He is
wrong; this is not Jubiter, but long lost Jake,
on the run and terrified for his life.

"It was a confidence-game," Jake starts,
and tells his story. He and two pals,
Bud Dixon and Hal Clayton, robbed a
St. Louis jewelry store of two diamonds
valued at twelve-thousand dollars. Jake and
Hal both bought little disguises for use
during a get-away, but Bud just bought
himself a screwdriver. That night, aboard a
riverboat, all three tried to stay awake,
guarding the stolen gems from each other,
but when Bud fell asleep, Jake and Hal
snatched the diamonds and tiptoed up to
the hurricane deck. The plan was to throw
Bud overboard when he came looking for
them, but he never showed up. Around
dawn, they realized that, instead of diamonds, they had stolen pieces of sugar.
They returned to the cabin with a new
plan, to take Bud ashore the next night, get
him drunk, take the diamonds, and bump
him off. Jake, however, remembering the
screwdriver, realized that Bud had hidden
the diamonds under the steel plate of his
boot heel.

The next night, the three found a tavern
in a Missouri town. Bud drank until he
passed out. After searching him, Jake suggested that the diamonds must be in Bud's

stomach, and offered to run to a drug store to "fetch something that'll make them di'monds tired of the company they're keeping." In a shrewd maneuver, he managed to walk out of the tavern wearing Bud's boots without Hal noticing. Instead of running to a drugstore, he ran to the river and climbed aboard the sternwheeler, sure that the diamonds were in the boots. The plan would have worked, except that the boat lay in dock for repairs, long enough for Hal and Bud to track Jake. Now all three outlaws are on board, and Jake is cornered "like a rat in a trap."

Tom, Huck, and Jake eventually manage to sneak on shore during a rainstorm. They split up, but make plans to meet by the sycamores right back of Uncle Silas's "tobacker field." The next evening, however, when Tom and Huck reach the sycamores, they find a scene of confusion. They see a couple of men run into the trees, hear screams for help, then watch as two men tear up the road, followed by two other men. Then, the boys see Jake Dunlap's ghost, walking up the road wearing the stolen boots. When they finally arrive at the farm, the boys cannot help noticing that Uncle Silas is restless, pacing and sighing. A slave knocks on the door and delivers the message that "Marse Brace" is looking for Jubiter. This interruption sends Uncle Silas into more agitation.

The next day, the boys decide to explore, out behind the sycamores. Tom is hoping the corpse is still wearing the boots. To their surprise, instead of finding a dead man, they find Jake sitting on a log, wearing a disguise. "Me and Huck's mighty glad to see you again," Tom tells Jake, who just motions with his hands and mutters nonsense.

In the next three days, the stranger becomes a curiosity as villagers become increasingly concerned by Jubiter's disappearance, openly speculating that he may have been murdered. Tom, aching for more adventure, has his heart set on finding the corpse, if there is one, and being celebrated for the discovery. On Sunday morning, he and Huck slip out of the house and, with the help of the blacksmith's bloodhound, find an arm sticking out of a muddy grave in a tobacco field. When Uncle Silas hears the news, he collapses, confessing, "I done it!" Wracked with guilt, he tells his family how he had become agitated with Jubiter and hit him over the head with a stick. The sheriff barges into the house and arrests poor Uncle Silas for the murder.

When the trial begins, Huck writes that the "lawyer for the prostitution" laid out his case and began calling witnesses; they tell a neatly coordinated story about Jubiter's murder at the hands of Uncle Silas who leaps to his feet and confesses again. Everyone is riveted to Uncle Silas, until Tom shouts, "A murder was done, but you never had no hand in it!" Tom weaves a story about the stolen diamonds, the recent troubles with Brace Dunlap, and the various characters he and Huck witnessed racing down the road the night they got to town. It is a long, convoluted story; and an accurate one. Tom tells the packed courtroom that Jubiter is not dead at all, but is sitting right there in the midst of them, then he rushes the slow-witted Jubiter and tears off the disguise, revealing the truth. Jake was murdered, Tom says, and buried by Brace. The crowd goes wild with excitement.

There is one more detail to be divulged; Tom dramatically exclaims, "Your Honor, there's a thief in this house." Enjoying the prolonged theatricality, Tom instructs Jubiter to put his foot on a chair.

He then unscrews the heel-plate and holds up the two missing diamonds for all to see. The judge proclaims the case closed, and the sheriff arrests Brace Dunlap and the witnesses he paid to falsely testify. Everyone returns to Uncle Silas's church and praises his sermons, though, to Huck, they are "the blamedest jumbledest idiotic sermons you ever struck, and would tangle you up so you couldn't find your way home in daylight."

This is the end of the story, except for one thing. When Tom is given the two-thousand dollar reward, he hands over half of it to Huck and never tells anybody, which, Huck writes, "didn't surprise me, because I knowed him."

## The Story behind the Story

Detective stories were all the rage in 1893 when Twain wrote this book. With the real life Jack-the-Ripper terrorizing London, the world seemed to crave a character like Sherlock Holmes, smarter than the average police officer. Arthur Conan Doyle's detective had first appeared on the scene in an 1887 "shilling shocker," but it was after the publication of the third story featuring the Baker Street bachelor that Sherlock Holmes became a household name. That was in 1891. Two years later, with his ear to the ground, Twain began writing the book that would eventually be titled *Tom Sawyer, Detective*.

# The Man That Corrupted Hadleyburg

· · · · · · · · · · ·

**Setting: Hadleyburg (Anytown, U.S.A.)**
**Period: Unspecified**

For three generations Hadleyburg has maintained its reputation as the most honest town around, and the people are damn proud of it. Smug, even. Honesty may be the town's strong suit, but hospitality is not. One day, someone offends a stranger, and the offense is not forgotten. For a year, the scorned man broods as he travels, unable to forget the insult. In revenge, he devises a plan to "corrupt the town."

Late one night, six months after making his decision to seek retaliation, the stranger returns to Hadleyburg and stops at the home of the old bank clerk, Edward Richards, whose wife, Mary, sits reading the *Missionary Herald* by lamplight. Edward is away, but the stranger only wants to leave something for him: a heavy sack with a note attached. The polite stranger departs, saying only that he will never again return to Hadleyburg now that his task is done. Mary cannot resist looking at the sack or reading the note, which begins:

*TO BE PUBLISHED: or, the right man sought out by private inquiry – either will answer. This sack contains gold coin weighing a hundred and sixty pounds four ounces.*

In the note, the stranger explains that, almost two years ago, his gambling obsession had nearly ruined him, but one kind person in Hadleyburg took pity on him when he was desperate and gave him twenty dollars with a word of advice. Encouraged, he stopped gambling. Now, the Hadleyburg native is to be rewarded with gold coins. The letter outlines how this can be accomplished: inside the sack is a sealed envelope containing the helpful remark. The person who is to receive the reward must first be able to recite that remark. An inquiry may be published in the local paper, with these instructions:

*Thirty days from now, let the candidate appear at the town-hall at eight in the evening (Friday), and hand his remark, in a sealed envelope, to the*

*Revd Mr. Burgess (if he will be kind enough to act); and let Mr. Burgess there and then destroy the seals of the sack, open it, and see if the remark is correct; if correct, let the money be delivered, with my sincere gratitude, to my benefactor thus identified.*

This is the set-up from which the story proceeds. The stranger has fabricated an incident, set a trap designed to unearth sins of omission and commission, the secrets and shortcomings of Hadleyburg's most respected citizens. As soon as Edward arrives home, he and Mary eye the sack of gold and reread the letter of instruction, then Edward rushes out of the house and hands over the document to the newspaper editor.

When Edward returns, he and Mary wonder who could have been so charitable to a degenerate gambler. The answer occurs quickly to both; most likely it was Barclay Goodson, recently deceased, and long despised. Goodson had been a disgruntled citizen of Hadleyburg, publicly ridiculing his neighbors as self-righteous hypocrites, albeit honest ones. Everyone had hated him, almost as much as they currently hate the minister, Rev. Burgess, the very man the stranger has selected to open the sealed envelope at the appointed time.

As it happens, the day of great temptation begins the very next morning, when everyone runs to the bank to see the sack of gold. In the days that follow, the heads of the nineteen principal households in Hadleyburg wonder aloud what the magic words might be. During the next three weeks, guilty secrets rise to the surface, and one by one, the people of Hadleyburg become unglued. The plot thickens when Mary and Edward receive a letter from Howard L. Stephenson, a stranger, who has heard about the mystery in Hadleyburg. He claims that he was visiting Goodson the night he handed a destitute foreigner twenty dollars and made his remark. Later, Goodson said how much he despised the proud people of Hadleyburg, except one:

*I think he said you — am almost sure — had done him a very great service once . . . and he wishes he had a fortune, he would leave it to you when he died, and a curse apiece for the rest of the citizens.*

Mary and Edward continue to read the letter from Stephenson, who writes that, with Goodson now deceased, Edward should take the reward: Goodson would have wanted it. To that end, Stephenson divulges the key to the mystery, the exact wording of the remark: YOU ARE FAR FROM BEING A BAD MAN: GO, AND REFORM. Mary is ecstatic and asks Edward to tell her about the "great service" he once did for once-ornery-now-dead Goodson, but he remains silent, unable to recall doing anything. Mary and Edward have no idea that the same secret-disclosing letter has been delivered to the eighteen other principal households.

In the days that follow, Reverend Burgess is handed sealed envelopes wherever he goes, until, at last, he is holding envelopes from all nineteen of Hadleyburg's most respected and prominent men. Friday night, the Town Hall fills with a curious crowd, all eyeing the sack of gold. The minister makes a brief speech, about honesty, then pulls the first envelope from his pocket and reads aloud from its contents: "The remark which I made to the distressed stranger was this: 'You are very far from being a bad man: go, and reform.'"

The minister explains that, if these words match the words on the envelope inside the sack of gold, the reward will go to its author, Mr. Billson. Instead of applause, the entire crowd seems stunned and paralyzed. This was not the name anyone expected to hear. "*Billson!* oh, come, this is too thin!" the people begin to whisper.

The minister opens the sack of gold, finds the enclosed envelope, opens it and removes two folded notes. One bears the instruction that it is not to be read until all the letters addressed to the Chair, if any, have been read. The other note is marked "The Test," and it is this note that the minister reads aloud. This note explains that the "remark" actually consisted of two parts. The first part is not important. It was the second part that must be remembered – all fifteen words. And the entire remark is this:

*You are far from being a bad man. Go, and reform – or mark my words – someday, for your sins, you will die and go to hell or Hadleyburg – try and make it the former.*

The minister has more envelopes to open and letters to read. There is one from a Mr. Pinkerton and one from Gregory Yates and another by Nicholas Whitworth. Each letter begins with the first half of the remark. It is now obvious that each has made false claims for the reward. When several of the "Nineteeners" try to leave the hall, shouts go up, "The doors, the doors, close the doors!" More letters are opened, more town leaders are red-faced. Now, as each letter is opened, the crowd recites in one voice, "You are f-a-r from being a b-a-a-a-d man." When eighteen letters have been read aloud, their writers mocked, Mary and Edward await their humiliation; theirs is the only remaining letter. To their relief, however, the minister claims that he

has no more letters to read. All eyes turn to Edward, as he is proclaimed the only honest town leader. The elderly couple is baffled, newly wary, and speechless as undeserved praise rolls their way.

Finally, the minister unfolds the second note he found in the sack of gold and reads it. It says that, if there is no claimant, the gold should be divided to all the honest town leaders. The audience groans and laughs. Then the minister reads the crucial postscript, exposing the whole exercise as a hoax.

*CITIZENS OF HADLEYBURG: There is no test-remark – nobody made one. There wasn't any pauper stranger, nor any twenty-dollar contribution, nor any accompanying benediction and compliment – these are all inventions.*

The letter explains how the stranger had returned to town, studied its citizens, learned their secrets, then set his trap and baited it. He has only one goal: "I am hoping to eternally and everlastingly squelch your vanity and give Hadleyburg a new renown."

After the letter is read, the sack of gold is opened. It holds nothing but gilded disks of lead. The people decide to auction it off and give the money to the only prominent man in town who, they erroneously believe, did not take the bait. After the auction and some complicated financial maneuvers, the story ends with the stranger awarding Edward close to forty-thousand dollars and a note acknowledging him as an honest man. The minister writes a note too, in which he acknowledges saving Edward from shame, because Edward had once helped him.

Now, Edward is more miserable than ever, knowing that he is far from honorable.

"I can't bear it," he confides to Mary, and throws both notes into the fire. A few days pass, during which the Richards, now rich in both financial security and guilty secrets, grow delirious and sick, muttering confessions to their nurses. Within days, both are dead, the last to fall "prey to the fiendish sack."

Soon thereafter, Hadleyburg changes its name; never mind to what, the reader is told.

**The Story behind the Story**

Mark Twain wrote this morality tale quickly, in December 1898, while he was in Vienna, scribbling it on the stationery of the Metropole Hotel. Still grieving the death of his daughter Susy and struggling with finances, he was in a mood to write of disillusionment, indulge his pessimism, and expose the human inclination toward pride and deceit.

One curious note, according to Twain scholar R. Kent Rasmussen, in the 1952 western *High Noon*, the lawman played by Gary Cooper defends a smug, self-important town against outlaws, even though its principal citizens have forsaken him. The name of the town is Hadley*ville*, inspired by Twain's infamous Hadley*burg*.

# Last Words and More
# Last Words

. . . . . . . . . . .

doggy-paddling in the churning waters of the Mississippi and grabbing brother Henry; grinning in the saloons and mining camps of the Wild West; showing up early for infant son Langdon and, later, for daughters Susy in Hartford and Jean in Redding; teasing sweet Livy year after year until he finally came for her in a villa outside of Florence. Twain would try to talk behind Death's back more than once, attempting to contact his brother Henry and his daughter Susy. Twain's most famous death quote, in all its variations, was made in a note written in May 1897, thirteen years before his demise:

On a hot summer night in Missouri, when he was only three years old, "Little Sammy" Clemens sleep-walked into the bedroom of his dying sister and plucked at her bed covers, a gesture all properly superstitious Victorians recognized as a sign of impending death. This was Sam Clemens's introduction to old man Death, who, as it turned out, would tag along on the path of life, lurking behind every corner in Hannibal;

*James Ross Clemens, a cousin of mine, was seriously ill two or three weeks ago in London, but is well now. The report of my illness grew out of his illness. The report of my death was an exaggeration.*

Being on such intimate terms, Twain incorporated death into his daily wit and wisdom and eventually came to long for it.

© Tom Tenney

WATERSON MARK TWAIN JOURNAL ©1988

"WHEN I REFLECT UPON THE NUMBER OF DISAGREEABLE PEOPLE WHO I KNOW HAVE GONE TO A BETTER WORLD, I AM MOVED TO LEAD A DIFFERENT LIFE."
—Pudd'nhead Wilson's Calendar

The country home I need is a cemetery.

Travel has no longer any charm for me. I have seen all the foreign countries I want to see except heaven and hell, and I have only a vague curiosity as concerns one of those.

I have never greatly envied anyone but the dead.

Isn't this life enough for you? Do you wish to continue the foolishness somewhere else?

Let us endeavor so to live that when we come to die even the undertaker will be sorry.

Each person is born to one possession which outvalues all his others – his last breath.

Oh Death, where is thy sting! It has none. But life has.

Life: we laugh and laugh, then cry and cry, then feebler laugh, then die.

But such is human life. Here today and gone tomorrow. A dream – a shadow – a ripple on the water – a thing for invisible gods to sport with for a season and then toss idly by.

Life was not a valuable gift, but death was. . . . Death healed the bruised spirit and the broken heart, and gave them rest and forgetfulness; death was man's best friend; when man could endure life no longer, death came and set him free.

Poor old Methuselah, how did he manage to stand it so long?

All say, "How hard it is that we have to die" – a strange complaint to come from the mouths of people who have had to live.

Whoever has lived long enough to find out what life is, knows how deep a debt of gratitude we owe to Adam, the first great benefactor of our race. He brought death into the world.

Death, the only immortal who treats us all alike, whose pity and whose peace and whose refuge are for all – the soiled and the pure, the rich and the poor, the loved and the unloved.

Pity is for the living, envy is for the dead.

I think we never become really and genuinely our entire and honest selves until we are dead – and not then until we have been dead years and years. People ought to start dead, and they would be honest so much earlier.

All people have had ill luck, but Jairus's daughter and Lazarus the worst.

No real estate is permanently valuable but the grave.

A distinguished man should be as particular about his last words as he is about his last breath. He should write them out on a slip of paper. . . . He should never leave such a thing to the last hour of his life and trust to an intellectual spurt at the last moment to enable him to say something smart with his last gasp and launch into eternity with grandeur.

At his own demise, Twain, sedated with morphine, was in and out of a dream state for days. One of his last recorded remarks was: "Isn't there something I can resign and be out of all this?"

# The Lost Man

· · · · · · · · · · · ·

(1904–10)

When Livy Clemens died, the last nail was put in the coffin of the "happy family" once described by daughter Susy. At the funeral in Elmira, Clara had to be restrained from flinging herself into her mother's grave and was soon carted off to a sanitarium. She spent the next year, cut off from all contact with her father. Two weeks after the funeral, a horse Jean was riding bolted in front of a carriage: the horse was killed in the accident, and Jean was knocked unconscious and severely bruised. For the rest of her abbreviated life, she would suffer increased seizures and erratic, sometimes violent, behavior. Like a nightmare from which he could not wake, the pitiless summer of '04 held one more loss for Twain: his sister Pamela died.

Twain might have faced the great raging storm like a withered King Lear, stripped of his family, mad with grief, flailing his thin fists on the barren heath; but he didn't. He turned to New York City for solace, renting an apartment on Fifth Avenue, just a few blocks north of Washington Square in the Village. Then, he picked up his pen and wrote, short pieces and bizarre ones, full of rage against an apathetic god. He wrote from a dog's point-of-view and then from a horse's. He wrote of seeing the world, newly made in the Garden of Eden.

He spent his mornings smoking in bed and dictating his memories, toward the creation of an autobiography. He did not fuss with accuracy. "When I was younger I could remember anything, whether it happened or not," he said, "but I am getting old, and soon I shall remember only the latter." Endlessly fascinated by his own life, he framed his life experiences as stories. He wrote: "I am the human race compacted and crammed into a single suit of clothes, but quite able to represent its entire massed multitude in all its moods and inspirations."

Twain had a plan for his autobiography:

*Start it at no particular time of your life; wander at your free will all over your life; talk only about the thing which interests you for the moment; drop it the moment its interest threatens to pale, and turn your talk upon the new and more interesting thing that has intruded itself into your mind meantime.*

At first, he dictated to Isabel Lyon, the attractive, devoted forty-something who had first been employed as Livy's personal secretary. With Livy gone, "the Lyon" watched over the den in the heart of the city-jungle. She organized the household, played hostess, supervised the servants, did the accounting, escorted her employer to various public functions, and took dictation. Lyon doted on Twain, whom she fondly called "the King."

Dinner at the White House in November, 1905, as the guest of Teddy Roosevelt, may have been momentous in the life of this son of humble Hannibal, but it paled in comparison with the dinner a few weeks later at Delmonico's in New York City, honoring Twain on his seventieth birthday. A forty-piece orchestra played, while the distinguished guests feasted, offered toasts, and gave five hours of speeches. None of the speakers could get the crowd going like Twain himself, who recounted the rules by which he lived:

*As an example to others, and not that I care for moderation myself, it has always been my rule never to smoke when asleep, and never to refrain when awake. . . . As for drinking, I have no rule about that. When the others drink I like to help.*

Not long after Twain's birthday bash, Albert Bigelow Paine, an energetic forty-year-old, visited Twain and found the author smoking in a bed littered with books and papers. When Paine mentioned an interest in writing a biography, he was startled to hear Twain's casual reply, "When would you like to begin?" From that moment, Paine was a part of the household and became Twain's most faithful (albeit starstruck) friend, traveling companion, and amanuensis; sorting letters and papers, taking notes in no less than two-hundred-and-forty-two dictating sessions, and playing billiards in the evenings when work was done. Engaging his "methodless method," Twain dictated half-a-million words. He scribbled in the margins of the transcribed pages, giving contradictory instructions about when certain passages could be published: seventy-five years after his death, one century, five-hundred years.

Early in 1906, Twain took up a new hobby; collecting young girls. With his own daughters either dead or distanced, he took one last look at his youth and the golden days when precocious sweethearts pouted through his afternoons. He called his collection "Angelfish" and fashioned a club called the "Aquarium." By the end of that year, Twain began appearing in his "dontcareadamn suit," strolling up and down Fifth Avenue, relishing the crowds that gathered to get a look at him. Fan mail arrived from all around the globe. Remarkably, one letter was simply addressed to "Mark Twain, Godknowswhere." The post office delivered it.

In June 1907, Twain made his last trans-Atlantic voyage, collecting a couple Angelfish along the way and delighting in the exuberant welcome he received from the stevedores upon docking – "my own class," he called them. He dined with George Bernard Shaw (a self-proclaimed "Huckfinnomaniac") and James Barrie (creator of Peter Pan). At Oxford, Twain was awarded an honorary degree. Lord

Curzon, the chancellor of the university, said, "Most amiable, charming and playful sir, you shake the sides of the whole world with your merriment," as the crowd stood and cheered. With the degree came a crimson and gray robe, which Twain would thereafter wear whenever he liked.

In the popular imagination, Twain's final years are nothing but bleak depression and bitterness. The truth is, much was sweet, even intoxicating, in those last years, but the bitterness left an aftertaste. For all the joy he seemed to get out of his celebrity status, he began referring to his lonely apartment as "The Valley of the Shadow." When Paine bought property in Redding, Twain did too. He hired an architect to build an eighteen-room Italian-style villa. In June 1908, he moved in, site-unseen, and named the house "Stormfield."

Twain took the advice of Ralph Ashcroft, a British entrepreneur, and registered the name "Mark Twain," then gave Ashcroft power-of-attorney. The following year, Twain was present at the wedding ceremony when Ashcroft married Isabel Lyon. Behind the scenes, Clara Clemens had grown paranoid and jealous of Lyon. She fanned rumors of various crimes and misdemeanors, accusing the newlyweds of theft and dishonesty. Twain had been taken advantage of one too many times. He did not wait for proof that the allegations had merit. By mid-April, he had fired Lyon and Ashcroft and turned them out of his home. Egged on by Clara, he called Lyon "a liar, a forger, a thief, a hypocrite, a drunkard, a sneak, a humbug." Lyon never spoke a harsh word about Twain, and no proof of wrongdoing was ever found.

Twain invited his youngest daughter to live with him at Stormfield, and, belatedly, the two fashioned a deep bond. There was more to Jean than illness: she had devoted herself to the cause of animal rights and, at Stormfield, proved herself to be a helpmate, caretaker, and friend. In October 1909, Twain donned his Oxford robe for the wedding of Clara and her long-time love, Ossip Gabrilowitsch, the pianist she had met in Vienna. Soon after the wedding day, the newlyweds sailed for Europe while Twain sailed for Bermuda. Now, the hand of Fortuna seemed to grow tired on the wheel of fate: she gave it one last downward spin.

Twain returned from Bermuda a few days before Christmas, but Jean found him oddly disinterested in the holiday that had always been the family's favorite. Determined to remedy his ill mood, she decorated Stormfield with garlands and trimmed the tree. On the morning before Christmas, Katy Leary found Jean dead in her bathtub. She had suffered a seizure and heart attack. Twain was too weak to travel to Elmira for his daughter's funeral. Instead, he spent the next few days writing an essay, "The Death of Jean." He was ready to put down his pen.

Twain had written of himself, "My temperament has never allowed my spirits to remain depressed long at a time." He returned to sunny Bermuda where his irrepressible spirit surfaced one last time. He penned "Advice to Paine," offering suggestions on the proper etiquette when entering heaven; played golf with Woodrow Wilson; and added an Angelfish to his Aquarium.

Sky-watchers were anticipating the return of Halley's comet when Twain's doctors sent for Paine and equipped him with morphine and hypodermic needles, should the ailing author need them on his return to the States aboard the *Oceana*. Twain was too weak to smoke, though he tried. Forty-eight hours later, he was wheeled down the gangplank in New York City and transported directly to Stormfield. After Clara and her husband arrived, a deathwatch began. Twain's speech was so slurred that he had to write notes to communicate. One to Clara began, "You didn't tell me but I have found out that you. Well, I . . . " and the note drifted off. Twain may have learned that Clara was five months pregnant. (She would give birth to Twain's only grandchild, Nina, in August, on the anniversary of Susy's death.) He died at sunset on April 21, just as Halley's comet was becoming visible.

The next day, Twain's body, dressed in a suit of white cashmere, was taken to Brick Presbyterian Church in New York City where four-hundred people attended a brief service conducted by the Reverends Henry Van Dyke and Joe Twichell. After the last "amen," the doors of the church were opened, and over three-thousand mourners, rich and poor, lettered and illiterate, shuffled by the open coffin, paying silent homage to the man who had kept the world laughing through its tears. Later, Twain's body was transported to Elmira, where his casket was lowered into the ground in a driving rain.

THERE IS A TIME TO LAUGH AND
THERE IS A TIME TO WEEP

# Extracts from Adam's Diary

· · · · · · · · · · ·

Setting: Garden of Eden and environs
Period: Beginning of human history

Adam's diary starts on a Monday, with the arrival of Eve, "a new creature." A gruff Stone Age guy, Adam is not at all pleased, but wishes that "it would stay with the other animals." This is Eden, witnessed first-hand, where everything is new, even the disturbing word "we." The new creature is constantly using that word and naming things. She has named the great waterfall

on the estate "Niagara Falls" (not a bad setting for the great "Fall" to come). The new creature, who eats too much fruit, has named herself Eve. Adam is glad when Eve makes friends with the snake, "because the snake talks, and this enables me to get a rest."

The snake has advised Eve to eat from the forbidden tree, and this greatly concerns Adam, who warns Eve that such an act might introduce death into the world. Foreseeing trouble, he attempts to escape, riding his horse.

*About an hour after sunup, as I was riding through a flowery plain where thousands of animals were grazing, slumbering, or playing with each other . . . all of a sudden they broke into a tempest of frightful noises, and in one moment the plain was in a frantic commotion and every beast was destroying its neighbor. I knew what it meant – Eve had eaten that fruit, and death was come into the world.*

Eve's action has serious consequences, as Adam had predicted. They lose their property and must now wear clothing and do work.

In an entry marked "Next Year," Adam notes that Eve has caught a new creature which she carries about and has named "Cain." At first, they think it might be a fish. Later, they are persuaded that it is a kangaroo. For a time, Adam's entries are primarily on the topic of the "unclassifiable zoological freak." It is little, noisy, and seemingly untamable, suffering "little storms of sorrow and passion." Adam wants to let it go, but Eve won't let him. The next entry, written five months later, begins with a definitive statement: "It is not a kangaroo." Now Adam suspects that the Cain creature may be a bear. He is perplexed by Eve's devotion to the creature and wonders if she has lost her mind.

Four months later, Cain is still thought to be a bear, but a new species, one that can imitate speech. It says, "poppa" and "momma." Adam has been looking for other talking bears, primarily in the area Eve calls Buffalo. Remarkably, while he is away on a search, Eve somehow catches another Cain-like creature without even stirring from the home estate. "I never saw such luck!" Adam notices that the older creature

is tamer now and can laugh and talk like the parrot. In fact, it may be a parrot. Eve is calling the new creature Abel.

Ten years pass. In the intervening years Adam has learned that the creatures are called boys. There are also some girls now. Most significantly, he writes that he was wrong about Eve: "It is better to live outside the Garden with her than inside it without her."

## The Story behind the Story

Twain worked and reworked this story, publishing a number of variations under a number of titles. Asked to submit a humorous piece to a souvenir publication for the 1893 Buffalo World's Fair, he reworked an earlier version, this time placing Eden at Niagara Falls. He titled it, "The Earliest Authentic Mention of Niagara Falls, Extracts from Adam's Diary." In April 1904, Harper's published it in book form with comical illustrations by Fred Strothmann. As if carved into stone slabs, cave-man style, the faux-Egyptian hieroglyphics and illustrations depict Adam in a Dutch boy haircut, smoking cigars and reading the newspaper.

# Eve's Diary

· · · · · · · · · · · ·

**Setting: Garden of Eden and environs**
**Period: Beginning of human history**

Adam's diary is blunt, gruff, crude, and comical. He grumbles as he observes the world and wonders about creation as he puffs his cigars. By contrast, Eve's diary is lyrical, poetic, eloquent, and filled with awe and passion on every page.

At first, Eve is alarmed that the world, created in a hurry, is a bit untidy. The mountains are in ragged condition, the plains cluttered with rubbish, the nighttime sky in disarray. She worries about the moon, which "got loose last night, and slid down and fell out of the scheme – a very great loss; it breaks my heart to think of it. . . . It should have been fastened better."

Eve finds comfort in nestling among the tigers, whose breath is sweet because they live on strawberries. "Experiment" is Eve's word for human. She is curious when she discovers that there is another Experiment, and follows it around, but continues her task of naming things. On an entry marked "Thursday," Eve writes in her journal that she has experienced her first sorrow, when "he" obviously avoided her company. Several days later she notes that, to please

"him," she has tried to get apples from the tree, though they are forbidden. So far, she has failed. One morning, she tells him her name, but he is not interested. Lonely, she gazes into a pool and finds a water nymph who talks only when Eve talks, slips away when Eve reaches out to her, and is timid on dark nights, but willing to meet when the moon is full.

Eve works at "improving the estate," delights in flowers, and ponders the man who continues to avoid her. One afternoon, she discovers fire. At first, she is afraid of it, but then finds it strangely beautiful. She suspects that "he" would not care for it, but only ask what it is good for. Her revery is interrupted by flames that reach the sky. Later, she concludes, "Fire is beautiful; some day it will be useful, I think." Because it was uncontrollable, Eve has learned a new thing: fear. "I wish I had never discovered it: it gives me dark moments, it spoils my happiness."

Animals follow Eve, acres of them in a "furry expanse" and above her are "storms of sociable birds and hurricanes of whirring wings." Calling herself the "first traveler," she explores the world, with the animals as her traveling companions. The animals are friendly to each other, and they understand when she speaks to them, though she can't make out a word they say to her. In *Adam's Diary* there was no mention of God, though he wrote obsessively about his children. In *Eve's Diary*, there is no mention of the children, but some talk of God and of the meaning of life and the universe and everything.

> *At first I couldn't make out what I was made for, but now I think it was to search out the secrets of this wonderful world and be happy and thank the Giver of it all for devising it.*

Just before the Fall, Eve is mostly worried about meteors. She has observed that some of the best stars melt and run down the sky. She worries that they will all melt, in time.

After the Fall, Eve remembers the lost Garden as if it were a dream. Her diary ends with her contemplation of death. She hopes that she and Adam, now in love, will die together. Failing that, she prays that she will die before Adam, writing, "life without him would not be life; how could I endure it?" The text ends with an entry from Adam's diary, written at Eve's grave: "Wheresoever she was, *there* was Eden."

### The Story behind the Story

Twain wrote this story in 1905 as a tribute to Livy, for the Christmas issue of *Harper's*. In June, 1906, he expanded the story and turned it into a small book, with intricate illustrations by Lester Ralph. Unlike the comical cartoons used in *Extracts from Adam's Diary*, Ralph's line drawings are elegant and graceful. They depict Adam and Eve, tiny against the looming landscape of the Garden and unselfconsciously naked. Because of the nude illustrations, the book was banned from the Charlton Library in Massachusetts. Twain entertained reporters by describing the librarians' careful examination of the offensive artwork:

*It appears that the pictures in Eve's Diary were first discovered by a lady librarian. When she made the dreadful find, being very careful . . . she examined the horrid things in de-* *tail. . . . Then she took the book to another librarian, a male this time, and he, also, took a long time to examine the unclothed ladies.*

The two diaries were eventually combined into one publication and have long been popular gift books, used occasionally as party favors at wedding receptions.

# Angelfish in Pigtails

. . . . . . . . . . . .

Mark Twain had seen angelfish on a visit to Bermuda, in all their vibrant colors. These flashy reef fish have compressed bodies, small mouths, and streamer-like extensions that flutter like ribbons in the waves. At night they hide in the nooks and crevices of the reef, but by day they swim in shallow waters, bold and fearless, sometimes forming harems around a dominant male. The metaphor was irresistible to the author who, like an aging Tom Sawyer longing for just one more glance and giggle from Becky Thatcher, sought the company of school-aged girls, craving their purity and youth. A celebrity who rarely found reason to postpone gratification, Twain knew what he wanted. His preference was not new; in 1858, during his days on the Mississippi River, he had become infatuated with a fourteen-year-old girl on a steamboat docked in New Orleans.

In the last four years of his life, when he made the acquaintance of a girl he liked, she became an "Angelfish," a member of his Aquarium Club. Twain's secretary, Isabel Lyon, said:

*His first interest when he goes to a new place is to find little girls. . . . Off he goes with a flash when he sees a new pair of slim little legs appear; and if the little girl wears butterfly bows of ribbon on the back of her head then his delirium is complete.*

This is enough to raise a blush or an eyebrow of a modern reader, steeped as we are in concerns about pedophilia. Twain's daughter, Clara, insisted that her father limit his contact with the girls,

and, after his death, fought hard to suppress any mention of them in biographies and published memoirs. Twain and his Angelfish had all the makings of a scandal, but Twain's relationship with the young girls was apparently platonic and avuncular.

In early 1906, Twain met fifteen-year-old Gertrude Natkin as he was leaving Carnegie Hall. He immediately began an intense correspondence with her, calling her his "dream grandchild." Four months after they met, Gertrude turned sixteen. Twain wrote to her:

*So you are 16 today, you dear little rascal! Oh come, this won't do. . . . Ah what has become of my little girl? I am almost afraid to send a blot [kiss], but I venture it. Bless your heart, it comes within an ace of being improper! Now, back you go to 14! – then there's no impropriety.*

As he sailed across the Atlantic to receive his honorary degree from Oxford, Twain met an eighteen-year-old who looked remarkably like Susy. Without shame, Twain latched on, pursuing Carlotta Welles with more than a little desperation. He called her Charley and, as she began obviously avoiding him, he sent her messages, including one early morning note attached to his calling card:

*Charley, dear, you don't know what you are missing. There's more than two thousand porpoises in sight, and eleven whales, and sixty icebergs, and both Dippers, and seven rainbows, and all the battleships of all the navies, and me. SLC.*

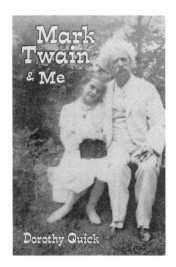

Mark Twain & Me

Dorothy Quick

Dorothy Quick was eleven when she met Twain on board the S.S. *Minnetonka* on the return trip. She proved his faithful companion on the voyage and corresponded with him until the day he died. An enthusiastic Angelfish, Dorothy wrote a memoir titled *Enchantment: A Little Girl's Friendship with Mark Twain* (1961), later retitled *Mark Twain & Me*.

By 1908, there were a dozen girls in his "Aquarium" whose names and ages he recorded in a notebook. Thirteen was the average age, but a few were as young as eleven. Twain formulated club rules and requirements for membership, including sincerity, intelligence, and a good disposition. He gave each of the chosen girls an angelfish pin to wear and named himself "the Admiral." When he moved to his new home in Redding, he jokingly referred to it as "Innocence at Home" and made the billiard room the official "club headquarters." Any Angelfish who went more than three months without corresponding with the Admiral could be summarily suspended from the exclusive club. In his letters, he pleaded with the girls to visit him, and many did, arriving with their mothers to spend weekends and holidays as Twain's house guests.

Frances Nunnally was sixteen when she met Twain onboard a ship headed for England in 1907, the same trip during which the Susy look-alike rebuffed the author. Twain enjoyed Frances's company during the voyage, and they spent some time together in London. Two years later, Twain spoke at Frances's high school graduation in Baltimore. It was his last public speech.

# Short Works of the 1900s

. . . . . . . . . . .

1900    **"As Regards Patriotism"**(Essay)
Patriotism has become a religion, Twain contends. If people were trained
to think for themselves, they might develop a genuine love of country, but
as it stands now, a cut and dried version of devotion to the country's flag is
forced on each citizen.

1900    **"Two Little Tales"** (Short story)
In this six-degrees-of-separation story, the narrator encourages a frustrated
inventor by telling a parable, "How the Chimney-sweep Got the Ear of the
Emperor."

1901    **"To the Person Sitting in Darkness"** (Essay)
In this essay, hailed as "a landmark of social-political satire," Twain names
missionaries as apologists for government forces and big business; con-
demns the bloodthirsty empire-building of the president, czar, emperor, and
kaiser, and their trinkets of civilization – glass beads, guns, hymn books,
gin; and laments acts of aggression taken against the poor in China, Cuba,
South Africa, and the Philippines. The Person Sitting in Darkness, Twain
writes, is sure to notice the corpses of massacred peasants. Condemning
U.S. imperialism, he ends with the suggestion that, if the U.S. continues
to spill the blood of people we claim to be liberating, we should design a
new flag, "with the white stripes painted black and the stars replaced by the
skull and crossbones."

1901    **"The Dervish and the Offensive Stranger"** (Essay)
This meditation in dialogue form is about good intentions that have harmful
results and evil deeds that produce favorable results. Columbus's discovery
of the New World (good) resulted in the subjugation and near extinction of
the Indian culture and population (bad); while the French Revolution
drenched the country in blood (bad), but brought about wonderful reforms
(good).

1901     **"Corn-pone Opinions"** (Essay)
Twain heard a slave say: "You tell me whar a man gits his corn pone, en I'll tell you what his opinions is." He interprets this to mean that religious beliefs and political opinions are simply "a matter of association and sympathy, not reasoning and examination."

c. 1901    **"The Lost Napoleon"** (Essay)
In 1891, as Twain sailed down a river through southern France, he saw a mountain range that looked just like Napoleon Bonaparte lying on his back.

1902     **"A Double-Barrelled Detective Story"** (Novella)
This grim spoof of the Sherlock Holmes phenomenon begins in Virginia with a scene of brutality, where newlywed Jacob Fuller spends three months torturing his pregnant wife before skipping town. The young woman recovers and changes her name to Stillman; when her son is born, she vows to use him as a tool for revenge. Most of the story takes place when Archy Stillman is a young man, in hot pursuit of the man who tortured his mother. Trouble is, he has located the wrong Jacob Fuller.

1902     **"The Belated Russian Passport"** (Short story)
In this satire of bureaucracy, a timid Yale student is persuaded by an aggressive extrovert into extending his European visit for a side trip to Russia. The Yalie anticipates trouble, for good reason: he does not have the proper documents.

1902     **"Does the Race of Man Love a Lord?"** (Sketch)
Twain argues that it is human nature to honor power. The boys in a gang worship the one who can fight off the rest, just like millions of Chinese citizens worship an emperor.

1902     **"The Five Boons of Life"** (Short story)
In the "morning of life," a good fairy arrives with a basket of gifts: Fame, Love, Riches, Pleasure, Death. She cautions a young man that only one of these gifts is truly valuable and weeps when he does not have the wisdom to choose Death.

1903     **"A Dog's Tale"** (Short story)
"My father was a St. Bernard, my mother was a collie, but I am a Presbyterian." This humorous opener is deceiving; by story's end we will have a devastating story, narrated by a dog named Aileen, about the horrors of medical experimentation on animals. Read as both an allegory on slavery and a parable about cruelty to animals, the story was distributed in pamphlet form by the National Anti-Vivisection Society of Britain.

1904     **"The $30,000 Bequest"** (Short story)
One day, happily married Saladin (Sally) and Electra (Aleck) Foster receive a letter from Sally's only living relative, Tilbury, informing them that his death is imminent and that he is leaving Sally an inheritance of $30,000. Tilbury's death is never reported; for several years, the Fosters live in an elaborate fantasy of riches to come, until reality intervenes.

1905   **"Adam's Soliloquy"** (Sketch)
Twain channels the spirit of Adam, who is wandering through the dinosaur exhibit in New York City's Museum of Natural History; neither he nor Eve have any recollection of dinosaurs. Adam muses on a conversation with Noah who, when asked about the extinct reptiles, "colored and changed the subject."

1905   **"The Czar's Soliloquy"** (Sketch)
The Czar contemplates his naked body in the mirror and thinks about the power of clothing to disguise human frailty. Weeping at his own hypocrisy, he gets dressed.

1905   **"A Horse's Tale"** (Novella)
After Twain was asked to help with a campaign against bullfighting, he wrote this story, told in the voice of Buffalo Bill's favorite horse, Soldier Boy. The horse and the commander's orphaned niece, Cathy, are inseparable. The story ends badly for both in a blood-drenched bullring in Spain.

1905   **"What Is Man?"** (Essay)
Twain repeatedly wrestled with the question of nature vs. nurture. This essay is fashioned as a debate between an Old Man (O.M.), who claims that human beings are shaped by environment and a Young Man (Y.M.) who counters this argument. "You and I are but sewing-machines," the O.M. says; "We must turn out what we can." He further instructs that there is only one constant; we act to secure our own happiness.

1905    **"King Leopold's Soliloquy: A Defense of His Congo Rule"**
(Political Tract)
After being contacted by the Congo Reform Association, Twain wrote
this satirical essay, which helped focus international attention on the atroc-
ities. In the essay, King Leopold, put into power with the cooperation of
European nations, reads aloud from pamphlets which expose his reign-of-
terror, pausing only to kiss his crucifix. Pacing alone in his room, the king
curses the reprinted photographs that show some of the fifteen-million
slaughtered citizens and mutilated children. He takes comfort in the
conjecture that most readers will be repulsed by such graphic material and
turn away.

undated **"Bible Teaching and Religious Practice"** (Essay)
Twain compares the Bible to an antiquated drugstore, which has stocked
the right medicines but pushed the wrong cures.

1909    **"The New Planet"** (Sketch)
Having read that astronomers have observed "perturbation" in Neptune's
orbit and anticipating the discovery of a new planet, Twain has fun with the
word "perturbate."

1909    **"A Fable"** (Short story)
An artist has painted a picture meant to be viewed in a mirror. His artistically
sophisticated house-cat is impressed, but other animals stand between the
picture and the mirror and see only themselves.

1909    **"Is Shakespeare Dead?"** (Essay)
This essay addresses the greatest unsolved mystery in literary history; the
true identity of the playwright who authored the work attributed to the
fellow from Stratford. With his usual wit, Twain outlines the main points
of the authorship question and concludes that, as with Satan, everything
written about Shakespeare is conjectural.

1909    **"That Day in Eden"** (Short story)
Satan writes in his diary, remembering a strained conversation he had with
Adam and Eve in the garden and his inability to explain concepts such as
pain, fear, good, and evil. While they talked, Eve ate the apple and became
modest, then handed the apple to Adam. Satan watched the couple walk
away, "bent with age."

1909    **"The Turning Point of My Life"** (Essay)
In this essay, published two months before his death, Twain rejects the
notion of one "turning point" in life. In a one-thing-leads-to-another chronicle, he recounts a number of links in the chain of his literary life, which he
traces back to the Garden of Eden.

1909    **"The Death of Jean"** (Essay in diary format)
Written just four months before his own death, Twain begins with the anguished howl, "Jean is dead!" and recounts the events of his youngest
daughter's death on the day before Christmas. It is a tormented tribute to
her twenty-nine years, which ends, "How poor I am, who was once so rich!"

# The War Prayer

· · · · · · · · · · ·

Setting: A Christian church in an unspecified nation
Period: Sunday morning during a time of
war

Illustration by John Groth

Young soldiers are marching off to war in
new uniforms amid "a fluttering wilderness
of flags," while drums beat and bands play.
In every breast there burns "the holy fire of
patriotism." On Sunday morning, wor-
shipers fill a church. Prominent among
them are the young men who will leave the
next day for the front; visions of glorious

battles fill their heads. Beside them sit their
parents, full of pride for their sons. After a
Scripture reading and a hymn, the pastor
offers a passionate prayer, asking God to
shield the young men in battle, make them
invincible, and grant them honor and glory.

While the preacher prays, a white-
haired stranger, whose eyes burn with an
unearthly light, walks silently up the main
aisle of the church. Everyone strains to see
him, while the preacher concludes his
prayer: "Bless our arms, grant us the victory,
O Lord our God, Father and Protector of
our land and flag!" Opening his eyes, the
minister is surprised to see the otherworldly
elder in front of him.

With an air of quiet authority, the
stranger waves the parson aside and surveys
the stunned congregation. When he
speaks, his voice is deep and solemn. "I
come from the Throne," he says, "bearing a
message from Almighty God!" The stranger
assures the congregation that God has
heard their prayers and the long petition of
the minister. God will grant everything that
was asked, he says, but only if it is still de-
sired after being fully interpreted. Every
prayer, the stranger continues, is really two
prayers, one uttered, the other not. With

that, he begins to give voice to the unuttered prayer behind the petition for victory.

At first, the words are familiar: he prays for the cherished young men, who will go forth to smite the foe. Then, the true meaning of this prayer is interpreted by the truth-telling messenger.

*O Lord our God, help us to tear their soldiers to bloody shreds with our shells; . . . help us to drown the thunder of the guns with the shrieks of their wounded, writhing in pain; . . . help us to wring the hearts of their unoffending widows with unavailing grief.*

The prayer is a wish list from Hell, the flip side of "protect our boys and make them victorious" spelled out in bloody detail. Still articulating the inventory of curses wished on the enemy population, God's messenger ends his prayer with these words:

*Make heavy their steps, water their way with their tears, stain the white snow with the blood of their wounded feet! We ask it, in the spirit of love, of Him Who is the Source of Love, and Who is the ever-faithful refuge and friend of all that are sore beset and seek His aid with humble and contrite hearts. Amen.*

After a pause, the stranger asks the congregation for their answer, saying, "Ye have prayed it; if ye still desire it, speak! The messenger of the Most High waits."

The story ends here with the statement: "It was believed afterward that the man was a lunatic, because there was no sense in what he said."

Illustration by John Groth

## The Story behind the Story

This antiwar fable was meant to make patriotic churchgoers wince, and it made publishers cringe. After writing the piece in 1905, Twain submitted it to *Harper's Bazaar* where it was rejected as "unsuitable." Like several other of his outspoken, reformist writings, it was published post-humously, in 1923, in *Europe and Elsewhere*, a collection of short pieces edited by Albert Bigelow Paine. "The War Prayer" was brought into print again in a 1972 collection, *A Pen Warmed-up in Hell*, edited by Frederick Anderson, then editor of the *Mark Twain Papers*. At the time, the U.S. was involved in an unpopular war in Vietnam. On college campuses across America, students passed mimeographed copies of Twain's story from hand to hand and read it aloud at antiwar demonstrations, prayer vigils, and speak-ins. It has since been kept in the public consciousness via the Internet and in at least two television dramatizations.

The character of the holy stranger was inspired by an eccentric, self-educated Midwesterner Twain wrote about in *Life on the Mississippi*. Henry Clay Dean was an ordained Methodist minister and lawyer, known for his powerful oratory. According to Twain, people who didn't know better thought that this man, whose torn trousers were "a world too short," was an escaped lunatic until they heard him speak; then they thought he was an escaped archangel.

# Letters from the Earth

. . . . . . . . . . .

Setting: The cosmos and planet Earth
Period: Spanning millions of years

God, bored with the vastness of empty space, decides to do some creating and invites three angels to witness the dramatic display. Satan, Gabriel, and Michael watch as God flings fistfuls of stars, planets, and moons across the universe. The cosmic light show is awe-inspiring, but what most impresses the three is that God has chosen to introduce the concept of the unsupervised, self-regulating Law of Nature.

God creates a great variety of animals and assigns each a primary characteristic (to the tiger is given ferocity; the rabbit, timidity). Though God calls this "an experiment in Morals and Conduct," Satan is alarmed that, by design, there is murder all along the food chain. The "masterpiece" of God's creation is the human being. Each person is given, in varying degrees, a range of qualities: courage, cowardice, ferocity, gentleness, fairness, justice, cunning, treachery. Mission accomplished, God sends the animals and humans to a little globe called *earth*.

When Satan is overheard making sarcastic remarks about creation, he is tem-porarily banished. He decides to visit earth and see how the experiment is going. What he finds there will provide him with enough amusement to last for an eternity. In his first letter from earth, Satan tells his celestial sidekicks that humans hold several bizarre notions, including that they are the "noblest work of God," and that God actually listens to their puny little prayers, even though there is not a shred of evidence. In the second letter, Satan describes the Christian concept of heaven, which excludes activities people most enjoy (sexual intercourse and intellectuality) and includes what they most loathe (harp-playing, hymn-singing, socializing with people of different races and nationalities).

In his third letter, Satan begins to untangle some of the curious notions to be found in the Christian Bible, such as the nonsensical story of Adam and Eve, who were unfairly expelled from the Garden after they succumbed to their God-given, natural curiosity. In his fourth letter, Satan contemplates Cain and Abel, who had sex with their sisters and begot some nephews and nieces. After the "pleasant labor of populating the world," God was disappointed with humans and decided to drown all but a few. For the rest of the fourth letter and throughout the following five letters, Satan rips into the myth of Noah, who did not know how to build a boat, let alone save the animals. Consequently, some became extinct, while others, like the fly, the primary carrier of typhoid fever, were saved. Noah also saved cholera and lockjaw germs.

In the ninth letter, Satan reports that, after the Universal Flood was over, Noah got out of the Ark, planted a vineyard, and promptly got drunk. "This person had been selected from all the populations because he was the best sample there was. He was to start the human race on a new basis." In the tenth letter, Satan writes that, when the Deity realized that death brought about an end to human suffering, he corrected his mistake by assuming the name of Jesus Christ.

After a few diversionary comments about masturbation, its inevitability, and the pointless prohibition of it, Satan writes his eleventh and final letter. He notes that human history "in all ages is red with blood, and bitter with hate" but that human violence and cruelty are nothing when compared to the violence and cruelty of God the Father Almighty.

## The Story behind the Story

Twain wrote "Letters from the Earth" in October and November 1909, the months between his daughter Clara's wedding and his daughter Jean's death. He died six months later.

Albert Bigelow Paine chose not to touch the controversial writing, agreeing with Clara that its publication might tarnish Twain's image. After Paine's death in 1937, Bernard DeVoto became literary editor, but not executor, of the Mark Twain Estate and immediately challenged Clara's efforts at censorship. A serious scholar, DeVoto valued Twain's irreverent writings and boldly assembled a book featuring "Letters from the Earth" as the title piece. DeVoto was no match for Clara, however, and failed to receive the necessary permission for its publication. Frustrated at being kept on such a short leash, he quit the job after only eight years. He was dead by the time Clara finally consented to publication of the book he had assembled. Henry Nash Smith, then editor of the Mark Twain papers, oversaw publication of *Letters from the Earth* in 1962, which made the *New York Times* bestseller list.

# Seeker and Skeptic

· · · · · · · · · · ·

## Mark Twain and Religion

*I never had but two powerful ambitions in my life. One was to be a pilot, & the other a preacher of the gospel. I accomplished the one & failed in the other, because I could not supply myself with the necessary stock in trade – i.e., religion.*

(letter to Orion, 1865)

According to popular belief, in the last decade of his life, overwhelmed by personal tragedy, Mark Twain succumbed to bitterness and cynicism, turned away from God, gave up on religion, and unleashed his despair and bitterness in blasphemous writings. The notion of this late life transformation is open to debate, however. Some students of Twain hold that he was *born* skeptical and that he spent his entire lifetime juggling bitterness and hope, doubt and faith.

### Hungry Sam and the Spiritual Smorgasbord

Young Sam Clemens freely tasted from a menu of faith offerings in holy, hellish

Hannibal. His stern father was a "free-thinker," who favored rationalism over religion and was bound by a strict moral code of right and wrong. If his father was all "head," his mother was all "heart." She sought solace and guidance where she could, especially after three of her children died before reaching age ten. She dragged Sam and his remaining siblings to Methodist and Presbyterian churches, where they sat through long sermons about an angry god and an eternal Hell. Twain's readers would share in his early church experience through the restless observations of Tom Sawyer who, dressed in his starchy Sunday clothes, is both "exceedingly improved and uncomfortable."

Sam learned his Bible verses by rote at Sunday school and got a second dose in the classroom where the Good Book was built into the curriculum. Hannibal, a frontier town on the busy Mississippi, attracted its share of prophets and proselytizers. When the spiritualism craze swept the country, he saw the mediums come to town with their seances. The month before he turned nine, Sam watched members of the Millerite sect climb a hill outside of town to wait for the end of the world. He heard visiting speakers lecture on witchcraft.

While Ralph Waldo Emerson led the intellectual New England Transcendentalists in writing eloquent tracts on the worth of the individual, the "Second Great Awakening" erupted, spewing Christian camp meetings throughout the rest of the country. If Tom Sawyer takes us to boring, buttoned-up, soul-killing church services, Huck Finn provides us with a front-row seat at the revivals, invigorated by hand-clapping, foot-stomping gospel songs. Drama was guaranteed; the gullible wept, prayed, and swooned over pretend pirates, who repented and got "saved."

When Sam became a cub pilot on the Mississippi, he immersed himself in the dense writings of the world's great thinkers; Carlyle, Plutarch, Shakespeare. It was there, floating down the river, that he picked up Thomas Paine's *The Age of Reason* and read the blasphemous deconstruction of God, the Bible, and of Christianity itself. During this same period, Sam's desperate prayers for the life of his sweet brother, Henry, victim of a steamboat explosion, went unanswered. Was anyone listening? If so, was it indifference or sadism that made the Big Anyone ignore such a heartfelt petition to spare his innocent brother? Like a hungry man at a banquet, Sam Clemens was pulled toward all things spiritual; but he was destined to remain hungry.

**God and Prayer**

When a fan rushed forward to kiss his hand, gushing, "How God must love you!" Twain politely quipped, "I hope so." As soon as the woman was out of earshot, however, he murmured to his friends,

"I guess she hasn't heard about our strained relations."

Twain may have longed for an abiding faith in a benign deity, but he could never claim it, nor, he suspected, could most others. When President Theodore Roosevelt threatened to banish the motto IN GOD WE TRUST, Twain mused to Andrew Carnegie that it was a beautiful motto, simple and direct. Then he added, "I don't believe it would sound any better if it were true."

Twain struggled with various notions of God throughout his life, but was consistently hostile to the idea of an interventionist God, who actively cares about or interacts with human beings. Especially irksome was the notion of prayer, a concept he repeatedly debunked, albeit playfully. In *Letters from the Earth*, Satan, visiting the planet, finds the whole notion of prayer quaint and ridiculous. With the tone of "you're not going to believe *this*!" he writes home to angel-pals Michael and Gabriel that humans believe that they are the "Creator's pet" and that the Maker actually listens to their crude flatteries and pathetic petitions.

"Letter from the Recording Angel," written in the style of a bureaucratic business letter from a heavenly agent to a coal dealer in Buffalo, is an invoice, tallying God's response to two categories of prayer: Public Prayers (those uttered at prayer meetings, Sunday school, family worship) and Secret Supplications of the Heart. A number of prayers have been dismissed on technicalities (contradictions, competing requests, restatements of divine purpose). Other prayers have either been granted or postponed for future consideration.

In *The War Prayer*, a heavenly messenger appears to a congregation as the pastor is fervently praying that God will protect their sons in battle and bring them home victorious. The messenger interrupts the prayer with word that God is listening, and wishes confirmation that the petitioners understand the full implications of their request. The robed stranger then clarifies the unspoken portion of the prayer:

*Help us to tear their soldiers to bloody shreds with our shells; help us to cover their smiling fields with the pale forms of their patriot dead; help us to drown the thunder of the guns with the shrieks of their wounded, writhing in pain.*

In dozens of essays and stories, Twain railed against the one who created the fly. In "Thoughts of God" he wrote:

*The planning of the fly was an application of pure intelligence, morals not being concerned. Not one of us could have planned the fly, not one of us could have constructed him; and no one would have considered it wise to try, except under an assumed name . . . yet billions of persons have excused the Hand that made him.*

The fly, Twain repeatedly points out, has caused widespread and indiscriminate misery, spread disease, pestered the dying, settled in soldiers' festering wounds, afflicted unoffending cows and hardworking horses. Yet, no one dares condemn the Maker for this curse, but, instead, heaps praises on the Creator. In "Little Bessie," a three-year-old converses with her mother about the nature of God and reasons her way through the facts of creation, as she has been taught. She concludes that, because God made the disease-bearing fly and gave the fly its nature, "God is a murderer." Similarly, in *Letters from the Earth*, God is called "the Great Criminal," because, having created myriad diseases, he stands idly by while innocent people suffer in agony.

In numerous stories, Twain pondered why a loving Creator would design and promulgate germs and flies or why Noah would have taken such pains to save them in the flood. In "Adam's Soliloquy," the first man remembers questioning Noah about some of the animals that did not make it onto the Ark, such as the dinosaur, and about the choice to preserve the fly, mosquito, locust, and cholera germ, to which Noah responded defensively, "On the whole, I think we did very well, everything considered. We were shepherds and farmers."

## The Bible

The Bible was a book Twain knew well and read often, and there are hundreds of biblical allusions in his work. Loving and loathing the Good Book, he appreciated that it was multifaceted, writing in *Letters from the Earth* that, in addition to some noble poetry and a few clever fables, it also had "blood-drenched history; and some good morals, and a wealth of obscenity; and upwards of a thousand lies." In "Bible Teaching and Religious Practice," Twain likens it to an antiquated drugstore, which has stocked the right medicines but pushed the wrong cures.

*The homoeopath arrived on the field and made him abandon hell and damnation altogether, and administered Christ's love, and comfort, and charity and compassion in its stead. These had been in the drug store all the time, gold labeled and conspicuous among the long shelfloads of repulsive purges and vomits and poisons, and so the practice was to blame that they had remained unused, not the pharmacy.*

Biblical characters regularly appear in Twain's works: Cain and Abel, Moses, Solomon, Jesus, and the Virgin Mary. Certain characters, however, play an especially large role in Twain's exploration of the nature of God and of humanity, most notably Adam and Eve, Noah, and Satan. In *The Diaries of Adam and Eve*, Adam is a harmless curmudgeon, grumbling his way through Eden, bothered by Eve and the strange little creatures named Cain and Abel who disturb his peace. Eve, by contrast, is full of wonder at creation, enraptured by the power to name each new thing she sees. In "That Day in Eden," Satan writes in his diary about the day he tried to explain to Adam and Eve various concepts such as fear, death, eternity. The two remained carefree and clueless until they ate from the Tree of Knowledge. The change was instantaneous and dramatic.

The world's first mother protests the expulsion from Eden in "Eve Speaks," questioning the harshness of the punishment.

*We knew no more then than this littlest child of mine knows now, with its four years – oh, not so much, I think. Would I say to it, "If thou touchest this bread I will overwhelm thee with unimaginable disaster, even*

*to the dissolution of thy corporeal elements," and when it took the bread and smiled up in my face, thinking no harm, as not understanding those strange words, would I take advantage of its innocence and strike it down with the mother hand it trusted?*

If Twain was forgiving of Adam and Eve, he also had compassion for Satan, a notion he borrowed from his mother, who maintained that Satan was the one sinner most in need of prayers and Christian understanding. In "The Chronicle of Young Satan," one of the "Mysterious Stranger" variations, Satan's nephew (also called Satan), visits earth. He seems to be callous toward suffering, but maintains that it is simply because he has no moral sense, unlike humans who do, though they have engaged in untold wars, murders, and massacres since the day Cain killed Abel, and will continue to slaughter each other in the future.

## The Church and Organized Religion

A lifelong churchgoer, Twain saved his most vitriolic comments for organized religion. *The Innocents Abroad*, Twain's travel memoir of the *Quaker City* cruise to the Old World, overflows with mocking scorn toward his pious fellow-passengers, Protestant "pilgrims" who steal every chance they get; he gladly counts himself as one of the "sinners." From their very first stop in the Azores, Twain finds "Jesuit humbuggery" flourishing in cathedrals. By the time the ship reaches Italy, Twain is articulate in his contempt for the Roman Catholic Church and its victims, who can be found begging in the shadows of Europe's most impressive and costly cathedrals, while fat and happy priests come and go. Italy, he writes, "is today one vast museum of magnificence and misery." His observations of the Holy Land, are equally scathing. In Jerusalem, Twain writes about the assumed site of the crucifixion of Jesus, describing it as grand and venerable and full of claptrap sideshows.

*History is full of this old Church of the Holy Sepulchre – full of blood that was shed because of the respect and the veneration in which men held the last resting place of the meek and lowly, the mild and gentle, Prince of Peace!*

In most of Twain's novels, the church is a place of hypocrisy, superficial morality, and the abuse of power. Presented as comic relief in the books featuring Tom Sawyer and Huckleberry Finn, the church is far less benign in *A Connecticut Yankee in King Arthur's Court*. Hank, the Yankee, names the Established Church a political machine, "an enemy to human liberty." His plan to dissolve the power of the church is to undermine it by introducing cleanliness, education, and freedom. Visiting the beautiful but dreaded Morgan Le Fay in her palace,

Hank is appalled when, just moments after she murders a page for a trifling offense, the queen is called to prayer. Hank writes: "I will say this much for the nobility: that tyrannical, murderous, rapacious and morally rotten as they were, they were deeply religious."

In *Personal Reflections of Joan of Arc*, the Maid suffers at the hands of conniving bishops and power-hungry Catholic priests who speak of faith but have none and who make deals with political devils. Twain let history condemn the church, straying little from actual trial transcripts and historic accounts. While he disdained the church, Twain could admire people of faith. In "The Turning Point of My Life," he fantasized Martin Luther and Joan of Arc in Eden, claiming that they would not have succumbed to temptation.

In numerous stories, Twain mocked trite Sunday school lessons, in which good behavior is rewarded and bad behavior punished. Time and again in his short fiction, the undeserving and malicious are treated with extra breaks, whereas the hardworking and sincere meet with hardship and heartache. Long-winded, "whangdoodle" preachers come in for serious ribbing throughout Twain's writings, and literal

THE CHURCH, THE KING, THE NOBLEMAN, AND THE FREEMAN.

interpretations of Scripture are dismissed out of hand.

Despite his written ridicule of all things religious, Twain was a churchgoing man, never more than when he courted Olivia Langdon. A person of strong faith, her parents had been instrumental in establishing an independent Congregational church in Elmira, when they and several dozen other parishioners broke off from the First Presbyterian Church, which upheld the "Bible defense of slavery." To persuade Livy that he was a religious man, Twain made the acquaintance of the Reverend Joe Twichell. An open-minded and progressive thinker who valued questions of faith over trite and pious answers, Twichell became Twain's best friend for life. The two established a weekly routine of hiking, praying, and discussing matters of faith.

Twain grew up hearing the slaves sing and, for the rest of his life, would often sit at the piano, singing spirituals to his own accompaniment. In an early letter, Twain named "Even Me" as his favorite hymn. Beseeching all three aspects of the Trinity for forgiveness, this hymn is a prayer that "showers of blessing," the "thirsty soul refreshing" would fall on the sinning singer. "Even me, even me, let some drops now fall on me."

What Twain really thought of church services can be surmised by his depiction of Sunday as a time of enforced and deadly boredom. In "The Enchanted Sea Wilderness," a ship is pulled into a vortex called the Devil's Racetrack; its calm and deadly center is known as Everlasting Sunday, a place where ships drift, corpse-laden and lost. In *Extracts from Adam's Diary*, the entry for Sunday is noteworthy for its brevity, reflecting Adam's longsuffering, stiff-upper-lip endurance of the day, with the repetition of two simple words: "Pulled through."

## Human Nature

In the age-old debate about nature vs. nurture, Twain leaned heavily toward nurture. In "The Turning-Point of My Life," he wrote:

*I see no great difference between a man and a watch, except that the man is conscious and the watch isn't, and the man tries to plan things and the watch doesn't. The watch doesn't wind itself and doesn't regulate itself – these things are done exteriorly. Outside influences, outside circumstances, wind the man and regulate him. . . . Some rare men are wonderful watches, with gold case, compensation balance, and all those things, and some men are only simple and sweet and humble Waterburys. I am a Waterbury.*

Similarly, in "Corn-pone Opinions," he maintains that beliefs, religious and political, are shaped by environment. People become Republican or Democrat, Moslem or Christian by association and

desire for acceptance, not by examination of the issues. Sadly, the result is not enlightenment or salvation, but merely conformity.

In "What Is Man?" starry-eyed Young Man is lectured by pragmatic Old Man, who builds a strong argument that, from the cradle to the grave, a human is shaped by the environment. The great Shakespeare, had he been born in Turkey, would have produced something "up to the highest limit of Turkish influences." Had he been born in France, his work would have been inspired and shaped by French influences. Had he been born on a barren rock in the ocean, he would have had no influences and therefore would have produced nothing.

At Eve's Grave – Adam: Wheresoever she was, there was Eden.

# No. 44,
# The Mysterious Stranger

· · · · · · · · · · ·

**Setting:** Austria
**Period:** 1490

This is Tom Sawyer meets *The Twilight Zone*, Huckleberry Finn meets Harry Potter. We begin in Hannibal, except that it is not Hannibal at all; it is Eseldorf (German for "Assville"), described as "a paradise for boys," a sleepy village in medieval Austria. The hearts and minds of the townsfolk are up for grabs in a competition between Father Adolf, the zealous Catholic priest who once met the devil face-to-face, and Balthasar Hoffman, a magician who, behind closed doors, dresses in a black velvet robe decorated with stars and moons. Both the priest and the magician are in the business of super-stition and manipulation.

Our Everyman-narrator is August Feldner, a teenaged apprentice printer. He lives in the Castle Rosenfeld with the fam-ily of the master printer, Heinrich Stein, a balding dreamer who loves books. The mas-ter's money-hungry wife, Frau Stein, has a passion for bringing sinners to God. August and the magician live with the Steins, as do

Frau Stein's daughter from a previous marriage and the master's widowed invalid sister and her angelic, teenaged daughter. There are also some castle employees, in-cluding Katrina, the cook and housekeeper; servants; and a number of printers who work in the print shop, located in the castle tower.

One day, a young stranger appears; he is willing to work for food and lodging. Immediately, Frau Stein is hostile, but old Katrina takes the hungry boy under her wing. He has an exceedingly odd name, Number 44, New Series 864,962, and is both feared and resented, but he proves to be a tireless worker with remarkable skills. It takes some time for August to find the courage to befriend the soft spoken outcast; eventually, however, the two boys become pals and face the print shop bullies together.

Tensions escalate in the shop until the workers go on strike, demanding that the master send 44 away. The strike comes at a critical time: two hundred Bibles have been commissioned from Prague and the job is due in mere hours.

Just then, a journeyman printer arrives to save the day. No one knows the real name of the wanderer, only his nickname, Doangivadam. It takes a quick sword fight and no-nonsense negotiation, but Doangivadam has almost managed to force the boys to end the strike, when news comes that something astonishing is happening inside the print shop: the presses are whirling and the job is getting done by invisible beings.

Everyone assumes that this magic is the work of Balthasar, but it is 44. He teaches August how to make himself invisible and creates a series of Duplicates, hard-working copies of the print shop slackers. The big job is done on time, but the appearance of the Duplicates has increased the bullies' loathing of 44. When they demand that Balthasar destroy the magical meddler, 44 suddenly bursts into flames and vanishes.

August, alone, grieves the loss of his remarkable friend, whose ashes are buried in unhallowed ground, but when August returns to his room, he is astonished to find 44 waiting for him. Resurrected, 44 pulls out all the stops; he produces sumptuous foods from around the world, including some from America, which has not yet been "discovered." Death and resurrection have loosened 44's tongue, and he expounds on the secrets of the universe. August, a rapt audience, struggles to make sense of what 44 tells him about the two selves: the Workaday-Self, which, clogged with flesh, tends to dull business, and the Dream-Self, which, being spirit, is not hindered by time or space. No. 44 is, himself, not human: "The difference between a human being and me," he says, "is as the difference between a drop of water and the sea, a rushlight and the sun."

Time is a human construction, confining to 44 who can dip into the spectrum of past, present, and future at will. The reason he visits earth is because he finds human beings amusing and because he enjoys the element of surprise. He is, he reminds August, only a boy who likes to do boy-things, like show off and astonish people with "stunning dramatics."

While 44 and August indulge in long conversations about the universe, Father Adolf pursues Balthasar, sure that he is responsible for the increasingly disrespectful and audacious actions of the Duplicates, who are now dating. No. 44 stirs things up by appearing in the guise of Balthasar and working real magic. Like a space alien Tom Sawyer on acid, 44, the all-powerful prankster with a short attention span, amuses himself by creating an artificial eclipse, making time flow backward, and arranging an Assembly of the Dead. Skeletons march by, including Charlemagne, Cleopatra, King Arthur, Pharaoh, Noah, Adam, and Eve and "the Missing Link."

Abruptly, 44 announces that he must go and will not be back. August suggests that they will meet again in the afterlife, but 44 breaks the news that there is no afterlife.

*It is true, that which I have revealed to you: there is no God, no universe, no human race, no earthly life, no heaven, no hell. It is all a Dream, a grotesque and foolish dream. Nothing exists but You. And You are but a Thought – a vagrant Thought, a useless Thought, a homeless Thought, wandering forlorn among the empty eternities.*

With that, 44 vanishes.

## The Story behind the Story

Check your bookshelf. If you have a book entitled *The Mysterious Stranger* by Mark Twain published before 1969, it is a literary hoax. Twain had tried at least three times to write this story of a magical, young stranger. In one version, "The Chronicle of Young Satan," the stranger is Satan, who visits Eseldorf in 1702 and plays with people's lives. In another variation, "Schoolhouse Hill," a boy named "Quarante-quatre" (forty-four) visits Missouri in the 1840s and befriends Tom Sawyer and Huck Finn. Twain left these "Mysterious Stranger" manuscripts, unfinished, in his desk drawer, but continued to play with the themes.

After his death, Twain's literary executor, Albert Bigelow Paine, and Frederick Duneka, a journalist, reworked the "Chronicle," made vast editorial changes and deletions, extensively rewrote the story, added or significantly changed central characters, and then tacked on the ending from "No. 44." The result was a fabricated novella, *The Mysterious Stranger, A Romance*. In 1916, it was published as a book by Mark Twain. The deception was not discovered until 1963, when scholar John S. Tuckey exposed the hoax. Putting a positive spin on the whole charade, Tuckey wrote:

*A false "Stranger" has thus been parading before the world while the real one has remained hidden and unknown. If Mark Twain's surviving spirit has the human scene in view, the prank-loving humorist is probably enjoying the resulting confusion.*

Twain had worked on *No. 44, The Mysterious Stranger*, commonly referred to as the "print shop version," in fits and starts at the close of his life. Following Tuckey's remarkable revelation, an authoritative text of Twain's last novel was finally published in 1969.

To date, no one has been able to explain the significance of the number forty-four or what Twain meant by naming his character "Number 44, New Series 864,962."

# Life After Death

· · · · · · · · · · · ·

## The Mark Twain Industry

Death may have come for Sam Clemens as Halley's comet sped away, but it did little to slow the Mark Twain industry. When he died, *Adventures of Huckleberry Finn* had been translated into German, Danish, Dutch, French, Russian, Swedish, Polish, Czech, and Ukrainian. Within a few years, new translations appeared in Lithuanian, Japanese, Spanish, Hebrew, Finnish, Norwegian, Estonian, Portuguese, Latvian, Slovene, SerboCroatian, Greek, Indonesian, and Rumanian.

### On the Trail of Mark Twain

MISSOURI

- *Mark Twain Birthplace State Historic Site*
  A red granite monument marks the original location of the birthplace of Sam Clemens in the village of Florida. The two-room shack still exists, but has been moved to the Mark Twain State Park, near the Mark Twain Lake. (*www.mostateparks.com/twainsite.htm*)

- *Mark Twain Boyhood Home and Museum*
  All across America, Mark Twain's name appears on schools, libraries, diners, and shops, but in Hannibal there is the Mark Twain Boyhood Home and Museum (*www.marktwainmuseum.org*), which opened in 1935, the centennial of Twain's birth. President Roosevelt flipped a switch in the White House that lit up the Mark Twain Lighthouse, an event covered on live radio broadcasts across the country.

- *"Tom Sawyer Days"*
  Hannibal has long been considered "America's Hometown." We not only know its streets and its people, but we want to *walk* those streets and *be* those people, thanks to Twain's re-creations. Since 1956, the people of Hannibal and the tourists who flock there have celebrated "Tom Sawyer Days" every year around the Fourth of July, crowning new Toms and Beckys. *Life* magazine once dubbed the festival "an orgy

of wholesomeness," with its pageants, parades, and contests in fence-painting and watermelon-seed-spitting.

• *Gateway Arch Riverboats*
St. Louis boasts sightseeing cruises on-board two paddlewheel riverboats, the *Becky Thatcher* and the *Tom Sawyer*. (*www.steamboats.org/traveller/ stlouis.shtml*)

IOWA

• *National Mississippi River Museum & Aquarium*
Located in Dubuque, this museum includes a National Rivers Hall of Fame with a nod to Twain's contributions to the lore and love of the great river. (*www.mississippirivermuseum.com/ nrhf.htm*)

NEVADA

• *Mark Twain Bookstore*
Located in Virginia City, this store/museum specializes in first editions, rare Twain items, and boasts "the largest stock of in-print and out-of-print Mark Twain (Samuel Clemens) books and materials in America." (*www.marktwainbooks.com*)

• *Territorial Enterprise Historical & Educational Foundation (TEF)*
The TEF, another Virginia City site, celebrates Twain's days as a writer in the Wild West. (*www.territorial-enterpirse.com/ foundation/about1.html*) In "Literary Pilgrimages: Mark Twain," Terry Ballard wrote, "At the Territorial Enterprise offices, there is a toilet seat in the printing room with the sign MARK TWAIN SAT HERE." (*http://faculty.quinnipiac.edu/ libraries/tballard/mtpilgrimages.htm*)

CALIFORNIA

• *The Mark Twain Project and Papers*

Lauded as a national treasure, the Project is based in the Bancroft Library of the University of California at Berkeley (*http://bancroft.berkeley.edu/MTP/*) and is devoted to publishing and preserving the massive quantity of Twain's papers and works and making them available to the reading public and to scholars.

• *"Jumping Frog Jubilee"*
Calaveras County claimed the *Frog* as its own in 1928. Today the Jubilee draws over forty-thousand every May. (*www.frogtown.org*)

• *"Huck Finn's Country and Bluegrass Jubilee"*
This Jubilee has been celebrated in the Mojave Narrows Regional Park since 1976, with fishing, raft-building, and grown men in straw hats plucking fiddles. (*www.huckfinn.com*)

NEW YORK

• *The Mark Twain Room of the Buffalo and Erie County Public Library*
During the years Twain lived in Buffalo, he was a member of the library. Today the library displays parts of the original manuscript of *Adventures of Huckleberry Finn*, the Norman Rockwell prints from the 1940 edition, Twain publications, portraits, and the walnut mantel which was once part of his house on Delaware Avenue. (*www.buffalolib.org*)

• *The Center for Mark Twain Studies, Elmira College*
Established in 1983, the Center assists students at all levels, "teaches teachers to teach Twain," and sponsors an international conference every four years. (*twaincenter@elmira.edu*) Also on campus are the Mark Twain Exhibit, his famous octagonal study, a statue of the author, and an Archive, located in the Gannett-Tripp Library.

- *Elmira History Museum*
Located in the Mark Twain building in downtown Elmira (currently a luxury apartment building), the museum displays memorabilia from the old Mark Twain Hotel, including a mural of Huck and Jim.
- *Mark Twain's Grave*
Woodlawn Cemetery, Elmira, where his wife's family is buried, is also where Twain's grave is located.
- *14 West 10th Street, Manhattan*
There is a bronze plaque commemorating Twain's residence at this pretty Greenwich Village address. He is rumored to haunt the stairwell. *The Daily News* dubbed this address THE HOUSE OF TERROR in 1987, after police discovered Hedda Nussbaum, battered but still alive, and the body of six-year-old Lisa, murdered by her father, Joel Steinberg.

CONNECTICUT

- *The Mark Twain House and Museum, Hartford*
A tour of the famously outlandish house at 351 Farmington Avenue is well worth visiting. Next door is the home of Harriet Beecher Stowe and behind it is the sleek and modern Mark Twain Museum. Opened in 2003, the museum features a film by Ken Burns; an orientation exhibit; photos; artifacts; a gallery with rare manuscripts, photos, and artifacts; a café; and a gift shop. (*www.marktwainhouse.org*)
- *The Mark Twain Library, Redding*
Twain lived in Redding for the last few years of his life, in a home he called Stormfield (which later burned to the ground). While there, he founded a library, was elected its first president, and raised funds for a building. Shortly after

his death, the building he envisioned was opened. Today, the "Mark Twain Room" holds a collection of books by and about Twain and volumes from his personal collection. Additions have been built around the original site, expanding the library into a modern institution. (*www.marktwainlibrary.org*)

BERMUDA

- *Fairmont Hamilton Princess Hotel*
Of Bermuda, Twain wrote, "You may go to Heaven if you want to. I'd druther stay here." He entertained fans with readings and reminiscences while staying here, and guests can still pose for photos beside a bronze Twain, seated on a teak bench.

CYBERSPACE
Mark Twain is alive and well on the World Wide Web. Here are a few of the sites:

- for quotations and newspaper collections (*www.twainquotes.com*)
- Jim Zwick's extensive site with links to other resources (www.boondocksnet.com)
- "Mark Twain Resources on the World Wide Web" also maintained by Jim Zwick (*http://web.syr.edu/~fjzwick/twainwww.htm*)
- PBS website (*www.pbs.org/marktwain/learnmore/links.html*)
- Mark Twain's Mississippi River (*http://dig.lib.niu.edu/twain/*)
- Mark Twain in His Times; by Stephen Railton at the University of Virginia, has manuscripts, reviews, articles, images (*http://etext.lib.virginia.edu/railton/index2.html*)
- Mark Twain Album; a fun site with old photos doctored by R. Kent Rasmussen (*http://pages.prodigy.net/arkent/_import/pages.prodigy.net/arkent/index9.html*)
- Mark Twain: a little bit of everything, listing numerous websites and suggested

activities for students (*http://42explore.com/twain.htm*)

## And the Award Goes To

• *Kennedy Center Mark Twain Prize for American Humor*
Established in 1998, the first of these awards was presented to Richard Pryor, chosen because, like Twain, he was a social critic whose commentary on the human condition inspired laughter and tears. Others winners have included Whoopi Goldberg, Lily Tomlin, Steve Martin, Neil Simon, and Billy Crystal. (*www.kennedy-center.org/programs/specialevents/marktwain/*)

Mr. Punch toasts Mark Twain

• *Mark Twain Creative Teaching Award*
The Mark Twain Museum in Hannibal gives this award for K-12 teachers who effectively introduce Twain to their students. Teachers are invited to submit lesson plans. The award ceremony is held during Hannibal's annual "Tom Sawyer Days." (*www.marktwainmuseum.org/content/education/teachers*)
• *Mark Twain Poetry Award*

The Poetry Foundation is the publisher of *Poetry* magazine, the oldest monthly devoted to verse in the English-speaking world. The award is given "in the hope that American poetry will in time produce its own Mark Twain." (*www.poetryfoundation.org/foundation/awards*)
• *Mark Twain Award*
The Missouri Association of School Librarians sponsors a children's choice award for a favorite book. The award, presented annually, is the result of a vote taken by Missouri students in grades four through eight. (*www.maslonline.org/awards/books/MarkTwain/*)

## Encore! Encore!

Twain was more than a writer, he was a colorful presence with a slow drawl, expectant pause, a cigar, and, eventually, the identifiable white suit. All of this made him easy to copy. What is more, he left behind a seemingly endless supply of material, guaranteed to get a response. Because of this, he lives again through an army of impersonators who take to the stage and coax their audiences into listening and laughing.

Top billing belongs to Hal Holbrook, the actor who has most successfully impersonated Twain since working on an honors project at Denison University shortly after World War II; by 1954, he had developed a solo show. In 1959, Ed Sullivan saw him and introduced him to a nationwide audience. As Twain, Holbrook took to the stage in New York City, then began touring the world, becoming the first American actor to go behind the Iron Curtain. In 1966, after returning to New York, he won a Tony Award for Best Actor. In 1967, with a ninety-minute CBS television special of *Mark Twain Tonight!*, he appeared before his largest audience: an estimated thirty-million viewers. In both 1977 and 2005, he brought Twain back to the Broadway stage. Holbrook has developed over sixteen hours of prepared material; he puts together an evening's performance from a long menu of set pieces. Holbrook lets the Twain persona unfold: stand-up comic, social critic, story-teller, philosopher.

In 1986, McAvoy Lane, already a Twain devotee, was inspired by a recording of Holbrook's performance to develop the "Trial of Mark Twain," inviting students to defend or negate the charge that the author was a racist. He speaks in the voice of Mark Twain in a lively courtroom drama and has traveled the world as the "Ghost of Mark Twain" (*www.ghostoftwain.com*). In 1992, he wrote *Hooked on Twain* (Trends Publishing). There are hundreds of other Twain impersonators throughout the United States. Many of them are listed on *www.gigmasters.com/Impersonator/MarkTwainImpersonator.asp* arranged by city and state.

There are also several Twain robots and virtual reproductions. At Walt Disney World in Orlando, Florida, Ben Franklin and Mark Twain, audio-animatronic figures, share the stage, narrating two hundred years of American history. In 1993, the "Virtual Mark Twain Story" was revealed at the Virtual Reality Expo. (*www.chops.com/Characters/Virtual_Mark_Twains_Story.htm*)

## Sell! Sell! Sell!

During his lifetime, Twain lent his name and his image to advertisers who needed help in promoting their products. The slogan, MARK TWAIN: KNOWN TO EVERYONE; LIKED BY ALL, was a godsend to merchants who piggybacked their products on the author's popularity. Twain loved it. Since the 1870s, his image has been used to sell everything from cigars to sewing machines, from pizza to plumbing services.

HARRIS & MOXLEY,

DEALERS IN

White & Fancy Goods,

SEWING MACHINES, &C.

12 Main Street, New London, Conn.

J. Emerson Harris,          Francis G. Moxley.

Twain scholar Shelley Fisher Fishkin, in *Lighting Out for the Territory,* found some irony in the ways Twain's image has been used by entrepreneurs:

> *Mark Twain's unfailingly poor judgment in the investing field evidently failed to trouble the founders of the Mark Twain Investment Company in Kansas City, Missouri. And his inability to hold on to whatever money he made doesn't seem to have bothered the Mark Twain Bank of St. Louis.*

Though he famously passed up the opportunity to invest in the telephone, the Mark Twain Rural Telephone Company was founded in 1952. On their Web site (*www.marktwain.net*) it is possible to read that "Mark Twain provides its customers with local and long distance phone service." By the 21st century, Mark Twain Communications was serving the Northeast Missouri area with dial-up access, DSL, and wireless high-speed Internet services.

Twain devotee Jim Zwick, writing about collectibles, reports that "there might be anywhere from 150 to more than 300 Mark Twain items listed at eBay."

# WHAT CAN COMPARE WITH LIFE'S SIMPLE PLEASURES?

Samuel Langhorne Clemens-Mark Twain, 1905

BASS HELPS YOU GET TO THE BOTTOM OF IT ALL.

## Clubs and Societies and Publications

- The *Mark Twain Journal*
  Said to be the oldest American journal devoted to one author, the *Journal* began as a quarterly in 1936. Now published twice a year, it is currently edited by Thomas A. Tenney of the English

Department at The Citadel in Charleston, SC. (*www.marktwainjournal.com/*)
- *The Mark Twain Circle of America*
  Formed in 1986 at the annual Modern Language Association (MLA) meeting in New York, the Circle meets annually at the conventions. It publishes a newsletter, the *Mark Twain Circular,* as well as the *Mark Twain Annual,* featuring criticism and pedagogy related to Twain and his works. (*www.winthrop.edu/english/twainannual/signup.htm*)
- *The Mark Twain Circle of New York*
  Founded in 1926 by Ida Benfey Judd as the Mark Twain Association of New York, the Association regrouped and changed its name in 1999. Its Web site is maintained by Twain expert Peter Salwen, who has led walking tours of Twain landmarks in New York City. (*http://salwen.com/mtahome.html*)

- *The Mark Twain Forum*
  This is an e-mail discussion group on all things Twain: news, papers, book reviews. It was launched in 1992 and continues to serve several hundred members. It maintains a home page "TwainWeb." (*www.twainweb.net*)

Used by permission of Tom Tenney

Logo of the *Mark Twain Journal*

# Left in the Desk Drawer

. . . . . . . . . . .

## The Unfinished Works

*"If I write all the books that lie planned in my head, I shall see the middle of the next century."*

~ Mark Twain

With a mind on fire and a pen warmed up in Hell, Mark Twain wrote almost every morning, regardless of weather or health. His output was galactic, but, like most other mortal writers, he left some stories in his desk drawer, barely started or not quite finished.

- **Autobiography of a Damned Fool**: Twain's older brother Orion is barely disguised as the inept apprentice printer named Bolivar in this mock and mocking family saga.
- **Captain Simon Wheeler, Detective**: Twain toyed with this amateur detective in both novel and play form, but could never get the story right. It involved a man who rode on horseback from Kentucky to Missouri, intending to settle a family feud. In the play version (*Cap'n Simon Wheeler, The Amateur Detective*), the murder weapon is a Protestant hymnal.

- **Captain Stormfield's Visit to Heaven**: Twain reworked variations of this story and worried that it was blasphemous. Though he never finished it, *Harper's* brought out a portion of the writings as a Christmas gift book in October 1909, making it the last of his books published in his lifetime. In the story, Captain Stormfield has died aboard his ship and, for thirty years, has been racing through space like a comet, "pointed straight as a dart for the Hereafter." When he arrives at heaven, he lands in the wrong district: it takes awhile for the clerk to find earth on a map of the universe where it is more properly known as "Wart." Eventually, Stormfield is given his wings, halo, harp, and hymnal. Before long, he realizes that only newcomers waste their time sitting on clouds: the true heavenly reward is an eternity of study.
- **Chronicle of Young Satan**: It was all blood, sweat, and tears for Twain when it came to writing **The Mysterious Stranger**. In the end, he had four different versions of the novel; none finished. In this variation, set in Austria in 1702, a

stranger appears: he is a sixteen-thousand-year-old angel named Satan. An insightful critic of humanity, he performs amazing tricks, such as recreating the moment Cain killed Abel, and mocks bloodthirsty humans.

- **The Enchanted Sea Wilderness**: When a brig sailing for Australia catches fire, a loyal St. Bernard is instrumental in saving the crew, but hard-hearted Captain Cable refuses to let the dog into the lifeboat. Later, Cable takes control of a ship whose captain has died; before long, the ship gets trapped in the dead center of a maelstrom, "Everlasting Sunday."

- **The Great Dark**: This story begins with a father and two daughters looking through a microscope at a drop of water. Suddenly, the Superintendent of Dreams appears, and the family finds itself aboard a ship, sailing across that drop of water.

- **Huck Finn and Tom Sawyer among the Indians**: Tom, Jim, and Huck, bored with life in Missouri, head west, joining the Mills family, whose three grown sons teach Tom and Huck to ride, rope, and shoot. The story turns macabre when Indians massacre the family and abscond with Jim.

- **Innocents Adrift**: Twain intended to write a whole book about sailing through France in 1891. Instead, he wrote an essay titled "Down the Rhone" and left it at that.

- **A Murder, a Mystery, and a Marriage**: Twain, failing to find other writers to join him in creative collaboration, wrote this bizarre little murder mystery, set in a Hannibal-like small town. Lost and then tied up in court battles for years, the story was first published in book form in 2001.

- **The Quaker City Holy Land Excursion**: Twain drafted only two quick scenes of this satirical play based on his experiences aboard the *Quaker City*.

- **The Refuge of the Derelicts**: Those defeated by life gather together, sitting drooped in their chairs, each lost in dreams of the past and what might have been.

- **Schoolhouse Hill**: In another variation on *The Mysterious Stranger*, Tom Sawyer, Sid, Huck Finn, and Becky Thatcher are in school one day when a new boy arrives. He is the extraordinary son of Satan, returned to earth to correct some of his father's misdeeds.

- **The Secret History of Eddypus**: In this dystopia, Twain imagines the world suffering under the domination of Mary Baker Eddy and her Christian Science religion.

- **Three Thousand Years Among the Microbes**: A magician has accidentally turned a man into a cholera germ. Here, the germ tells, in his own words, about life inside the bloodstream of an unwashed tramp. From a germ's point-of-view, the beggar's ravaged body is a "grand and awe-compelling" planet. After a lengthy discussion with a Yellow-fever germ named Benjamin Franklin about the vitality and interconnectedness of everything, the microscopic narrator posits a theory:

*Man is himself a microbe, and his globe a blood-corpuscle drifting with its shining brethren of the Milky Way down a vein of the Master and Maker of all things.*

- **Tom Sawyer's Conspiracy**: Set in pre-Civil War America, Tom Sawyer, dreading a slow summer, proposes that Huck and Jim join him in starting a "civil war," but the only thing his friends will agree to is a "conspiracy" to create an abolitionist scare.

- **Which Was It?**: An arrogant slaveholder has robbed and murdered while trying to save his dwindling fortunes and someone else has been accused of the crime. A wronged ex-slave suddenly appears; he knows the truth and the tables seem about to be turned.

- **Which Was the Dream?**: A senator and his happy family endure a series of disasters and, before long, the senator is stripped of all wealth and power. He is charged with a series of crimes. Just as the word *forgery* is spat at him, the narrator wakes up. Was it a dream?

# Stage and Film Adaptations of Twain and His Creations

. . . . . . . . . . . .

PLAYBILL®

BROOKS ATKINSON THEATRE

HAL HOLBROOK

MARK TWAIN TONIGHT!

WWW.PLAYBILL.COM

## MARK TWAIN AS A CHARACTER

*The Adventures of Mark Twain*: 1944, feature film
Screenplay by Alan LeMay, Directed by Irving Rapper
(Dramatization of Twain's life, with sequences rearranged for audience appeal.)
*Mark Twain Tonight!*
(Solo show of Twain impersonation developed and performed by Hal Holbrook — see page 203.)
*Mark Twain: Beneath the Laughter*: 1979, television drama
Screenplay by Gill Dennis and Larry Yust (also directed)
(Twain, played by Dan O'Herligy, relives some unsettling moments and suffers the Christmastime death of his daughter, Jean.)
*The Adventures of Mark Twain*: 1985, feature claymation film
Screenplay by Susan Shadburne, Directed by Will Vinton
(Twain pilots a steamboat-shaped airship in an attempt to catch up with Halley's Comet. Tom, Huck, and Becky are his nervous passengers.)
*Mark Twain and Me*: 1991, Walt Disney Television
Screenplay by Cynthia Whitcomb, Directed by Daniel Petrie
(Based on the memoir of Dorothy Quick, Twain, played by Jason Robards, befriends an eleven-year-old girl.)
*Sam and Joe*: 1994, two-act play
Written by Ed DeJean
(Based on the lives of Samuel Clemens and Rev. Joseph Twichell.)
*Mark Twain and the Laughing River*: 1996, Chicago, video, CD
Composed, written, performed by Jim Post. Accompanied on cello and piano by Janet Post
*Better Than It Sounds: The Musical Mark Twain*: 2001, NYC
Written, directed, and narrated by Peter Salwen
(Music Twain loved and loathed: popular songs, tunes from the pre–Civil War minstrel shows, African-American spirituals, and songs with lyrics by Twain.)
*Mark Twain, a Film*: 2002, Documentary, "American Lives" series, PBS
Directed by Ken Burns
*A Musical Tribute to Mark Twain*: 2005, Walnut Creek, CA
(A musical journey along the Mississippi River with comments about Twain.)

## MARK TWAIN'S FICTIONS

The Celebrated Jumping Frog of Calaveras County
*Best Man Wins*: 1948, Columbia Pictures feature film
Directed by John Sturges, Edgar Buchanan as Jim Smiley
(Clara Clemens Samossoud and the estate of Samuel L. Clemens brought a lawsuit against Columbia, but the court ruled that the story was in the public domain.)
*The Notorious Jumping Frog of Calaveras County*: 1980, live-action and animated, aired by HBO

Produced by Severo Perez, Directed by Dan Bessie, Adaptation by Ellen Geer
*The Notorious Jumping Frog of Calaveras County*: 1981, ABC-TV
  Directed by Robert Chenault
*The Notorious Jumping Frog of Calaveras County*: 1999, film
  Directed by Robert Chenault
  (A school teacher asks troublemaker Jimmy Smiley to read and report on Twain's story.
  Jimmy learns a lesson about cheating.)
*Jump: A Frogumentary*: 2005, Coolbellup Media, Inc., film
  Produced and directed by Justin Bookey
  (Three frog teams and a solo jockey prepare for the annual competition in Calaveras
  County.)

## A Connecticut Yankee in King Arthur's Court

*A Connecticut Yankee in King Arthur's Court*:1921, silent film
  Directed by Emmett J. Flynn, Starring Harry Myers as the Boss, "Martin Cavendish"
  (While reading a book on chivalry, Martin Cavendish is knocked unconscious by a
  burglar and dreams of Camelot.)
*A Connecticut Yankee*:1927, musical
  Music and lyrics by Richard Rodgers and Lorenz Hart
  Broadway (1927–28); London (1929); Broadway revival (1943)
*A Connecticut Yankee*:1931, first sound film
  Directed by David Butler, Will Rogers as Hank Martin, Maureen O'Sullivan as
  Alisande, Myrna Loy as Morgan le Fay
  (A radio repairman is knocked out by a crazed customer and finds him-self in merry
  Olde England saying, "Can you tell me where the helleth I am?")
*Connecticut Yankee*:1949, first color film/ musical
  Directed by Tay Garnett, Bing Crosby as Hank Martin, Rhonda Fleming as Alisande
  (Set in 1912, a singing mechanic finds himself in Arthur's England.)
*Connecticut Yankee*:1952, Studio One television play
  Tomas Mitchell as Boss, Boris Karloff as Merlin
*Connecticut Yankee*: 1954, Kraft Television Theatre
  Starring Edgar Bergen as the Boss
*A Connecticut Yankee*:1955, television musical
  Eddie Albert as Martin Barrett, Boris Karloff as King Arthur
  (Martin Barrett is knocked out when his fiancée hits him over the head with a bottle
  of champagne. He dreams of Camelot.)
*A Tennessee Rebel in King Arthur's Court*:1960, television play/ Ford Startime series
  Starring Tennessee Ernie Ford as the Boss
*Connecticut Yankee*:1970, animation, CBS-TV
*A Connecticut Rabbit in King Arthur's Court*: 1978, animation
  (Retitled for home video as *Bugs Bunny in King Arthur's Court*)
  Directed by Chuck Jones
  (Bugs Bunny goes back in time and is mistaken for a "dwagon" by Sir Elmer of Fudde.
  Daffy Duck is King Arthur.)

*Connecticut* Yankee: 1978, PBS-TV
    Starring Paul Rudd as the Boss
*Unidentified Flying Oddball:* 1979, Disney adaptation
    (Renamed *The Spaceman and King Arthur*)
*A Connecticut Yankee in King Arthur's Court:* 1989, NBC-TV
    Directed by Mel Damski, Starring Keshia Knight Pulliam as Karen Jones
    (A modern twelve-year-old girl falls off a horse and wakes up in Camelot.)
*Army of Darkness:* 1993, horror film
    Directed by Sam Raimi
    (A man is sent back to the medieval age to use modern technology to fight a "horde
    of undead.")
*Young Connecticut Yankee in King Arthur's Court:* 1995
    (While fixing an electric guitar, a teenager is zapped back in time.)
*A Knight in Camelot:*1998, TV movie
    Directed by Roger Young, Whoopi Goldberg as Dr. Vivien Morgan, Michael York as
    King Arthur
    (A computer researcher is accidently sent back in time to King Arthur's court with
    her laptop.)

## The Death Disk

*The Death Wafer:* 1902, dramatization by Mark Twain, staged at Carnegie Hall
*The Death Disk:* 1909, silent film

## A Double-Barrelled Detective Story

*A Double-Barrelled Detective Story:* 1965, independent film
    Adapted by Adolfas Mekas

## Eve's Diary and Extracts from Adam's Diary

*The Diaries of Adam and Eve:* 1988, Public Television's "American Playhouse"
    Starring David Birney and Meredith Baxter Birney

## The Facts Concerning the Recent Carnival of Crime

*Mark Twain's Carnival of Crime:* 1988, television adaptation
    Starring Richard Henzel as Mark Twain

## The Gilded Age: A Tale of To-day

*The Gilded Age:* 1874, unauthorized dramatization by Gilbert B. Densmore
    Starring John T. Raymond as Colonel Sellers
*Colonel Sellers:* Twain's revision of Densmore's play
    Starring John T. Raymond

## The Heathen Chinese (poem by Bret Harte)

*Ah Sin, The Heathen Chinese:* 1877, play

(Twain collaborated with Harte on this four-act play about a Chinese laundryman in a California mining camp.)

## Adventures of Huckleberry Finn

*Huckleberry Finn:* 1902, musical stage adaptation of scenes primarily from *Tom Sawyer*
 Produced in Hartford, Philadelphia, Baltimore, Music and Lyrics by Klaw and Erlanger

*Huckleberry Finn:* 1920, silent film
 Lewis Sargent as Huck, George Reed as Jim
 (Shot on the Mississippi River)

*Huckleberry Finn:* 1931, first sound movie, Paramount
 Junior Durkin as Huck, Jackie Coogan as Tom, Clarence Muse as Jim
 (Becky Thatcher and Tom join Huck and Jim on the raft.)

*Huckleberry Finn:* 1939, MGM's adaptation
 Mickey Rooney as Huck, Rex Ingram as Jim, William Frawley as the Duke

*The Adventures of Huckleberry Finn:* 1960, MGM, first color adaptation
 Songs by Alan Jay Lerner and Burton Lane, Eddie Hodges as Huck, Archie Moore (boxing champion) as Jim

*Huckleberry Finn:* 1974, musical produced by Reader's Digest and United Artists
 Jeff East as Huck, Paul Winfield as Jim

*Huckleberry Finn:* 1975, ABC-TV
 Ron Howard (age twenty-one) as Huck, Donny Most as Tom, Antonio Fargas as Jim and Royal Dano as Mark Twain

*The Adventures of Huckleberry Finn:* 1981, NBC-TV
 Kurt Ida as Huck, Brock Peters as Jim

*Big River:* 1984, musical adaptation
 Music and Lyrics by Roger Miller
 (After opening in Cambridge, *Big River* moved to Broadway and won seven Tony Awards in 1985.)

*Adventures of Huckleberry Finn:* 1986, Public Television miniseries
 Patrick Day as Huck, Samm-Art Williams as Jim

*The Adventures of Huck Finn:* 1993, Disney feature film
 Directed by Stephen Sommers, Elijah Wood as Huck, Courtney Vance as Jim, Jason Robards as the King, Anne Heche as Mary Jane Wilks

*The Trial of Huckleberry Finn:* 1996
 Written by Wesley Britton
 (*Adventures of Huckleberry Finn* is put on trial to determine if the book is racist and deserving of censure. A black critic faces off against Twain and his lawyer, David Wilson. Huck has the last word.)

*Born to Trouble: Adventures of Huck Finn:* 2000, Documentary, PBS
 Produced and directed by Jill Janows, Written by Jill Janows and Leslie Lee, Narrated by Courtney B. Vance

(Considers questions of race, class, censorship and culture through the lens of Twain's masterpiece. Interviewees include David Bradley, Jocelyn Chadwick-Joshua, Shelley Fisher Fishkin, and James Miller.)

*Big River*: 2001, Deaf West Theatre, Los Angeles
    2003, Roundabout Theatre Company, off-Broadway
    (Scripted for spoken English and American Sign Language for a mix of hearing and deaf performers.)

*Huck and Holden*: 2006, Off-Broadway, NYC
    Script by Rajiv Joseph, Directed by Giovanna Sardelli
    (Holden Caulfield and Huck Finn, symbols of the American Dream, inspire a young Indian immigrant studying engineering in the U.S.)

### The Innocents Abroad
*Innocents Abroad*: 1983, PBS
    Craig Wasson as Mark Twain

### Letters from the Earth
*Letters from the Earth*: 2005, Off-off Broadway
    Created and performed by The Collapsable Giraffe
    (Earth has plenty of beer and topless women. Satan IM's his ex-buddies in heaven, while Adam is suicidal. Eve is a mannequin.)

### Life on the Mississippi
*Life on the Mississippi*: 1980, Public Broadcasting System
    David Knell as Sam Clemens, Robert Lansing as Mr. Bixby

### The Man That Corrupted Hadleyburg
*The Man That Corrupted Hadleyburg*: 1980, American Short Story series, public television
    Robert Preston as the stranger

### The £1,000,000 Bank-Note
*The Thousand Pound Bank Note*: 1920, silent film
    Directed by Alexander Korda
*"The £1,000,000 Bank-Note"*: 1949, on television series "Your Show Time"
*The Million Pound Note*: 1954, (Great Britain) first sound film adaptation
    (Released in the U.S. as *Man with a Million*)
    Gregory Peck as Adams
*Trading Places*: 1983, feature film
    Loose adaptation starring Eddie Murphy and Dan Aykroyd
*A Million to Juan*: 1994, film
    Directed by Paul Rodriguez
    (Loose adaptation, set in modern Los Angeles)

## No. 44, The Mysterious Stranger
*No. 44*: 1982, Austrian television adaptation
Chris Makepeace as August, Lance Kerwin as 44

## The Mysterious Stranger
*Mark Twain and His Angel*: 2000, Big Dance Theater, NYC
Directed by Paul Lazar and Annie-B Parson, Choreographed by Annie-B Parson, Script by Scott Renderer, Songs by Cynthia Hopkins

## The Prince and the Pauper
*The Prince and the Pauper*: c. 1881
Adaptation by Olivia Clemens for family production, starring Twain as Hendon
*The Prince and the Pauper*: 1889, Philadelphia, first professional stage production
Adaptation by Daniel Frohman and Abby Sage Richardson
*The Prince and the Pauper*: 1909, silent short film produced by Thomas A. Edison's company
*The Prince and the Pauper*: 1915, first feature-length film adaptation, Famous Players Company, Marguerite Clark played both Prince Edward and Tom Canty
*The Prince and the Pauper*: 1920
Directed by Alexander Korda
(Filmed in Vienna)
*The Prince and the Pauper*: 1937, Warner Brothers
First major sound film, Directed by William Keighley, Title roles played by identical twins, Bobby and Billy Mauch; Errol Flynn starred as Miles Hendon
*The Prince and the Pauper* notable international productions:
1943, Soviet Union; 1966, China; 1968, India; 1969, Ireland
*The Prince and the Pauper*: 1957, Du Mont television network
*The Prince and the Pauper*: 1959, Shirley Temple Theatre, television play
*The Prince and the Pauper*: 1962, Walt Disney Presents
(Three-part television production, later packaged as a feature-length film, starring Sean Scully in the title roles.)
*The Prince and the Pauper*: 1970, Australia, animated film
*Crossed Swords*: 1977, U.S./ U.K. production
Cast included Charlton Heston (Henry VIII), George C. Scott (Ruffler), Raquel Welch (Edith), Ernest Borgnine (John Canty), and Rex Harrison (Norfolk)
*The Prince and the Pauper*: 1990, Disney Company, cartoon starring Mickey Mouse
*Barbie as the Princess and the Pauper*: 2004, direct-to-video
(About a blond princess and a brunette pauper)
*Garfield: A Tail of Two Kitties*: 2004, 20th Century Fox animated film
Directed by Tim Hill; Bill Murray, voice of Garfield

## The Private History of a Campaign That Failed
*The Private History of a Campaign That Failed*: 1981, Public Broadcasting System television
　　Directed by Peter H. Hunt
　　(Incorporates *The War Prayer* as an epilogue.)

## The Tragedy of Pudd'nhead Wilson
*Pudd'nhead Wilson*: 1896, stage adaptation
　　Adaptation by Frank Mayo
*Pudd'nhead Wilson*: 1916, silent film
*Pudd'nhead Wilson*: 1983, Public Broadcasting System
　　Ken Howard as Wilson, Lise Hilboldt as Roxy

## Roughing It
*Roughing It*: 1873, musical, New York City
　　Adaptation by Augustin Daly
*A Mountain Blizzard*: 1910, silent short film by Thomas A. Edison's company
*The Pony Express:* 1925, silent film
　　Charles Gerson as Mark Twain
Story elements: 1959, "Bonanza" TV series (fifth episode) Howard Duff as Mark Twain
*Roughing It*: 1960, NBC-TV
　　Andrew Prine and James Daly as Mark Twain (younger/older)

## The Adventures of Tom Sawyer
*Tom Sawyer, A Play in 4 Acts*: 1885, adaptation by Mark Twain
　　Produced by Miles and Barton in Yonkers and Hartford
　　(The title role was played by an adult woman.)
*Tom Sawyer*: 1917, silent film
　　Directed by Jesse L. Lasky, Jack Pickford as Tom
*Huck and Tom*: 1918, silent movie
　　Directed by Jesse L. Lasky, Jack Pickford as Tom
*Tom Sawyer*: 1930, Paramount, first sound film adaptation
　　Jackie Coogan as Tom, Junior Durkin as Huck
*Tom Sawyer*: 1931, dramatization, New York
　　Paul Kester's adaptation (copyrighted in 1914)
*Tom Sawyer*: 1935, stage adaptation by Sara Spencer
*The Adventures of Tom Sawyer*: 1938, first color film of this novel
　　Produced by David O. Selznick; Tommy Kelly as Tom, Jackie Moran as Huck
　　(Notably, Hannibal was rejected as a film location because it no longer had a
　　19th-century look.)
*The Adventures of Tom Sawyer*: 1956, adaptation by Charlotte B. Chorpenning
*Livin' the Life*: 1957, Off-Broadway musical adaptation
*Tom Sawyer*: 1973, Reader's Digest and United Artists musical version for television
　　broadcast Songs by Richard and Robert Sherman and John Williams, Johnnie
　　Whitaker as Tom, Jeff East as Huck, Jodie Foster as Becky Thatcher

(Several scenes were shot in Missouri.)

*Tom Sawyer*: 1973, television adaptation
Josh Albee as Tom, Vic Morrow as Injun Joe, Buddy Ebsen as Muff Potter, Jane Wyatt as Aunt Polly

*Tom Sawyer No Boken*: 1980, Japanese TV series, animation
Broadcast by World Masterpiece Theater, Directed by Hiroshi Saitô

*Tom Sawyer*: 1982, Soviet television adaptation

*Rascals & Robbers: The Secret Adventures of Tom Sawyer and Huck Finn*: 1982, Fox Home Entertainment TV movie
Directed by Dick Lowry

*The Adventures of Con Sawyer and Hucklemary Finn*: 1985, ABC-TV
A "girls' version," starring Drew Barrymore and Brady Ward

*Tom & Huck*: 1995, Walt Disney Pictures
Directed by Peter Hewitt, Jonathan Taylor Thomas as Tom, Brad Renfro as Huck
(Promotional tag line: A LOT OF KIDS GET INTO TROUBLE. THESE TWO INVENTED IT.)

*Tom Sawyer*: 2000, MGM's animated feature film
Music by Christopher Klatman and Mark Watters
(Tom and Becky are cats, Huck is a fox. Voices provided by popular country music singers.)

*The League of Extraordinary Gentlemen*: 2003, film adaptation of a comic-book series
Directed by Stephen Norrington
(Sawyer is an American secret service agent sent by Theodore Roosevelt to ensure world peace by foiling the Fantom's evil plans.)

## Tom Sawyer Abroad

see *The Adventures of Mark Twain*

## Tom Sawyer, Detective

*Tom Sawyer, Detective*: 1938, Paramount film
Directed by Louis King, Billy Cook as Tom, Donald O'Connor as Huck

## The War Prayer

see *Mark Twain: Beneath the Laughter*
see *The Private History of a Campaign that Failed*

*The War Prayer Oratorio*: 1995, Ulster Choral Society, Kingston, NY
Music by Herbert Haufrch, Libretto by Mark Twain

*Mark Twain's War Prayer*: 2002, Radio Drama, WMNF-FM, Tampa
Produced by Matthew Cowley

# Best Loved Witty Sayings of Mark Twain

. . . . . . . . . . .

## Crossword Puzzle Answers

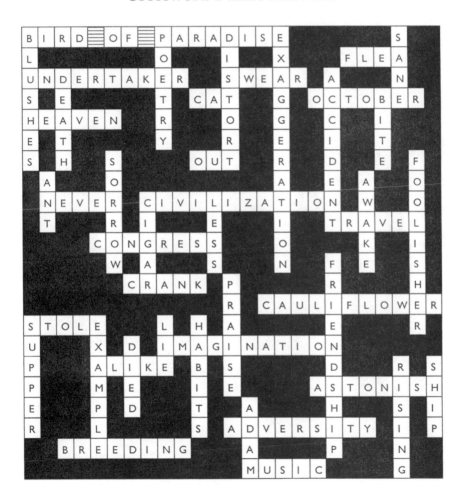